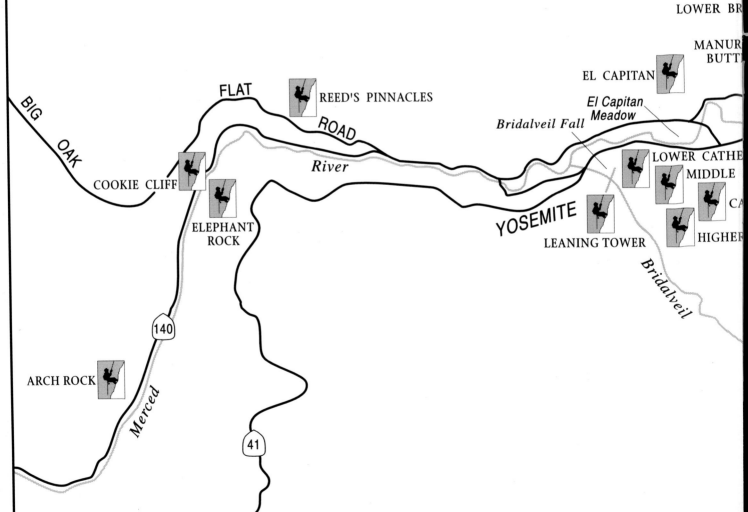

YOSEMITE VALLEY CLIMBING AREAS

EAGLE P

MIDDLE B

LOWER BR

MANUR
BUTT

EL CAPITAN

*El Capitan
Meadow*

Bridalveil Fall

FLAT

REED'S PINNACLES

ROAD

BIG

OAK

River

COOKIE CLIFF

LOWER CATHE

MIDDLE

CA

ELEPHANT
ROCK

YOSEMITE

LEANING TOWER

HIGHER

Bridalveil

140

ARCH ROCK

Merced

41

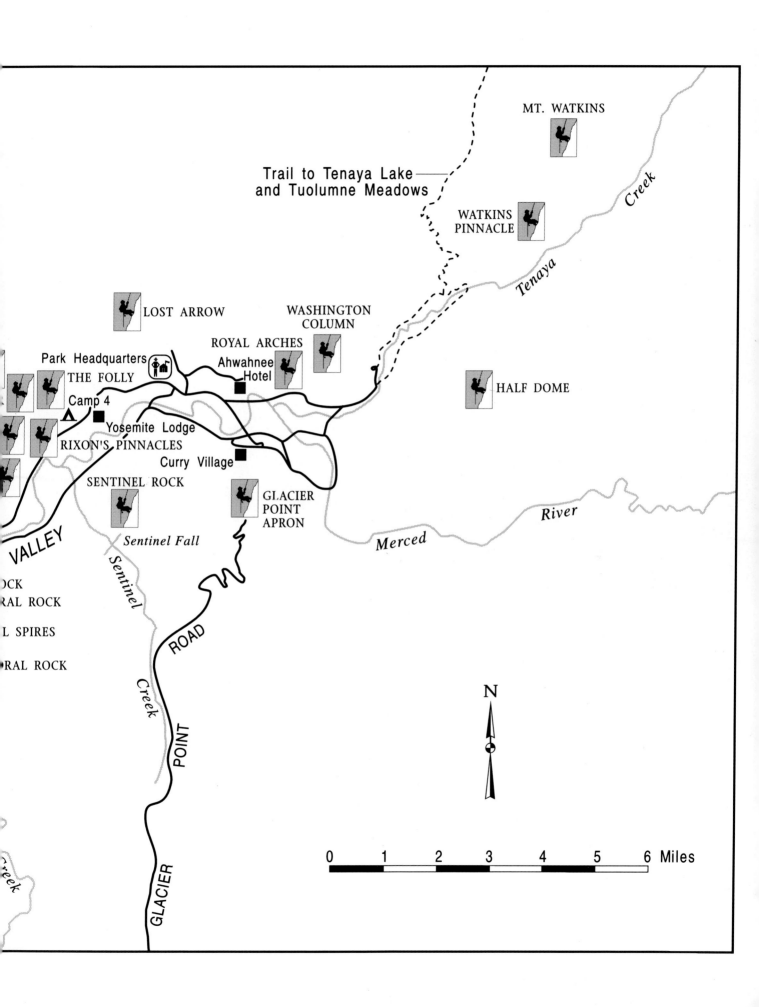

MT. WATKINS

Trail to Tenaya Lake
and Tuolumne Meadows

WATKINS
PINNACLE

Tenaya

Creek

LOST ARROW

WASHINGTON
COLUMN

ROYAL ARCHES

Park Headquarters

Ahwahnee
Hotel

HALF DOME

THE FOLLY

Camp 4

Yosemite Lodge

RIXON'S PINNACLES

Curry Village

SENTINEL ROCK

GLACIER
POINT
APRON

River

VALLEY

Merced

OCK

RAL ROCK

Sentinel Fall

L SPIRES

Sentinel

RAL ROCK

Creek

ROAD

POINT

N

GLACIER

0   1   2   3   4   5   6 Miles

DEFYING GRAVITY

DEFYING GRAVITY

*High
Adventure
on
Yosemite's
Walls*

GARY ARCE

WILDERNESS PRESS

For my wife BRENDA,

In gratitude for her unending support

and love;

and for CHRISTOPHER *and* MICHELLE,

that they may always live by the teaching

"Seek and ye shall find."

Copyright © 1996 by Gary Arce
Design and composition by Wilsted & Taylor
Cover design by Larry Van Dyke
Front-cover photo copyright © by Phil Bard
Maps by Barbara Jackson

Library of Congress Card Number 95-31974
International Standard Book Number 0-89997-185-7

Printed in Canada

Published by WILDERNESS PRESS
2440 Bancroft Way
Berkeley, CA 94704
Phone: (510) 843-8080
FAX: (510) 548-1355

Write for free catalog

Library of Congress Cataloging-in-Publication Data

Arce, Gary, 1959–
    Defying gravity : high adventure on Yosemite's
walls / Gary Arce. — 1st ed.
        p.   cm.
    Includes bibliographical references and index.
    ISBN 0-89997-185-7
    1. Rock climbing—California—Yosemite
National Park—Guidebooks.   2. Rock climbing—
California—Yosemite National Park—History.
3. Yosemite National Park (Calif.)--
Guidebooks.   I. Title.
GV199.42.C22Y6718   1995
796.5'0979447—dc20   95-31974
                                                    CIP

CONTENTS

PREFACE

The intent of this book is to provide a general outline of the development of rock climbing in Yosemite. It does not attempt to be a compilation of every single noteworthy route or climber. Indeed, some climbers may not find their favorite face climb or big wall included in this volume. In the process of research and editing, certain events and people stood out in my mind, and the text reflects this bias. However, I hope that this book will provide a useful overview of Yosemite climbing, allowing the reader to get a general sense of what has occurred in this extraordinary park, and who were some of the people involved.

The rating for a climb used in this book reflects the difficulty encountered on a climb's first ascent. Many of these ratings have changed over time. For example, the North America Wall on El Capitan originally carried a formidable rating of A5 in 1964. Subsequent ascents over the years have physically widened the cracks (due to piton placement, etc.) to such a degree that the route is now considerably easier. This is the case for many of the classic early climbs in the park. Ratings for free climbs reflect the general consensus expressed in current guidebooks, though whenever possible, these numbers also reflect the difficulty at the time of the first ascent. Changes have likewise occurred in these ratings over the years.

A number of individuals provided valuable support for this project, including John Bachar, the Bancroft Library, Phil Bard, Gary Bocarde, Jim Bridwell, David Brower, Peter Croft, Linda Eade (Yosemite Research Library), Greg Epperson, Chris Falkenstein, Morgan Harris, Bill Hatcher, TM Herbert, Tom Herbert, Mike Jones (material quoted from *Downward*

Bound [copyright 1975 by Warren Harding] used with permission of Menasha Ridge Press), Michael Kennedy, Don Lauria, Randy Leavitt, John Long, Elaine Maruhn, Marjorie McCloy, Leroy Radanovich, Rose Robinson, Galen Rowell, Royal Robbins, Steve Roper, Thomas Spence, and Allen Steck. Special thanks are offered to Tom Frost, George Meyers, and Billy Westbay, who patiently shared with me a wealth of information about Yosemite climbing, and generously allowed the use of many excellent photographs. Allen Steck, Royal Robbins, Galen Rowell, Jim Bridwell, and Peter Croft graciously agreed to read the original manuscript, and their insightful comments and suggestions are greatly appreciated. Tom and Caroline Winnett, and the staff of Wilderness Press, also deserve special thanks for their invaluable support and suggestions.

This book would not have been possible were it not for my mother, Stella, who always made the time to cart three rambunctious boys to Yosemite each year. Often accompanied by the intrepid Ames clan (Russ, June, Debbie, Pam, and Skip), my brothers and I spent many enjoyable summers learning about the park and about each other. Hikes up the Half Dome cables with my brother Dennis and alpine rambles in the Minarets with my brother Bob were particularly memorable, and left a lasting impression on me. I can never thank my family enough for what they have taught me, and for the sacrifices they have made on my behalf.

Finally, my deepest thanks are extended to my wife, Brenda, who has given me the encouragement and love to fulfill my dreams, and to my children Christopher and Michelle. In a world filled with peaks and valleys, they continue to be the true high points of my life.

Gary Arce
Victorville, California
June, 1995

FOREWORD

by ROYAL ROBBINS

Yosemite Valley is one of the preeminent rock climbing centers of the world. Of this there is no dispute. I would go further and suggest that, because of the scope, variety, accessibility, beauty, rock quality, length of climbs, and extended periods of fair weather, Yosemite reigns supreme atop the lone pinnacle of rock climbing excellence throughout the world.

Rock climbers know Yosemite as "The Valley." John Muir long ago aptly christened it "The Incomparable Valley." Who hasn't heard of Yosemite National Park? Who hasn't seen pictures of Yosemite Valley, or of the great monoliths that stand so serenely guarding the Valley's flanks? This stupendous gash in the Sierra Nevada has seen the playing out of many a human drama, one of the early ones being between the Yosemite Indians and the U.S. Army. This book chronicles the unfolding of another drama, a drama of vertical endeavor, of man pitted not against man, but against granite and gravity. It is quite a story, and might be said to start with John Muir's famous episode on Mt. Ritter, where he found himself trapped in a position familiar to climbers down through the ages—spread-eagled in the middle of a difficult section, unable to go either up or down. Luckily for us, Muir climbed safely out of his predicament, else we would have lost one of the greatest voices that ever sang the songs of things natural.

Muir's entrapment might also stand as a metaphor for the spirit of Yosemite climbing itself, which, through its history, has found itself caught in the struggle between the sublime and the ridiculous, unable to decisively go either up or down. As recounted in these pages, Yosemite climbing has been the scene of selflessness, generosity, courage, tenacity, and heroism, and also of envy, braggadocio, anger, fault-finding, ill-speaking, and other evils to which our race is heir. As a player in some of these events, I cannot claim a spotless record of virtue myself. I could say, "Well, we are only human," but that would give up the struggle for a higher reality which is why most of us took up climbing in the first place.

When I was 15 years old I borrowed a book from the library, a book about mountaineering called *High Conquest*, by James Ramsey Ullman. In that book was a picture of a climber on a steep rock face, somewhere high in the mountains. He was on the tips of his fingers and the toes of his boots, and his rope dropped straight from his waist into oblivion. The caption read, "Hard rock—thin air—a rope." In this apparently terrifying position, the climber looked calm, confident, and in charge. He was master of the situation. I instantly saw my future. I would become *that* climber. I would give my life to the mountains. I felt and responded to the dream of high enterprise, of brave deeds among the peaks. And so it happened that climbing became my destiny, much of it played out in the environs which form the locus of this narrative.

I was pulled toward the mountain way by more than that single picture. On the frontispiece of that book is a quote by the famous English mountaineer George Leigh-Mallory, who perished high on Everest: "Have we vanquished an enemy? None but ourselves." And so it is that the title of this book, *High Conquest*, refers not to the conquest of mountains, but to the conquest of ourselves. Near the end of his book Ullman observes, "For it is the ultimate wisdom of the mountains that a man is never more a man than when he is striving for what is beyond his grasp, and that there is no conquest worth the winning save that over his own weakness and ignorance and fear."

Since first reading those words and accepting the mountain way, I have seen Ullman's ringing words denigrated. I have seen the rise of cynicism, and mean-spirited competition poison the climbing community. I have seen lies told, and truth twisted. I have seen wrath and fury and hatred. I have seen vanity and egoism and self-promotion become mountains themselves. I have seen bullies and boors and loud-mouths. And I have seen climbers not only stuck in the mud, as we all are, but *wallowing* in it, glorying in excess, in license, in hardness of heart, in foulness of mouth, and in rejection of the idea of *goodness*.

But I have seen plenty of examples of the other side too. I have seen much evidence that climbing brings out the best in men. I have seen many high spirits who have kept the faith: Tom Frost, Chuck Pratt, Bruce Carson, Beverly Johnson, Chuck Wilts, John Mendenhall, Joe Brown, Layton Kor, Henry Barber, John Bachar, Paul Piana to name a few. And a special tribute to more recent bearers of the flame: Peter Croft and Lynn Hill, individuals so rare and special that, although their deeds are of the highest levels of achievement, their humility before the mountains is even greater.

Yes, the great climbers of the past spoke the truth—climbing is a high calling, a noble enterprise. Climbing *does* call forth the best from us. *It is Pride that calls forth the worst*. We seem to be entering an era in which our best will be on call, and Gary Arce finishes his history with optimism and hope. We climbers can each do our part by curbing our pride, raising our thoughts, and acting always with courage and charity.

Ullman finishes his book with this admonition, "It is not the summit that matters, but the fight for the summit; not the victory, but the game itself."

Enjoy this book, dear reader, and when you play the game, play it well.

CLIMB RATINGS

The ratings used in this book are based on a three-part system. The first part is called the Grade. This describes the overall length and severity of a route. Grade can be subdivided into six categories, represented by Roman numerals:

GRADE I: *very short climb requiring only one or two hours*

GRADE II: *short climb requiring about half a day*

GRADE III: *climb requiring most of a day*

GRADE IV: *climb requiring an entire day*

GRADE V: *long climb requiring two days*

GRADE VI: *very long climb requiring more than two days*

The second part of the rating system is called the Class. This describes how difficult the climbing is. Class is also subdivided into six categories, represented by numbers:

CLASS 1: *extremely easy, such as walking along a trail*

CLASS 2: *off-trail hiking or boulder hopping that occasionally requires the use of hands for balance*

CLASS 3: *climbing that requires the constant use of hands; the slope steepens so that some climbers will desire a rope for safety*

CLASS 4: *strenuous climbing with considerable exposure; very steep slopes mean that nearly all climbers will desire a rope for safety*

CLASS 5: *technical rock climbing where proper use of ropes and other climbing equipment is essential for safety. Class 5 is further subdivided by decimals (the so-called Yosemite Decimal System). These range from 5.0 (easiest, large holds for hands and feet) to the current maximum of 5.14d (extremely steep and difficult, tiny holds for hands and feet). From 5.10 to 5.14, the Class can be subdivided even more using the letters a, b, c, d. A climb rated 5.10c is harder than a 5.10a route, and both are harder than a 5.9 climb. Class 5 is also known as free climbing, because ropes and other equipment are not used for upward progress; they only catch the climber in the event of a fall.*

CLASS 6: *artificial or "aid climbing," where the use of equipment is necessary for upward progress*

The last component of the rating system is the Aid rating, used only for Class 6 climbs. The aid rating is subdivided into the following five categories:

A1: *extremely easy aid climbing, placements are very strong*

A2: *easy aid climbing, placements are relatively strong*

A3: *strenuous aid climbing, sometimes difficult to make good placements for upward progress*

A4: *difficult aid climbing; many placements are weak and may only hold body weight*

A5: *extremely difficult aid climbing, extremely weak placements, high potential for a long and dangerous fall. Sometimes referred to as "borderline death!"*

These three rating components are combined to provide a detailed description of a climb, with the Grade listed first, the Class listed second, and the Aid rating (if applicable) listed third. A route described as (IV 5.8 A2) means that the Grade is IV (an all-day climb), the Class is 5.8 (moderately difficult technical rock climbing), and the Aid climbing is relatively easy. A climb rated (VI 5.11 A5+) means be prepared for many days of intense, dangerous climbing—and make sure your life insurance is paid up!

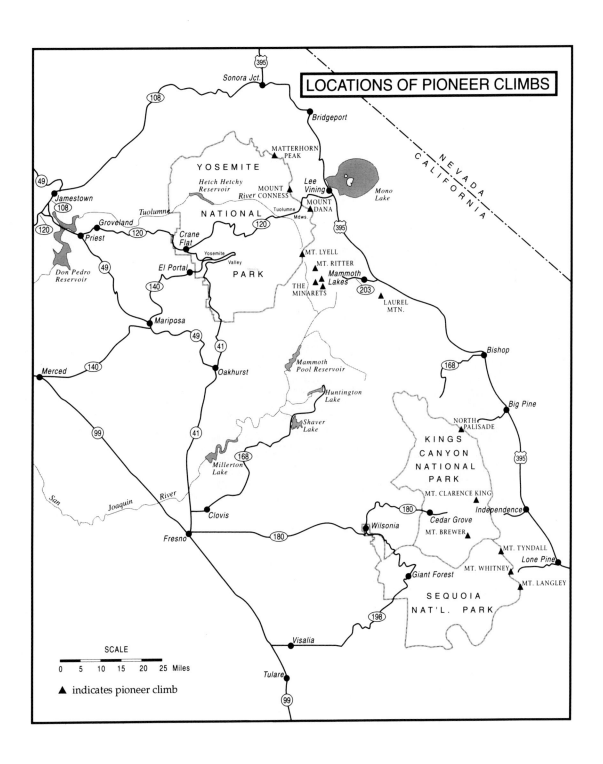

LOCATIONS OF PIONEER CLIMBS

SCALE

0 5 10 15 20 25 Miles

▲ indicates pioneer climb

El Capitan, the crown jewel in Yosemite's granite crown

THE
YOSEMITE

*Having once entered the
Valley, one is no longer left in
doubt as to the reason for its
fame. For no other valley is
so remarkably fashioned,
and no other valley holds
within so small a compass
so astounding a wealth
of distinctive features.*

FRANCOIS MATTHES

Towering cliffs, thundering waterfalls, verdant meadows, diverse wildlife— these are among the sights that draw approximately four million people each year to Yosemite National Park. Spanning nearly 1200 square miles of California's Sierra Nevada, Yosemite is rightly regarded as one of the crown jewels of the national park system. A stunning array of scenery and habitats lies between the chaparral foothills of El Portal and the icy summit of Mt. Lyell. The park is a refuge not only for vacationers but also for 230 species of birds, 80 species of mammals, and more than 1400 species of plants. The endangered peregrine falcon, the immense giant sequoia, and the elusive mountain lion all find sanctuary here. With 94% of the park classified as official wilderness, Yosemite is an important natural island in a rapidly shrinking world.

In contrast to the wilderness part of the park, Yosemite Valley bustles with activity. Nearly everyone spends at least some of their time in the park here, for the dramatic skyline of this narrow gorge is renowned throughout the world. Cliffs such as El Capitan, Half Dome, and Sentinel Rock soar far above the Valley floor. Their rugged outlines seem to embody our image of strength and permanence.

However, Yosemite's vertical landscape is much more than just the passive meeting of rock and sky. This unique gallery of sculpted cliffs and domes is an irresistible attraction to climbers throughout the world. The vertical realm has provided the stage for some of the most gripping dramas and most remarkable achievements in modern mountaineering. Those who have entered the arena have embraced both the sacrifices and the rewards of the sport. Their ranks include business professionals and scientists as well as drop-

outs and tramps. But despite the differing backgrounds of climbers, the
climbing experience produces many
shared emotions: fear, determination,
exhilaration, serenity. It also creates a
heightened awareness and appreciation
of the beauty so lavishly displayed in
Nature.

This book chronicles the continuing
development of rock climbing in Yosemite. It is a story of adventure, uncertainty, failure, and triumph—men and
women giving everything they have in
a quest for some highly personal goals.
Their determination to continually
attempt challenging new routes provides an eloquent example of the restless human spirit. But in the end, climbers' success or failure is secondary to the
insight they gain about themselves and
their environment. Many life-long
friendships have been forged through
the shared feelings and hardships of
climbing. This is hardly surprising.
For few activities are so demanding,
and yet so rewarding.

The First Climbers

For thousands of years before the
coming of white settlers, the Yosemite
region was home to Native Americans.
A subtribe of the Sierra Miwok, called
the Ahwahneechees, inhabited the Valley, which they called Ahwahnee (meaning "Place of the Gaping Mouth"). The
steep cliffs of Yosemite Valley formed a
mountain bastion that protected them
from other tribes. They had names for
all the familiar Valley landmarks, such
as El Capitan (To-to-kon-oolah, the
mythical leader of the First People),
Yosemite Falls (Cho-lock, "The Fall"),
Half Dome (Tis-sa-ack, an Ahwah-
neechee maiden), and Bridalveil Fall
(Po-ho-no, "Puff of Wind").

Under the leadership of Chief Tenaya, the Ahwahneechees thrived in
Yosemite. The bountiful resources

of the Sierra met all their needs. They
established a permanent village in the
Valley, as well as seasonal hunting/fish-
ing camps throughout the high country. In the course of their travels, the
Natives no doubt reached some of the
accessible Yosemite summits. The continued pursuit of game, scouting new
territory, or performing sacred rites
may have compelled them to venture far
above timberline. Although the Natives
seldom left any long-term trace of their
passage, later mountaineers have surely
followed in the footsteps of the original
Yosemite climbers.

Into The Valley

The destiny of the Ahwahneechees was
forever changed in 1833. In the autumn
of that year a weary group of mountain
men became the first non-Natives to
see Yosemite Valley. In late October a
party of fur trappers under the direction
of Joseph Walker was making its way
through the Sierra when they suddenly
found themselves gazing into Yosemite
Valley from the north rim. Although
the secret of Yosemite was now known,
the main attention the Sierra did receive
during this period was associated with
two of the most infamous events in the
history of the American West.

The first occurred over the winter
of 1846–1847, when a party of emi-
grants under the direction of George
and Jacob Donner became trapped in
the Sierra. With their wagons hopelessly mired in deep winter drifts and
their provisions exhausted, the snow-
bound pioneers began to die one by one
from the combined ravages of starvation
and hypothermia. The survivors were
forced to eat the flesh of their dead companions in a desperate attempt to stay
alive. Only half of the 89-member
group were eventually rescued.

The details of the Donner Party's
gruesome survival created a sensation

when news of it leaked out. However, this event was nowhere near as significant for the Yosemite region as the 1848 discovery of gold near Sutter's Fort. Seemingly overnight, California became the focus of the nation's attention, and the Sierra's western foothills teemed with the frenzied activity of gold-struck miners. No stream or gravel bar was too isolated or too remote to be forever changed by the destructive methods of hydraulic mining. And anything that interfered with the miner's potential bonanza, including the local Natives and their tribal territories, had to give way.

But the tribes did not remain passive for long. Seeing their streams and fishing grounds ruined, their forests destroyed, and their game killed off, they eventually began to strike back at the miners and settlers. These skirmishes soon escalated to the boiling point.

In response to the increasing violence near Yosemite, officials in Mariposa County organized the Mariposa Battalion to capture the local tribes and relocate them to reservations on the Fresno River. James Savage led a detachment of the battalion into the mountains in March 1851 bound for Yosemite Valley.

When they reached the Valley, the members of the group seemed surprisingly unimpressed by the scenery. However, the battalion doctor Lafayette Bunnell was deeply moved. He was astonished at the majesty and the enormity of the scene, and remarked that this mysterious valley was surely "a fit abode for angels of light." The battalion soon left Yosemite, having failed to capture the Natives.

In May 1851 a second expedition was dispatched to Yosemite. They eventually captured Chief Tenaya's band near the north shore of Py-we-ack ("Lake of the Shining Rock"), now known as Tenaya Lake. The starving Ahwahneechees were marched out of the mountains to a Fresno River reservation. They were later allowed to return to Yosemite, although Chief Tenaya was killed in 1853 during a quarrel with the Mono Indians.

In the ensuing years many changes would come to Yosemite. Yet the mighty cliffs would remain unyielding in the face of these changes. Slowly at first, then with increasing frequency, Yosemite's vertical world would tease climbers with fleeting glimpses of alluring challenges and stunning new horizons. The curious and the adventurous would look upon the huge walls and the majestic peaks with more than just admiration. They would want to be a part of the glorious scene—sometimes gathering data in the name of science, sometimes searching for personal enlightenment—but always pushing themselves to reach a distant summit.

And many such summits awaited their exploration.

Mt. Lyell (right), the highest peak in Yosemite

THE
PIONEER
CLIMBS

We climbed a peak over
11,000 feet high which we
named Mount Hoffmann,
after our topographer.
It commanded a sublime
view. Perhaps over 50 peaks
are in sight. . . . The scene
is one to be remembered
for a lifetime.

WILLIAM BREWER

In the early summer of 1863 a rugged group of men converged on Yosemite Valley. Josiah Whitney, William Brewer, and Charles Hoffmann formed the Sierra field crew of the California Geological Survey. The legislature had created the Survey three years earlier to investigate and map the young state of California. Since 1860 the men had been mapping other parts of the state. They now turned their attention to the Sierra.

Under the direction of Whitney, the crew spent eight days mapping the Valley and then set out for the little-known high country. A prominent peak to the north soon drew their attention. Hoping to learn more about the region, they climbed the mountain's southern slope. The panorama that greeted them was one of the best in the Sierra. Serrated peaks clawed the sky, bulbous domes billowed above the forest, and the distinctive outlines of Clouds Rest and Half Dome rose in the south. The view from the 10,850-foot summit was the first of many stunning vistas that the members of the Survey would enjoy. They named the peak Mt. Hoffmann. Although the difficulties of this ascent were minimal, it represented an important milestone—the first verified ascent of a major High Sierra peak.

The men then continued eastward, and soon spied a brooding red mountain beyond Tuolumne Meadows. Brewer and Hoffmann were eager to attempt its ascent. Upon reaching the summit, the pair could see along the Sierra crest for many miles. Tuolumne Meadows appeared as a tiny green pasture to the west, and the blue water of vast Mono Lake lay suspended like a mirage in the arid Great Basin. Deeply impressed by the surroundings, Brewer wrote, "It is not often that a man has the opportunity of attaining that height, or of beholding such a scene." They named the 13,053-foot mountain Mt. Dana, after the American geologist James Dana.

Still glowing from this ascent, Brewer and Hoffmann were soon off again. They followed the Lyell Fork of the Tuolumne River toward a snow-clad peak they had spotted from Mt. Dana. This peak proved much more difficult than their two earlier climbs. "We toil on for hours," Brewer wrote. "It seems at times as if our breath refuses to strengthen us, we puff and blow so in the thin air." Although they weren't able to reach the summit, the ascent still provided useful information on the regional geography. In honor of the renowned British geologist Charles Lyell, the peak was christened Mt. Lyell.

The following summer the Survey returned to the Sierra. A noteworthy addition to the group was Clarence King, a recent graduate of the Yale Scientific School. Young and energetic, King had spent the preceding months with the Survey studying the gold fields of the Sierra foothills. The distant views he obtained of the high peaks to the east stirred his restless spirit and left a powerful impression. His impassioned description of them aroused Whitney's curiosity, and he dispatched a field party under the direction of Brewer to explore the range south of Yosemite. This would prove to be one of Whitney's most important decisions.

In June 1864 the party set off across the torrid Central Valley for the unexplored mountains of the Kings River region. Upon reaching the high country, Brewer and Hoffmann lost no time in once again scrambling up as many peaks as possible. On July 2 they set off to ascend a large conical peak that soared above their camp. From the summit of the peak, which they named Mt.

Brewer (13,570 feet), a dazzling panorama of mountains and canyons greeted them. "The view was yet wilder than we have ever seen before," Brewer exclaimed. "Such a landscape! A hundred peaks in sight over 13,000 feet—many very sharp—deep canyons, cliffs in every direction almost rivaling Yosemite, sharp ridges almost inaccessible to man, on which human foot has never trod—all combined to produce a view the sublimity of which is rarely equaled, one which few are privileged to behold."

More important than the view, they could see several peaks in the distance that were even higher than Mt. Brewer. Two of the peaks they named Mt. Tyndall and Mt. Williamson, and the highest of them all they called Mt. Whitney, in honor of their leader.

When they returned to camp and recounted their findings, King was captivated by the thought of climbing Mt. Whitney. The peaks represented much more to him than mere data points for scientific knowledge. There was great challenge and adventure among those lofty summits, and he had to be a part of it.

He lay awake that night, planning how to ask Brewer for permission to leave the group and attempt the peak. The next morning, after inviting the group's packer Richard Cotter to join him, King laid out his plans to Brewer. "It was a trying moment for Brewer," said King, "because he felt a certain fatherly responsibility over our youth, a natural desire that we should not deposit our triturated remains in some undiscoverable hole among the granites. He freely confessed that he believed the plan madness, and Hoffmann too told us we might as well attempt to get on a cloud as to try the peak."

But after much discussion Brewer

The field party of 1864: Gardner,
Cotter, Brewer, and King

finally consented. So the two eager
explorers hurriedly assembled their
provisions, rechecked the new hob-
nails on their boots, and then embarked
on one of the great adventures in the
history of Sierra mountaineering.

Their approach to Mt. Whitney traversed some of the most difficult terrain in California. For two days the
pair struggled through unknown canyons, straddled knife-edged ridges,
tied handkerchiefs together for rope,
and endured frigid bivouacs among the
high peaks. At times they seemed over-
whelmed by the enormity of their undertaking and by the solitude of their surroundings. "With an aspect of endless
remoteness burns the small white sun,"
King wrote. "There is no sentiment of
beauty in the whole scene; no suggestion, however far remote, of sheltered
landscape. . . . Silence and desolation

are the themes which Nature has
wrought out under this eternally
serious sky. . . ."

King never missed an opportunity
to dramatize and embellish their experiences. He had a penchant for describing his travels in the most harrowing
terms—which was not uncommon
for writers of the day. As a result, his
description of the journey was a vivid
portrayal of vulnerable adventurers
ascending slopes of hopeless difficulty
while valiantly suppressing fears of
being "hurled over the brink of a preci-
pice" and "dashed" to pieces on the
jagged rocks below. Their journey was
portrayed as a noble quest of almost
medieval proportions, and of course
the pair somehow prevailed over all
obstacles.

When King and Cotter reached
the base of their objective, they made
rapid progress on the mountain's lower
slopes. But near the summit they were
stopped by a blank wall of rock with a
huge, sinister icicle in front of it. Since
King was "animated by a faith that
the mountains could not defy us," he
chipped small holds in the ice and gingerly made his way up.

After this daring maneuver they
easily reached the mountain's windswept summit. At first it was an incredibly triumphant moment. But the magic
of the moment suddenly disappeared
when they looked around and discovered they had climbed the wrong mountain! Instead of being atop Mt. Whitney
(14,494 feet), the highest peak in the
state, they were actually on the summit
of Mt. Tyndall (14,018 feet), six miles
to the north. Trying to suppress their
disappointment, the two errant climbers nursed their wounded pride and
struggled back toward their distant
camp.

Their return journey was also something of an epic, as they tried a different

route in the hope of finding easier going. Instead, the way was every bit as difficult. When Cotter's boots fell apart, he had to cover his feet with old flour sacks and continue on as best he could, leaving bloody tracks across the snowfields.

In spite of this setback, King remained determined to be first atop Mt. Whitney. Over the next nine years he made several more attempts but repeatedly failed. On one attempt he again made a crucial error on the approach and ended up on a peak too far south (Mt. Langley—14,042 feet). Sadly for King, the summit of Mt. Whitney was finally reached in 1873 by three fishermen from Owens Valley.

Although King was not the first to stand on Mt. Whitney's rocky summit, he ranks as one of the most important early explorers of the range. His surveys covered many areas that were previously unknown, and his dramatic and colorful writing introduced the Sierra to a wide audience. At times his descriptions could be excessively flamboyant. Yet behind the dramatization of his capricious adventures was a mountaineer completely enamored with the Sierra. On one occasion, standing beneath the towering east face of Mt. Whitney, he expressed these emotions: "I can never enter one of these great hollow mountain chambers without a pause. There is a grandeur and spaciousness which expand and fit the mind for yet larger sensations when you shall stand on the height above." Countless climbers coming after him, themselves captivated by the majesty of the scene, have felt likewise.

King would soon venture north from the Whitney region, bringing to Yosemite both his surveying skill and his thirst for adventure.

While the California Geological Survey was tackling the rugged Sierra, more serious battles were occurring in the eastern US. The Civil War was exacting a horrible toll on both lives and property, and President Lincoln was under enormous strain. Yet in the aftermath of the Union victories at Gettysburg and Vicksburg, the President found time to consider an extraordinary legislative bill. The provisions of the bill would create a state park composed of Yosemite Valley and the Mariposa Grove of giant sequoias. The land would be granted to the state of California for public use, resort, and recreation, and would be inalienable for all time. A number of people worked tirelessly for passage of the bill, including Galen Clark, Thomas Starr King, Frederick Law Olmsted, Israel Raymond, and Senator John Conness.

The persuasive lobbying of these influential citizens, together with Carleton Watkins' outstanding photographs of the Yosemite region, convinced President Lincoln to sign the bill. The Yosemite Grant became official on June 30, 1864. It was the first natural preserve in the country, established eight years before Yellowstone. A Board of Commissioners was formed by the governor to manage the Grant, and Galen Clark was appointed the resident Guardian.

In the fall of 1864 Clarence King and Richard Cotter pushed north from the Kings River region toward the newly created park. They planned to continue the mapping begun the previous year and to precisely determine the boundaries of the Grant. During October the pair surveyed and climbed virtually all of the major summits around Yosemite Valley.

Two years later King returned to Yosemite with James Gardiner. In July they made the first ascent of Mt. Clark (11,522 feet), a notable peak southeast of the Valley. At one point during the climb a short headwall momentarily blocked further progress. A key hand-hold lay just out of reach, so the climbers decided to make a short jump for it. King described the situation with his characteristic flair: "Summoning nerve, I knew I could make the leap. But the life and death question was whether the debris would give way beneath my weight and leave me struggling in the smooth recess, sure to fall and be dashed to atoms." As usual, King somehow managed to avert an untimely death and victoriously reached the summit.

In the autumn they turned their attention toward another unclaimed mountaineering prize—Mt. Conness (12,590 feet). They made their ascent from Young Lakes and reached the summit on September 1. The aesthetic outline of Mt. Conness, rising regally above the thick forest, is still a sought-after goal by modern mountaineers.

The climbs accomplished during this period ranged in difficulty from Class 2 to Class 3. Yet in coming years, the standards for hard climbs would begin their relentless rise. One man in particular, an energetic Scotsman, would be instrumental in this trend. In addition to his many climbing achievements, his enthusiastic voice would tirelessly proclaim the beauty and the importance of Nature. Through his selfless example, a powerful movement of environmental awareness would begin. It all started in 1868.

The Sierra Prophet

In the spring of 1868 a young inventor and amateur botanist sailed into the placid waters of San Francisco Bay. John Muir's presence in California resulted from a series of chance occurrences. While Muir was working in an Indiana wagon-wheel factory, a sharp-pointed file accidentally pierced his right eye and nearly blinded him. Forced to recover in a darkened room, isolated from the forests that he loved so much, Muir resolved to waste no more time in the hollow pursuit of money. Instead, he would search for the riches that only wilderness could offer. "I might have become a millionaire," he later said, "but I chose to become a tramp."

When his sight returned, Muir set off on a 1000-mile walk to the Gulf of Mexico in 1867, hoping eventually to explore the great tropical rainforest of the Amazon Basin. Unable to find a suitable ship heading south, he decided instead to make a trip to the central Sierra Nevada. He had heard rumors of a spectacular gorge called Yosemite Valley—where waterfalls fell from the sky like manna from heaven, and majestic cliffs seemed to have been hewn by the mountain gods themselves. With nothing better to do, he wanted to see if the place really lived up to its reputation. Unknown to Muir, this spur-of-the-moment jaunt would forever change the direction of his life.

After docking in San Francisco, Muir set out on foot on April 1, 1868 for the Sierra and his rendezvous with destiny. From the top of the Coast Ranges at Pacheco Pass he caught his first glimpse of the Sierra on the eastern horizon. He was dumbfounded by the majesty of the sight, exclaiming that the Sierra "was so gloriously colored and so radiant, it seemed not clothed with light but wholly composed of it, like the wall of some celestial city." From that moment he felt "that the Sierra should be called, not the Nevada or Snowy Range, but the Range of Light."

His enthusiasm only increased when he reached Yosemite Valley. He proclaimed, "The Valley looks like an immense hall or temple lit from above. But no temple made with hands can compare with Yosemite. Every rock in its walls seems to glow with life . . . as if into this one mountain mansion Nature had gathered her choicest treasures!"

Muir's first visit to Yosemite was very brief. It wasn't until 1869 that he could explore the region more thoroughly. In that year he accepted a summer position supervising a flock of sheep north of the Valley. This allowed him numerous opportunities to slip away and study the magnificent landscape all around.

One feature that immediately caught his attention was Cathedral Peak (10,911 feet). He described it as "one of

Nature's cathedrals, hewn from the living rock . . . nobly adorned with spires and pinnacles." Through the summer he studied the natural history of the area, sketched the landscape in his notebook, and eagerly awaited a chance to climb the peak "to say my prayers and hear the stone sermons."

His chance finally came on September 7. He climbed the mountain's eastern slope to a high ridge, then traversed around to the south side of the upper tower. An exposed crack, more difficult than any yet tried in the Sierra, loomed ominously in front of him. Yet Muir carefully squirmed up the crack and reached the summit about noon.

Looking around, Muir could hardly believe his eyes. A stunning panorama of peaks, ridges, lakes, and meadows exalted his spirit and captivated his senses. "How wild everything is!" he exclaimed, "wild as the sky and as pure! . . . This I may say is the first time I have been at church in California!"

In contrast to his predecessors, Muir described his adventures in extremely humble terms. Although his Cathedral Peak climb was more difficult than anything else yet attempted in North America, Muir noted that the summit was reached only after he had "loitered by the way to study the fine trees," flowers, and birds. He never indulged in embellishments or undue theatrics. Had Clarence King been along, his account of the same ascent surely would have involved a sensational life-or-death melodrama. But Muir found Nature to be a patient teacher and a generous provider, and he never failed to enjoy the infinite charm of the natural world. Where King would observe "no sentiment of beauty" among the high summits, Muir would invariably see a "glorious array of white peaks deep in the sky, every feature glowing, radiating

John Muir

beauty." In an era still obsessed with Manifest Destiny and conquering the western frontier, Muir's approach was far ahead of his time.

Muir not only enjoyed the comfortable summer days, but also climbed trees during furious storms, rejoiced in a winter avalanche ride, and boulder-hopped on talus blocks still quivering from a massive earthquake. And although his excursions into the back-country would commonly last many days, he simply tossed some bread and tea into his pockets and "jumped over the back fence."

Late in 1869, as winter approached and the sheep left the mountains, Muir was hired by Valley innkeeper James Hutchings to build and maintain a small sawmill below Yosemite Falls. Muir later built a tiny cabin near the mill and, in keeping with his need always to be close to Nature, diverted a small stream through one corner of the structure. From this base Muir ventured into the mountains at every possible opportunity, studying the regional flora and geology, and formulating plans to climb as many of the surrounding peaks as he could.

Of all the peaks in the area, Muir considered the towering hulk of Mt. Ritter (13,157 feet) to be particularly captivating. In October 1872, after guiding some artists to the wild country above Tuolumne Meadows, Muir set off alone for the peak that he called "the king of the mountains" in this part of the range.

As he came to grips with the north face of the untouched giant, Muir found the climbing to be unexpectedly serious. He recalled that "after gaining a point about halfway to the top, I was brought to a dead stop, with arms outspread, clinging close to the face of the rock, unable to move hand or foot either

up or down. My doom appeared fixed. I *must* fall. . . . My mind seemed to fill with a stifling smoke. But this terrible eclipse lasted only a moment, when life blazed forth again with preternatural clearness. I seemed suddenly possessed of a new sense. The other self—ghost of bygone experiences, Instinct, or Guardian Angel—call it what you will—came forth and assumed control. Had I been borne aloft upon wings, my deliverance could not have been more complete. I found a way without effort, and soon stood upon the topmost crag in the blessed light."

The following year Muir traveled south from Yosemite. He and Hutchings had not been getting along well, so Muir quit the sawmill and became the Sierra's first climbing bum. He wandered into the mountains west of Lone Pine and claimed an exhilarating prize—a new route on the stunning eastern escarpment of Mt. Whitney. In contrast to the circuitous route pioneered by the Owens Valley fishermen, Muir climbed a steep chute (now called the *Mountaineer's Route* —Class 3) which rose in a single elegant sweep almost directly to the top of California's highest peak. As usual, Muir could not suppress his boundless enthusiasm. He reveled at the expansive view along the craggy spine of the Sierra, noting that "well-seasoned limbs will enjoy the climb of 9000 feet required for this direct route, but soft, succulent people should go the mule way."

Muir would go on to establish other aesthetic routes in Yosemite and throughout the Sierra. These included a daring traverse along Fern Ledge beneath the thundering fury of Upper Yosemite Fall, as well as explorations in Tenaya Canyon and the Grand Canyon of the Tuolumne River. He ranks as both one of the top climbers and one of the best natural scientists of the era. His style of treading lightly through the wilderness, learning Nature's story along the way and constantly discovering new beauties, still provides modern climbers with an enduring role model. It is likely that no individual will ever match the impact on Yosemite that John Muir had.

During this period—the early 1870s—several prominent Yosemite summits had yet to be reached. One of the most obvious was Mt. Lyell (13,114 feet), the tallest peak in the region. Brewer and Hoffmann had first attempted the peak back in 1863, but difficulties had stopped them 150 feet from the top.

The actual summit was reached by John Tileston in August 1871. Climbing alone, with only some blankets and basic provisions, he began the ascent in late afternoon. As darkness approached he bivouacked near the base of the mountain. "I found some dry wood not far off, where some stunted pines grew in crevices of the rock, made some tea in a tin cup, and enjoyed the strange and savage scene all around me," he described. "Immense precipices, great masses of snow, the roar of water descending by many channels and cascades, the rattling down of loosened stones, and the novelty of my situation, alone in that wild place, made a scene which impressed itself on my mind."

Beginning early the next morning he followed the Lyell Glacier to a notch high on the mountain's northwest flank, then ascended the northwest ridge to the top. The roof of Yosemite had finally been climbed.

Certainly one of the most dramatic summits to still remain untouched was

The cables on Half Dome

the bald granitic crest of Half Dome. Josiah Whitney had declared that the summit was "perfectly inaccessible, being probably the only one of all the prominent points about the Yosemite which never has been, and never will be, trodden by human foot." But this declaration, like several other of Whitney's pontifications, was soon proven wrong.

In fact several individuals were engaged in the enterprise of climbing Half Dome. James Hutchings had initially approached the mountain in 1869, but he turned back below the main difficulties of the balding summit. Local resident John Conway was the first to make a serious attempt. With an eager group of boys he attacked the dome's northeast flank in 1871. They first hiked up a rounded shoulder of the dome to a point about 450 feet below the summit. Here the angle steepened to 45 degrees and the rock became exceptionally smooth. The fearless youths were then sent up the slippery face. They carried an assortment of metal spikes which they planned to hammer into cracks in the rock. If everything went well they would attach a rope to the spikes. The group did manage to climb upward a short distance and left a rope in place, but blank rock above prevented further progress.

Four years later the task passed to Scottish trail-builder George Anderson. Using Conway's old rope he quickly reached the blank section. Then he patiently drilled a succession of holes in the rock, five to six feet apart, into which he hammered eyebolts. He stood on one bolt while he reached up and drilled the next hole. The laborious job took many days to complete, but Anderson eventually reached Half Dome's summit. John Muir was particularly proud that a fellow Scotsman was first to reach the top.

This bold ascent was noteworthy for two reasons. First, Anderson's route would remain the only route to the summit of the dome for over half a century. Second, and even more important, this ascent marked the debut of extensive bolt placements on the American climbing scene. Future climbers would definitely have their hands full with bolting controversies—how many artificial bolts were justified for a given route? Although Anderson's ascent was widely praised at the time, the bolting genie was now out of its bottle.

Two years after his success on Half Dome, Anderson turned to another impressive objective—Mt. Starr King. He teamed up with James Hutchings and John Lembert for an attempt on the southeast side of the dome. This climb was significant because it featured one of the earliest known uses of specialized rock-climbing shoes in America. According to Hutchings, Anderson wore specially made moccasins, "the soles of which he had previously covered with turpentine."

Meanwhile, the energetic John Muir became involved in more pressing issues. In 1889, while touring the high country with magazine editor Robert Underwood Johnson, Muir was appalled at the damage done to fragile meadows and streams by homesteading and by sheep grazing. He noted with alarm that the "hoofed locusts" stripped the vegetation, trampled the soil, and defiled the streams. Although Yosemite Valley and the Mariposa Grove were protected as a state park, the magnificent high country was still vulnerable to development and exploitation.

The pair decided to try to stop the destruction by working toward the creation of a Yosemite National Park. The new park would incorporate the superb forests and peaks around the original Yosemite Grant, all the way from the western foothills to the crest of the Sierra. To achieve this ambitious goal, each man would play a crucial role. Muir wrote a series of articles in Johnson's *Century Magazine* to raise public concern about the damage being done. At the same time Johnson lobbied influential friends in the East to support the idea of a new national park. Their efforts, combined with those of other far-sighted people, resulted in the establishment of Yosemite National Park on October 1, 1890.

One particularly special part of the new park was the spectacular Ritter Range, southeast of Tuolumne Meadows. Besides the two dominating peaks of Mt. Ritter and Banner Peak, the region also contains a series of wild and jagged spires called the Minarets. When Muir himself sketched the original boundaries of Yosemite, he naturally included the stunning Ritter Range within the park. However, this superb climbing area was later excluded from the park, when Yosemite's boundaries were amended in 1905. Despite the exclusion, the Ritter Range would figure prominently in the training of some of Yosemite's most prolific climbers.

Along with several other concerned environmentalists, John Muir went on to form the Sierra Club in 1892. This influential group dedicated itself to studying and protecting natural resources. Whether by chance or by design, the former mountaineer and "tramp" emerged as a driving force in America's growing conservation movement.

During the remainder of the 1800s, the most remarkable ascent to occur was accomplished by Stanford professor Bolton Brown. In 1896 he set out for the unclimbed Mt. Clarence King (12,905 feet) in the Kings River region. Although he successfully reached the summit, the significance of the climb lies in the methods that he used.

Climbing alone in this remote part of the range, Brown pioneered the use of two important rock-climbing techniques which would later be used extensively in Yosemite: manipulating artificial chockstones in cracks, and using rope slings for direct aid.

On the upper part of the mountain, about 500 feet from the top, Brown was confronted by a steep, smooth cliff. He first tried to lasso a rock horn above, but the small pinnacle broke loose when he pulled on the rope. So he adopted a daring new strategy, which he described in this way: "I took the noose, and having tied a big knot in the rope end, threw it repeatedly until it caught in the crack. Then I climbed the rope. I did not dally with the job either, for every second I was afraid that the knot would pull through the crack. The operation was repeated several times. I finally looped the rope over an all-too-slight projection along the upper edge of the topmost block, and compelled myself to put one foot in it and stand up, dangling in that precarious sling, until I could get my arms on the top and squirm over." Modern guidebooks rate this section as 5.4. That Brown would even attempt such innovative methods during a solo ascent is a striking indication of his determination and his composure. It was nearly two decades before the peak was climbed again.

Several of the Sierra's most outstanding mountaineers also came to Yosemite around this time. One was James Hutchinson (not to be confused with Valley innkeeper James Hutchings). The talented Hutchinson was drawn to a slender, untouched summit in the northeast part of the park called Matterhorn Peak (12,279 feet). In 1899 he climbed the mountain's west flank, thus beginning an impressive list of Sierra first ascents. Often accompanied by the intrepid explorer and mountaineer Joseph N. LeConte, he later participated in pioneering routes to the top of North Palisade, Mt. Humphreys, Mt. Sill, Mt. Mills, Mt. Abbot, and Black Kaweah.

Another remarkable climber to make the pilgrimage to Yosemite was the soon-to-be-legendary Norman Clyde. Of all the mountaineers who have come to the Sierra, few have ever dominated the climbing scene as he did. In 1914 he climbed Parker Peak, just outside

Yosemite's east boundary, as well as Foerster Peak and Electra Peak. Accompanied by the renowned Tuolumne naturalist Carl Sharsmith, he later pioneered a route to the uppermost summit of the Echo Peaks.

After this mountain baptism Clyde ceaselessly explored some of the most remote and spectacular corners of the range. His exploits are the stuff of folklore. Estimates are that he made over 1000 ascents in the Sierra, usually alone. Former Sierra Club President Francis Farquhar noted that "for over 40 years he was the most ubiquitous climber in America and probably has more first ascents to his credit than anyone else in the country. Norman in his prime was a superb climber, whose strength and endurance have hardly been equaled by any other in the Sierra."

Powerfully built and intensely driven, Clyde was originally a high-school principal in the Owens Valley town of Independence. But an incident in which he allegedly blasted a few gunshots over the heads of some rowdy students brought an abrupt halt to his career. So he retreated into the mountains and nonchalantly established routes that remain classics to this day.

Summer or winter, under sunny skies or stormy tempests, Clyde was happiest when on one of his high mountain solos. "I have found much joy and inspiration in my splendid loneliness," he explained. "In such a life there is, of course, a good deal of adventure, some romance, and a certain amount of hardship. The more one learns to take care of himself, however, the less hardship there is!"

Amazingly, on his extended mountain wanderings he delighted in carrying a monstrous backpack. Often

Norman Clyde

weighing over 100 pounds, the mammoth pack would typically contain some iron cooking pots, a skillet or two, several pairs of boots, axes and rifles, a set of pistols, cameras, a few fishing rods, and assorted books in English and Greek. Although at times he had a fiery nature, Clyde was a gentle man who was content to sit quietly beside an alpine stream and peruse *The Iliad* in its original Greek. His love for the mountains often enticed him into climbing the same peak again and again. "Even repeated ascents continually reveal something new," he once remarked, "as no mountain is altogether the same on any two occasions." Clyde's unquestioned ability and eccentric style assure his place as one of the Sierra's most colorful characters.

In Yosemite Valley, two of the most prolific climbers of the day were Charles Michael and Walter Starr Jr. As the Valley's assistant postmaster, Michael had a perfect base from which to operate. During the 1920s he established new routes on Lower Brother, the Leaning Tower, and the Diving Board, to name a few. Although he was extremely modest and unassuming, his bold solos of Devil's Crag #1 and Michael Minaret were widely respected in the climbing community. Starr also reveled in solitary adventures among the great peaks, completing new routes on Mt. Humphreys, Mt. Williamson, Sawtooth Peak, and Mt. Sill. "Starr usually traveled alone," said Francis Farquhar, "for few could keep up with him on the trails, and few equaled him in the agility with which he climbed."

Much of what we know today about Yosemite and the High Sierra stems from the efforts of these adventurous pioneers. In the decades between the Geological Survey's ascent of Mt. Hoffmann and Walter Starr's backcountry rambles, much had been learned about the park's magnificent mountain landscape. The climbers of this era were completely self-sufficient and surprisingly confident. They thought nothing of making solo ascents at the highest levels of difficulty. Whether they were meticulous scientists like Brewer and Hoffmann, or whimsical vagabonds like Muir and Clyde, all contributed to building a mountaineering foundation that later climbers would revere.

The coming years would see the development of daring new techniques to surmount ever more complex and spectacular obstacles. But it is the pioneers who hold a special place in the history of Yosemite climbing. They were the ones who set the wheels in motion. For in terms of climbing the great peaks, they were there first.

3

THE VERTICAL FRONTIER

Yosemite Valley offers one of the finest localities in America for . . . concentrated rock climbing. Long enjoyed throughout the world as complete in and of itself, this sport does not require attainment of high summits, but tends to emphasize route-finding, whether on summits, walls, or aretes. For that reason, Yosemite has been a pure rock climbing mecca.

RICHARD LEONARD
AND DAVID BROWER

America during the 1930s was hardly characterized by an abundance of carefree leisure time. The country was languishing in the economic downturn of the Great Depression. Basic needs like food and shelter became increasingly difficult to satisfy. Productive farmland turned to dust, hundreds of banks failed, and entire towns were uprooted.

In the midst of this turmoil, the Sierra climbing scene seemed understandably slow. But beneath the surface a quiet revolution was underway. For the region's immense granite walls, ignored by previous climbers, started to attract attention. A significantly new attitude began to evolve. Young climbers did not automatically dismiss routes which simply *looked* difficult.

The confidence required for this new attitude started to emerge in 1931. In that year Francis Farquhar, editor of the *Sierra Club Bulletin* and later Club president, invited Robert Underhill to California. Underhill was highly respected at the time due to his impressive ascents of the Aiguilles du Diable and Mont Blanc in the Alps, and the Southeast and North ridges of the Grand Teton in the Rockies. Farquhar asked Underhill to teach a seminar on the basics of roped climbing and rope management.

This request was quite timely, for knowledge of the fundamental principles of rope handling and belays was still in its infancy. The first proper use of climbing ropes in the Sierra probably occurred the previous September, when John Mendenhall made an ascent of Laurel Mountain (11,812 feet), a large peak southeast of the Minarets. So California climbers, who were still lagging behind the technical advancements made in Europe, had much to learn.

Their eagerness to learn, combined with Underhill's expertise, produced rapid results. Underhill first taught a small group of Sierra Club climbers on the slopes of Mt. Ritter and Banner Peak. Some of the pupils then applied their new skills on ascents of Temple Crag and Thunderbolt Peak. The latter mountain was named by the first ascent team after a lightning bolt struck alarmingly close to them during the climb.

Despite this close call, enthusiasm and energy were running high. Underhill and several Club members next turned to the spectacular 2000-foot east face of Mt. Whitney. Although the mountain was often climbed via easy slopes on its backside, the towering east face had always been ignored. It seemed to be an impregnable fortress of hopelessly steep rock. However, the young rock climbers had other ideas.

Besides Underhill, the climbing team consisted of the indomitable Norman Clyde, plus Jules Eichorn and UCLA student Glen Dawson. Eichorn and Dawson were well acquainted with each other, having already shared ascents of Mt. Sill, Mt. McGee, The Dragtooth, Matterhorn Peak, Finger Peaks, Eichorn Pinnacle, and Matthes Crest. Now on Mt. Whitney they formed a powerful alliance with Underhill and Clyde.

In a remarkably fast ascent the climbers linked a series of ramps and crack systems together, arriving at the summit in only three hours. Even today many climbers cannot match the speed and route-finding skill of the first party. The *East Face* of Mt. Whitney (III 5.4) remains one of the true classics of the High Sierra.

Although the climb was completed quickly, it presented difficulties never considered by Brewer, King, or Hutchinson. It symbolized a completely new approach to climbing. Reaching a summit by a simple hike was no longer enough. Climbers began to purposely choose routes simply because they offered a challenge. Dawson explained, "More and more, we are becoming interested in new routes and traverses rather than in the ascents of peaks by easy routes."

During this same period an independent group of Bay Area climbers had similar feelings. On some small rock outcrops of the Berkeley hills, Richard Leonard spearheaded a movement that revolutionized attitudes and belay methods on vertical rock. He and his friends, known as the Cragmont Climbing Club, felt that the old commandment of "the leader must not fall" was a hindrance to becoming a better climber. They believed that falling was a crucial part of the learning process, and that the only way to become stronger and to develop better judgment was to climb to the point of falling off. But in order to do this safely, the climber had to have absolute confidence in the belay. And since the belay methods in use at that time were extremely crude, they first had to make improvements in belaying before they could try harder routes.

With this in mind they held numerous practice sessions on the Berkeley crags. Leonard, who had an analytical and thorough mind, placed meticulous emphasis on safety for the entire belay system. Each component and technique was scrutinized. If something looked questionable it was discarded and a better alternative developed.

The hip belay and the dynamic belay were two of the most important methods that Leonard and the Cragmont climbers developed. In the hip belay, the rope passes over the belayer's hips instead of the shoulders. This permits the belayer to support the weight of a fallen climber more safely. The dynamic belay, in which the rope passes slowly through a belayer's grasp during a fall, was also an important development, for it placed less strain on the belayer, the climber, and the equipment. Both of these developments were major advancements in climbing technique, and they gave a huge boost in confidence to the local climbers.

Then the Cragmont group set their sights on Yosemite. They reorganized and became part of the Sierra Club. Now known as the Rock Climbing Section (RCS), they scrutinized the vertical landscape of the park with boyish enthusiasm. Although all the major summits had been climbed, an extraordinary array of pinnacles and spires remained untouched.

Eichorn was one of the first to recognize this treasure trove of virgin rock. He first climbed a dramatic finger of rock on the flank of Mt. Hoffmann called *The Thumb* (I 5.5). After completing this ascent, he directed his energies toward the impressive Cathedral Spires in Yosemite Valley.

These needle-like pinnacles, consisting of a Lower Spire and a Higher Spire, each rise over 1900 feet above the Valley floor. Both pinnacles appeared formidable—well protected by overhangs and blank-looking rock. But in spite of the apparent difficulties, a strong party made preparations for an ascent of the bigger of the two spires. In addition to Eichorn, the team included Richard Leonard and Bestor Robinson.

The three climbers first came to grips with the Higher Spire during the summer of 1933. Easy slopes at the base of the spire's west and south flanks led upward to within 400 feet of the summit, so that was where they started the climb. However, their equipment was extremely primitive. Their pitons consisted of ten-inch nails from a hardware store, and the leader was only partly

protected by threading the climbing rope through crude slings attached to the nails. They climbed a short distance up the spire but were eventually forced to retreat due to the difficulty of the climb and the lack of proper equipment. This trip convinced Robinson that the ascent "would involve far more difficult climbing than anything that had previously been attempted by any member of the party."

In August, all plans were put on hold when Walter Starr Jr. was reported overdue from a climbing trip in the Minarets. The close-knit climbing community immediately converged on the area, searching the rugged summits and couloirs of the Ritter Range for their friend. As the days passed and Starr could not be found, their initial concern turned increasingly to despair. The search was finally called off on August 19, but a determined Norman Clyde remained behind, combing the area for clues. Several days later his search led him up Michael Minaret. It was there that he found Starr's body. He enlisted the help of Eichorn, and together they solemnly buried Starr on the rocky ledge where he lay. The untimely death of this brilliant climber was a severe blow to the spirits of California mountaineers.

Knowing that their dead friend would have wanted them to carry on, and hoping to put this tragedy behind them, the Cathedral Spire group set their sights back on climbing. But instead of immediately returning to the Higher Spire, they first completed a climb on Washington Column. Accompanied by Hervey Voge, they established a circuitous route to Lunch Ledge, 1000 feet up the Column's southwest side in September 1933. The ascent was the first technical rock climb (using ropes, pitons, and

Higher Cathedral Spire. The 1934 route climbed the sunlit face

The Cathedral Spires

formal belays) to be completed in the Valley (II 5.6). After this success the climbers returned to the Higher Cathedral Spire.

In November Eichorn, Leonard, and Robinson started up the spire for the second time. They now had European pitons and carabiners to work with. Since the route involved several traverses, Eichorn used the novel technique of leading with two ropes. This technique involves clipping each climbing rope into some, but not all, of the protection points on a pitch. The purpose is to allow each rope to travel from the leader's waist to the belayer in a straight line, thus lessening the rope drag. However, as darkness approached the climbers were only halfway up the spire's southwest face. With nightfall coming and their pitons running out, a retreat was again necessary. During the winter months they stockpiled pitons, carabiners, ropes, and other gear. They returned to the spire in April 1934.

Finally equipped with the proper tools, and utilizing the pitons left in place from the previous attempt, they rapidly regained their former high point. They enjoyed a brief lunch on a tiny ledge, watching transfixed as their orange peels dropped hundreds of feet to the talus far below. "Lunch over, we faced the most difficult stretch of the entire climb," Robinson recalled, "a long chimney too wide for bracing and, worst of all, ending in an overhanging wall devoid of cracks suitable for pitons."

Eichorn and Leonard swapped the lead several times on this intimidating section. Innovative piton placements became necessary, such as hammering them in sideways to span the wide cracks. At one point Leonard was confronted with a blank impasse above, while a tantalizing crack lay just out of reach off to the side. To reach the crack he was first lowered 20 feet on the rope. Then he swung back and forth like a pendulum until he was able to reach the crack. These pendulum traverses, along with the two-rope technique and unusual piton placements, were extremely bold practices at the time. Methods such as these would permit sections of seemingly impossible rock finally to be climbed.

The climbers continued upward to a ledge just below the final summit block. But the rock here looked impossible—Robinson described it as completely sheer, "without any convenient one-eighth-inch cracks designed for receiving pitons. How exasperating to be 40 feet below the top and no route in sight, especially with the sun setting! Hopefully, we followed this ledge to the south to see what we could see."

Around the corner they found a crack. "It was almost perpendicular, too small for handholds or footholds, but it would take pitons. Twelve pitons we drove into it and used them for the ascent without additional handholds or footholds. Then a ledge, a two-man stand, a little scrambling, and we were on the flat-topped summit" (II 5.5 A2).

They hurriedly took some pictures and then began the exhilarating rappels back to the ground. Robinson noted that their greatest satisfaction was having demonstrated "that by proper application of climbing technique extremely difficult ascents can be made in safety."

Several months later the same trio would also complete the first ascent of Lower Cathedral Spire (II 5.6 A1). On both of these routes they displayed exceptional levels of innovation, boldness, and determination. The new skills

which they had honed so carefully, along with their adventurous spirits, had led to the opening of an entirely new age—the age of modern Yosemite rock climbing.

A number of other climbers were also actively exploring the Sierra's magnificent landscape during this period. Besides Eichorn, Dawson, and Robinson, the main players throughout the 1930s were David Brower, Morgan Harris, Walter Brem, William Rice, Ken Adam, Kenneth Davis, Jack Riegelhuth, William Kat, Ralph Griswold, DeWitt Allen, Fritz Lippmann, Torcom and Raffi Bedayan, and Hervey Voge. Together this group blazed new routes throughout Yosemite, and regularly ventured into the high country from the Whitney region to the Sawtooth Range.

Brower in particular had an enviable list of new Sierra routes, including climbs of Mt. Abbot, Mt. Darwin, North Palisade, Mt. Sill, Center Peak, and North Guard, as well as numerous winter ascents. He was one of the top

(Left to right) Bestor Robinson, Richard Leonard and Jules Eichorn on the summit of Higher Cathedral Spire

climbers of the era, known for his mastery of delicate movements. "Back then it was easy to be a world-class climber," he joked, "because there were so few climbers in the world!"

In Yosemite, Brower and Harris formed a powerful team, combining their talents on new routes such as *Panorama Cliff* (III 5.4), *Lower Brother* (III 5.6), *Cathedral Chimney* (II 5.7), *Glacier Point Terrace* (II 5.2), and *Yosemite Point Couloir* (III 5.7). Brower would also take part in the landmark first ascent of New Mexico's Shiprock in 1939. "Dave was always a single-minded person," said Harris. "If he wanted to do something, you'd better get out of his way."

Following in the footsteps of John Muir, Brower went on to become one of the giants in America's conservation movement. He took one of the earliest color movies of the High Sierra, and this impressive film was instrumental in the successful campaign to establish Kings Canyon National Park. Brower also fought to create five other national parks, several national seashores, and a series of wilderness areas. His impassioned writings and lectures awakened many people to the need to treat the environment with respect and dignity. As a measure of his stature and influence, he was twice nominated for the Nobel Peace Prize.

But at this time, the early 1930s, Brower's conservation battles still lay in the future—in a world which would seem immeasurably more complex than it was in the early days of the RCS. For more than any other period of Yosemite climbing, the 1930s were a time of innocence and joyful exuberance. "It was marvelous to be a climber back then," Harris noted. "Everybody knew everybody else very well. There was no competition, probably because we weren't smart enough to be competitive! No

egos got in the way or had to be massaged. We were just a bunch of really good friends. I remember a lot of days when we weren't necessarily climbing, but just out exploring the Valley. We enjoyed a lot of lovely days, far from tourists, not doing anything particularly difficult, but just enjoying the beauty of Yosemite and enjoying each other's company. We were very much a family."

The climbers' basecamp at this time was Camp 9, the Organization Campground near the Ahwahnee Hotel. This was the original hangout of Valley climbers, most of whom were RCS members. It was here that they would rendezvous and prepare for their mountain excursions. And much preparation was needed, especially in terms of their equipment.

One of Harris' trips to the Lyell Glacier was typical of outings of this period. "I never had any money," he said, "so on that trip I made my own crampons. I just took some nails and pounded them through a couple of boards. Then I strapped these on my boots and climbed up the glacier. And they worked pretty good!"

On some occasions, getting to and from the peaks was even more memorable than the actual ascent. After one extended backcountry trip, Harris tried to bicycle from the Valley back to his home in Berkeley. The ride was routine for a while. But when he reached the hot foothills west of the park he could go no farther. It was simply too hot. So he sought relief, shade, and a milkshake in a roadside cafe. "Sitting right next to me was a motorcycle cop," Harris recalled. "The cop glanced over and said, 'You look tuckered.' I told him that I was indeed tuckered from riding my bike. So he said, 'How'd you like a tow? You got a rope?' So I got out my climbing rope and away we went. I still recall quite vividly passing cars going 45 miles per hour. Drivers couldn't believe what they were seeing! He towed me quite a ways and then insisted on buying me a basket of fruit. That sort of thing doesn't happen too much these days. But it was great fun!"

One year after the first ascent of Higher Cathedral Spire, Harris became interested in an especially bold type of route. He envisioned a climb that would ascend one of the main walls of Yosemite Valley, leading directly from the forest floor to the rim of the Valley. He found what he was looking for in the Royal Arches.

Royal Arches

The gracefully curving Royal Arches form a prominent landmark in the eastern end of the Valley. Harris noticed that immediately left of the Arches a series of ledges and cracks led about two thirds of the way up the wall. "As an avid birdwatcher I always had a pair of binoculars with me," he said. "Besides studying birds I was constantly studying the cliffs, looking for new routes. You could look in any direction and no one had ever been there before! Since Camp 9 was so near the Royal Arches, that was the formation that I focused on." Although most of the route looked reasonable, a troubling blank section separated the lower ramps from an upper set of cracks. The hardest part of the climb appeared to be crossing the blank area to link the upper and lower sections.

Accompanied by Ken Adam, Harris made an early probe of the Arches in 1935. The pair climbed only a short distance up the cliff and then descended. They returned the following spring and reached the blank section. To their relief a small ledge ran across the wall toward the upper crack system. The ledge appeared, as if by magic, exactly where it was needed. Buoyed by this

The 1936 route on the Royal Arches

unexpected find they used a pendulum traverse to swing across and reach the ledge. Having apparently solved the crux of the climb they descended to prepare for an all-out attempt.

In October Kenneth Davis joined Harris and Adam in an effort to complete the climb. The trio quickly reached the blank section and pendulumed across to the ledge. But to their dismay the ledge abruptly ended at a second blank section. Another pendulum enabled them to cross this obstacle, only to be confronted with a frightening dropoff.

But here again luck was with them, for a dead pine tree had fallen across the void to form a convenient bridge.

Like the ledge, the fallen log appeared exactly where it was needed. However, their convenient wooden bridge was far from stable. "Even on the first ascent that log looked old and shaky," said Harris. "We had no idea if it would hold or not. But I gave it a great bear-hug and started up. I wasn't particularly scared, but I was concerned that maybe I didn't belong there!"

Although the rotten log shifted and shook in an alarming way, it remained in place. All three climbers carefully squirmed across it, completing one of the classic free pitches in Yosemite.

Easier climbing then allowed them to rapidly gain height. Soon they reached a point just short of the rim. But as in the plot of a suspenseful movie, one final obstacle blocked their way. An overhanging wall directly above prevented any thought of going straight up. Being this close to the top, the climbers never even considered giving up—they could actually see the forested rim of the Valley directly to their left. But separating them from the rim was a smooth, fiercely exposed slab.

Since a traverse of this slab would avoid the daunting overhang above, Harris summoned his nerve and carefully started across. Although the slab was not steep, there were no cracks to hammer in pitons. So Harris had to proceed without protection. "In my little ol' tennis shoes, I remember feeling that this was right at the limit of what friction would take!" he said. To make matters worse, pine needles covered the smooth rock, making the footing even more treacherous. But Harris carefully brushed them aside and continued the delicate traverse. All the while, the yawning drop-off provided an uncomfortable reminder of his precarious position. Modern guidebooks rate this section as 5.4, but the smooth rock and lack of protection still cause climbers to approach the pitch with respect.

After Harris reached the safety of the trees, Adam and Davis then took their turns. Both completed the traverse without incident. The climb completed, the trio could finally relax and savor their accomplishment (III 5.6 A1).

Like the earlier ascent of Higher Cathedral Spire, the Royal Arches climb pioneered difficult new terrain. Both routes were significant departures from previous ascents. Both climbs required new techniques and a bold, innovative approach in the face of intimidating obstacles. But the climbers of the day were up to the task, and willing to push themselves and their equipment to more challenging levels.

Climbers of this period had taken the most important step toward success— they were willing to risk failure. And indeed they did fail on numerous occasions. However, they used these setbacks to improve their tools and their climbing skills. All the while, their insatiable appetite for new frontiers and new adventure propelled them ever upward.

In the years to come, climbers would hold on to these ideals as they continually searched for fresh challenges. Not surprisingly, Yosemite had a wealth of such challenges in store.

Climbers on the tip of Lost Arrow Spire

4

THE
SALATHÉ
ERA

*One cannot climb at all
unless he has sufficient urge
to do so. Danger must be
met—indeed it must be
used—to an extent beyond
that incurred in normal life.
That is one reason men
climb, for only in response
to challenge does a man
become his best.*

ANTON NELSON

In the years leading up to World War
II, Yosemite climbers began to consider
the next great leap forward. The recent
ascents of the Cathedral Spires and
Royal Arches had indicated that other
outstanding climbs awaited their attention. A number of untouched pinnacles
around the Valley continued to fascinate
many climbers, especially Richard Leonard. He soon came under the spell of
one particular formation—Lost Arrow
Spire.

Since the time of the Ahwahneechees, Lost Arrow Spire had held a
special attraction. The Ahwahneechees
believed that the gods had fashioned the
slender Arrow in remembrance of the
hunter Kos-soo-kah. Legend had it that
he fell to his death from the rim of the
Valley while trying to send a message on
an arrow to his lover far below.

But Leonard was unconcerned with
the tragic Native legend. Instead he
focused on the route to the summit,
and from a distance it looked both
direct and menacing. A deep chimney
on the Arrow's left side rose 1200 feet
from the base of the wall to a shadowy
notch, 250 feet below the Valley rim.
From there a team would need to locate
some weakness in the Arrow's formidable armor to finally stand atop the tiny,
sharp summit.

In 1935 Leonard decided to examine
the Arrow more closely by rappelling
from the Valley rim down to the notch.
But he described the exposed view he
obtained as "terrifying even for those
who had climbed the Cathedral Spires.
It was unanimously agreed that we
would never attempt it!" But "never"
is usually too long for a climber, and
two years later Leonard returned with
David Brower. The two Yosemite veterans probed the defenses of the great
chimney at the base of the wall. After
six hours of strenuous climbing they

reached a ledge called First Error, 350 feet up the chimney. Although they were making progress, they lacked adequate equipment for an all-out push and decided to retreat.

One of the most noteworthy ascents of this period occurred several years later, in late 1941. On a cool December morning, Torcom Bedayan and Fritz Lippmann were struggling to ascend the *West Arrowhead Chimney*. The dark chimney, choked with immense boulders, turned out to be a formidable problem. Lippmann later called the climb "a suicide route." Yet the significance of the ascent was not because of its difficulty (II 5.5 A1), or because it marked the beginning of a new era. On the contrary, the ascent marked the end of an era.

When the two climbers returned to the Valley floor, they learned what else had happened on that same morning— December 7—that carrier-based planes under the direction of Japanese Admiral Yamamoto had bombed the US Pacific Fleet at Pearl Harbor. In the coming years, America's attention would be riveted on such distant places as Leningrad, Guadalcanal, Normandy, and Hiroshima.

Not surprisingly, climbing activity in Yosemite was virtually nonexistent during the war. In a sense the war came to the Valley, for the Ahwahnee Hotel was used as a special hospital and recuperation facility by the US Navy. Many of the best local climbers answered their country's call and joined the military, some becoming highly respected officers. Among this group were Captain David Brower, Captain Raffi Bedayan, Major Richard Leonard, Lieutenant Fritz Lippmann, and Colonel Bestor Robinson. Although their main assignment was training US troops in the fundamentals of climbing and mountain travel, they also attempted various routes on the Matterhorn and Mont Blanc.

After the war, the plentiful supply of excellent climbing equipment was a major boon to Yosemite climbing. Nylon ropes, new pitons, and aluminum carabiners were now reasonably priced and widely available.

Postwar climbers, like their predecessors before the war, were very interested in Lost Arrow Spire, despite the fact that Leonard had described the route as being "the nightmare of all those who have inspected it closely." Climbers at the time also expressed considerable interest in the southwest face of Half Dome and the north face of Sentinel Rock. These three routes represented what many considered to be the "three great Yosemite climbs" of the era. All were considered great prizes, but no all-out attempts were immediately made.

Such a bold step would await the coming of an unassuming Swiss blacksmith. Seeking a remedy for marital and health problems, 47-year-old John Salathé adopted a vegetarian diet and decided to learn rock climbing. Because of his advanced age, thick accent, and odd diet, Salathé did not have the appearance of one who would revolutionize American rock climbing. Those who didn't know Salathé often mistook him for some oddball, prune-eating tourist. Even fellow climbers began to wonder about him when he would recount tales of his conversations with spirits and angels. Yet beneath his humble exterior, the fire of adventure burned with a visceral intensity.

Salathé's vertical education progressed rapidly after his meeting with Anton Nelson and several other climbers. Although not known as an exceptional free climber, Salathé quickly completed many of the established Valley routes. Soon he too was attracted to the "three great climbs," especially the Lost Arrow.

In August 1946 Salathé felt ready to attempt the Arrow. His plan was to rappel from the rim to the notch, and then climb the upper part of the slender pinnacle. He arranged to meet two companions on the rim but they never showed up. Undaunted, he decided to make a self-belayed solo attempt, something unheard of at that time.

After descending onto the boulder-strewn notch, Salathé scouted a tiny crack that led up one corner of the Arrow. He rigged up his self-belay system and pulled out a remarkable set of pitons. He had previously forged these new, high-strength pitons himself from a tough steel alloy similar to that used in Ford Model A axles. Unlike the soft conventional pitons other climbers used, Salathé's pitons could be driven into imperfect cracks without buckling. The new pitons were stronger and tougher than any other pitons available

at that time, and they would prove to be a powerful tool.

Methodically he climbed to a comfortable ledge which now bears his name, 75 feet above the notch. But rapidly approaching darkness forced an end to this attempt. He carefully retreated and made plans to return.

One week later he was back on the Arrow with John Thune. They soon reached Salathé Ledge and pressed on. Small cracks carried them upward and again Salathé's marvelous pitons proved themselves. The climbing was almost exclusively slow and tedious direct aid. Toward evening they reached a point just 40 feet from the top. However, the waning light and blank rock above dictated a descent. A series of time-consuming bolts would be needed, and drilling in the dark did not appeal to Salathé. Confident that their next attempt would reach the summit, the pair retreated.

But before Salathé could return, four others reached the summit using a bizarre rope maneuver. Anton Nelson, Jack Arnold, Fritz Lippmann, and Robin Hansen hiked to the rim with the intent of tossing a rope over the top of the spire, and then ascending the rope to the summit. After two days of flailing with their ropes and hardware, the group did manage to reach the top. But this contrived rope toss was not a true climb, even though the men had stood atop the spire. As Nelson himself later wrote, "Spectacular and effective though it was, this maneuver required very little real climbing." The controversial feat simply highlighted one fact: the Lost Arrow Spire still awaited a true ascent.

Instead of immediately returning to the Arrow, Salathé first attempted another of Yosemite's "great climbs"— the southwest face of Half Dome.

John Salathé in Yosemite

Scores of hikers had reached the summit since George Anderson drilled a route on the northeast side in 1875. Yet the bald southwest face, so prominent from the overlook at Glacier Point, had repelled previous efforts. Jules Eichorn, Bestor Robinson, Richard Leonard, and Henry Beers had attempted the route during the 1930s, but were stopped after gaining only a few hundred feet.

In October 1946 Salathé convinced Nelson to join him on Half Dome. The determined pair began near the center of the face and followed a series of difficult cracks and corners. Once again Salathé's pitons were placed in otherwise hopeless seams, thus eliminating the need for bolts. When darkness overtook them, the two climbers refused to give up. They huddled together through the night on a small stance, enduring Yosemite's first climbing bivouac. The climb was completed the next day (IV 5.7 A3), and it marked the first significant step forward since the 1934 ascent of Higher Cathedral Spire. Nelson noted that "the considerable exposure, the inspiring views, and the unsurpassed goal . . . make the climb a treat of the first magnitude."

Salathé and Nelson realized that they formed an excellent team. They both took climbing extremely seriously and meticulously planned their ascents. The next great challenge which attracted them was the Lost Arrow. However, this time they decided to attempt not just the tip of the spire, but the entire Lost Arrow Chimney.

From their previous experience they reasoned that the ascent would take about five days of sustained, difficult climbing. Salathé forged several new piton designs, including a huge "sky hook." To save weight they also planned to cut food and water supplies to an absolute minimum. Their meager diet would consist of raisins, dates, and nuts, while each climber would consume only three quarts of water during the entire five days. Few modern climbers would even consider attempting such a demanding route with such scant provisions.

During the summer of 1947, Salathé and Nelson made several attempts on the Lost Arrow Chimney. An effort over Memorial Day weekend was cut short by an intense thunderstorm. A two-day attempt in July succeeded in pushing the route above the First Error to the next prominent ledge, Second Error. However, the combined effects of intense heat, constant anxiety, and insufficient equipment eventually brought a halt to this attempt.

Other climbers then took their turn at the route. One of these was Chuck Wilts, a climber already well known from impressive climbs such as the 1944 first free ascent of *Higher Cathedral Spire* (II 5.8) and numerous new routes at Southern California's Tahquitz Rock. He later established the classic *Southeast Buttress* of Cathedral Peak (III 5.6) and the *South Face* of Rixon's Pinnacle (III 5.8 A2), and he developed a new type of piton called a knifeblade. The new pin, much thinner than other pitons available at the time, allowed climbers to utilize extremely narrow cracks and therefore avoid bolt placements. It was a major advance in direct aid climbing.

But on the Lost Arrow Chimney, the talented Wilts also came up empty. So Salathé and Nelson set about preparing for a final attempt. They acquired more hardware, yet still had only 18 pitons and 12 carabiners. As with their food and water supply, the pair were cutting it very close on climbing gear.

In September they started up the

Chimney for yet another attempt. The familiar lower pitches passed quickly. They climbed for 13 hours the first day and spent the night 650 feet up. Their progress slowed considerably in successive days as the difficulties increased. But tenaciously they continued moving up. Salathé cleverly used innovative piton placements in awkward cracks, and boldly led difficult pitches with limited protection. At one point he doggedly maintained the lead for eight straight hours.

In addition to the difficulty of the climb, both men also fought a constant battle to overcome hunger and thirst. Even the nighttime hours offered little relief, since their uncomfortable bivouacs permitted little sleep. Nelson recalled, "The hours before dawn that should have permitted the greater comfort of climbing were passed largely in talk. Food, sleep, and water can be dispensed with to a degree not appreciated until one is in a position where little can be had."

On the morning of the fifth day the climbers had just 40 feet to go. Above them stretched the blank, "flint-hard and flawless" section that had stopped Salathé the year before. But nothing would stop him this day. He placed a series of bolts up the blank rock and soon the two men were shaking hands atop the Arrow. The first big wall climb in the country was now complete (V 5.8 A3).

By every measure this ascent was a landmark achievement. The technical difficulties far exceeded anything yet climbed in North America. The considerable strain of living and working in a vertical environment was kept at a manageable level, even after successive days on the rock. Perhaps most importantly, the climbers displayed the commitment necessary to venture into the unknown and succeed. Their climb represented a true adventure, and they were sticking their necks out to attempt it. As Nelson later wrote, "We understood that rescue from an accident in the Great Chimney was not to be expected." But they also had confidence in their own judgment and ability. This powerful combination of commitment and confidence would continue to serve them well in Yosemite.

Sentinel Rock: Steck-Salathé

Of the "three great Yosemite climbs" that were recognized at the time, John Salathé had accomplished the first two. The third route, Sentinel Rock's north face, still reposed in ominous uncertainty. Here again Salathé would leave his mark.

In 1948, one year after climbing the Lost Arrow, Salathé and Nelson were in action once again. They established a short route on Sentinel's *Northeast Bowl* (III 5.8 A1), to the left of the true north face. Although this route was not on par with Half Dome or the Lost Arrow, it did pique Salathé's interest in the unclimbed north face. And he was not the only one to be interested.

Years before, many climbers had visualized a route on the right side of the wall. An obvious series of cracks and ledges ran up the 800-foot-high Flying Buttress. Above this buttress lay a steep, smooth section called the Headwall, which appeared to be a formidable obstacle. The final section consisted of a sinister-looking chimney system. The full package would surely be a considerable undertaking.

During the late 1940s a number of parties probed the shadowy wall, with varying degrees of success. Robin Hansen, Jack Arnold, and Fritz Lippmann reached a high point only 150 feet up the face before severe difficulties

Bill Long on an early probe of Sentinel's north face

stopped them. A 1949 attempt by Allen Steck, Phil Bettler, Jim Wilson, and Bill Long completed eight pitches, reaching 450 feet up the wall in two days of arduous climbing.

Then a major advance occurred in 1950 when Wilson and Bettler reached the top of the Flying Buttress, thus establishing the lower part of the route. But their description of the route above sounded ominous: blank rock, overhanging walls, and a horribly narrow chimney.

Yet the foreboding description did nothing to discourage Allen Steck. He loved new horizons and new adventures. At a time when most of his contemporaries were either holding down respectable jobs or attending college,

Steck was a bit of a rebel, doing questionable things like bicycling across Europe and sleeping in farmers' haylofts along the way.

Here in Yosemite, the ascent of Sentinel meant a great deal to him, and several factors compelled him to get more serious about it. First, he dearly wanted to make the first ascent because he was, in his words, "obsessed with the route." Second, the Wilson/Bettler attempt clearly showed that other motivated climbers were nearing success. "At that point," Steck explained, "I suddenly began to realize that maybe the wall was slipping away from me." And third, his familiarity with the rock had dispelled any demons of fear and self-doubt. "I'd been up on the wall before," he noted, "so I'd lost the awe of standing beneath it. Plus I was young and fairly stupid!"

Several weeks after Wilson and Bettler came down from the Flying Buttress, Steck recruited Wilson for an all-out attempt. But this campaign was short-lived. A falling rock severed one of their ropes on the second pitch, so the pair improvised a rappel and retreated.

Back on the ground, Steck remained focused on the north face. He planned to return for another attempt over the July Fourth weekend. But his climbing partner was committed to assisting a Sierra Club group in the Minarets. Trying to think of another partner, he recalled Salathé's impressive routes on Half Dome and the Lost Arrow. So he phoned Salathé with an invitation to join him on Sentinel. The energetic blacksmith, now 51 years old, was easily persuaded.

On June 30, 1950, the two climbers scrambled up a long series of ledges which led to the base of the north face. As the Valley simmered in the grips of a stifling heat wave, Steck and Salathé prepared mentally and physically for a multiday climb, carefully packing their equipment: 18 pitons, 15 carabiners, and 12 bolts.

They reached the top of the Flying Buttress in two days. Then for the next three days, they battled a continuing stream of difficulties on the remaining 700 feet of the route. Immediately above the Flying Buttress, Salathé placed six bolts in a grueling ten-hour lead. "That was a tough day for me," Steck joked. "The hardest part was staying awake at the belay!" But despite the slow progress, Salathé's lead on the Headwall pitch was the key to reaching the upper chimney system.

Yet the difficulties were far from over. At one point the sides of the chimney converged into a distressing, claustrophobic slot called the Narrows. This first appeared to be a hopeless barrier, but again Salathé engineered a solution. By boldly placing pitons upside-down and back-to-back, he climbed around the awkward chimney and onto the outside face. It was yet another of his brilliant leads.

As in the earlier epic on the Lost Arrow, the scorching summer heat was also a factor on Sentinel. Steck noted that "each afternoon at two the sun came from behind the wall and turned the face into a veritable furnace. Temperatures up to 105 degrees were recorded down in the Valley and there wasn't a breath of wind. We could watch swimmers down in the Valley, languishing in the cool waters of the Merced. . . . If only those swimmers would stop splashing! And this was only the third day! John never said much about it, but I knew he was thirsty. Standing there in slings, with his hammer poised, John would turn his head and say, 'Al, if I could only have just a little orange juice!' Up on that wall, oh what such a simple thing as a glass of orange juice would have been worth!"

Despite the heat and the long, difficult climbing, the weary climbers reached the summit around noon on the fifth day. Their determination and skill had led to another milestone in the development of Yosemite climbing (V 5.9 A3). But for Steck and Salathé, reaching the top was a bit anticlimactic. For they were so thirsty that they immediately began a hasty descent in search of water. "The overpowering heat cannot be described in simple words," Steck exclaimed. "We were out of our minds with thirst!"

In Steck's case, the descent was a little too hasty, for he took a wrong turn and ended up at a dangerous drop-off.

Allen Steck leading the 15th pitch on Sentinel Rock

He was so crazed with thirst, he briefly considered leaping off the 30-foot cliff in hopes of getting down quicker. "My judgment was numbed by the thought of water," he admitted.

Eventually they found a small stream and happily engorged their desiccated bodies. Only then did Steck feel that the climb was really over. "This was the climax of the climb," he wrote, "a supreme climax! And I can say, in retrospect, that it was well worth the effort!"

In the years following this ascent, Steck would go on to establish a number of outstanding routes in the Valley and the High Sierra. With partners such as Jim Wilson, Les Wilson, Dick Long, Bob Swift, and Willi Unsoeld, he would pioneer such aesthetic lines as *Yosemite Point Buttress* (IV 5.8 A2), *El Cap Tree* (III 5.6 A2), El Capitan's *East Buttress* (IV 5.7 A2), and the *South Face* of Angel Wings (V 5.8 A4). But it is the 1950 route on Sentinel's north face, now known as the Steck-Salathé route, that remains one of his finest achievements. "This is a technical age," he later noted, "and climbers will continue in the future to look for new routes. For there is nothing more satisfying than being a pioneer."

Meanwhile, the 51-year-old Salathé returned to Switzerland for a short time before eventually moving back to America. Although his climbing activity decreased after the Sentinel ascent, John Salathé left an enduring legacy on the Yosemite climbing scene. He is remembered as the driving force behind the classic big wall ascents of the 1940s and early 1950s. It was John Salathé who first opened the door into Yosemite's untouched gallery of huge granite walls. Others coming after him would decorate the gallery with a myriad of elegant new routes, but it was the gray-haired blacksmith who first set the process in motion.

For Salathé, however, more important than reaching each summit was the manner—the *style*—in which the climbs were completed. He never smothered a route with equipment or tried to bring the difficulties down to his level. On the contrary, he worked hard to build himself up to the level of each climb, whether by training to do without water or devising new tools to eliminate bolt placements.

Commitment, innovation, and vision characterized the approach of John Salathé. Future climbers, inspired by his style, would look to Yosemite's walls for dramatic new adventures. And they would not be disappointed.

5

THE GOLDEN AGE

*Climbing is a great game—
great not in spite of the
demands it makes, but
because of them. Great
because it will not let us
give half of ourselves—
it demands all of us.
It demands our best.*

ROYAL ROBBINS

At every stage in the development of rock climbing in Yosemite, a few individuals always rose above the existing levels of ability. Their bold actions have advanced the sport in exciting new directions. Visionaries such as John Muir, Richard Leonard, Allen Steck, and John Salathe are remembered for the dramatic impact they had on the prevailing attitudes of their time. A similar trend developed during the 1950s and 1960s. A small group of dedicated climbers had a profound effect on rock climbing around the world as they quietly established routes of exceptional difficulty and beauty.

Several of these climbers had their roots in Southern California. Inviting crags, such as Tahquitz Rock and Stoney Point, were much less intimidating than Yosemite's towering walls. So Southern California climbers felt comfortable challenging themselves on increasingly difficult routes. These cliffs were also much closer to Los Angeles, making it easy for climbers to spend many weekends and holidays there. A strong feeling of camaraderie evolved among the regulars and they soon formed a close-knit community.

One particular climber who would soon make a huge impact on Yosemite was a lanky teenager named Royal Robbins. Family problems at home had made him unusually independent at a young age, and he didn't seem to fit in well at school. But he had an overwhelming desire for adventure and challenge, and the friends he did have shared this longing.

Their hunger for adventure inspired them to learn as much as they could about rock climbing. Recalling his early training in Southern California, Robbins said, "We went out there with just a few pitons, plus some old clothesline or rotting hemp rope stolen from the

Royal Robbins (below) and Chuck Pratt on the traverse into the Black Dihedral, El Capitan

sides of trucks, and we tried to act like climbers." On one occasion at Stoney Point, Robbins managed to do a very good imitation of a climber taking a leader fall, and he ended up breaking his wrist. Yet two weeks later he was back on the rocks, climbing with a cast—a little humbler and a little wiser. Even at this young age, Robbins' determination was clearly evident.

When not climbing, Robbins and his friends hopped aboard freight trains in search of new adventures. They scrambled all over the moving boxcars and delighted in making daring jumps between cars as the train raced along. Ending up in some unknown place miles from home, and then hitchhiking back to Los Angeles was all part of the fun.

Through his climbing, Robbins found a perfect outlet for his adventurous spirit. He climbed the hardest routes with apparent ease, surprising many people with his natural ability and daring style. He improved so fast that he soon felt ready to try a new challenge. That challenge would consist of a striking 200-foot corner at Tahquitz called *The Open Book*. Previous climbers had always used direct aid at the difficult sections. But in 1952 Robbins boldly led the route completely free. Without realizing it, he had just completed the most technically difficult route in the country.

Like the innovative approach of the Cragmont climbers in the 1930s, the landmark ascent of *The Open Book* was made possible because Robbins adopted a fundamental change in his mindset about climbing. "The key to our success was due to one simple thing," he explained. "It was simply that we brought a different attitude to the game. We had faith in our equipment and we went up there willing to fall.

The old adage that 'The leader must not fall!' was outdated, but a lot of climbers at that time still clung to it. But we came from a different perspective, and this allowed us to climb closer to our true potential."

This ascent underscored the need for a new system for rating rock climbs. Up to this point, all technical rock climbs were rated simply Class 5, meaning that ropes, pitons, and proper belays were required for safety. However, some routes were clearly harder than other routes, so a more precise classification system was needed. Tahquitz climbers addressed this need by subdividing Class 5 climbing into precise numeric values, ranging from 5.0 for the easiest routes to 5.9 for the hardest routes. *The Open Book* was given the formidable

Royal Robbins climbing at Tahquitz Rock

rating of 5.9, the first route in America to be classified as such.

After this ascent many Tahquitz climbers followed Robbins' example and began to really push themselves. "Royal was the one we all leaned on," said TM Herbert. "The rest of us just tried to follow in his footsteps. He was without a doubt the outstanding climber of our era. And he did all those hard climbs in some goddammed high-top basketball shoes!"

In addition to their interest in difficult routes, these climbers also paid particular attention to the style of their ascents. The goal was to climb challenging routes quickly and easily. They soon applied this sporty approach to Yosemite's forbidding walls.

In 1953 Robbins, Jerry Gallwas, and Don Wilson arrived in the Valley intent on making the second ascent of Sentinel Rock's north face. In fact Robbins had first come to Yosemite in 1951. With two friends he had hitchhiked to the Valley, naively hoping to ascend some great routes. But the ambitious youngsters could scarcely get off the ground, and they returned to Southern California somewhat humbled. Now, two years later, the 18-year-old Robbins was older, stronger, and smarter, and felt ready to attempt the forbidding *Steck-Salathé.*

As a measure of the respect that Valley climbers had for the route, no one had yet attempted the coveted second ascent. But the L.A. teenagers not only completed the route in exemplary style, they also cut the climbing time from five days to two. "We did some pretty wild things on that climb," Robbins said. "We must have been infused with some sort of energy and ability which only comes rarely." They free-climbed much of the route and Robbins established an important variation directly

through the Narrows. At one point, as Robbins began a traverse, he naively grasped the rope and figured that he could easily swing across. "I had no judgment about such things in those days," he noted. "I took quite a swing and bounced about 150 feet across the wall. When I finally stopped I was pretty battered. But we were young and healthy and resilient . . . and we probably saved half an hour just doing that."

But what really impressed Robbins were the quality of the route and the extraordinary ability of the humble Swiss blacksmith. "Salathé's standards were exceptionally high," Robbins exclaimed. "He never took the easy way out. It was all we could do to just follow the route and try to figure out what he had done. That route is a work of art!"

The following year, 1954, a number of significant events occurred. First, another Tahquitz climber, sports-car enthusiast Warren Harding, came to Yosemite and began a pattern which would be repeated many times in the future—establishing difficult new routes on the Valley's huge walls. He first climbed the long *North Buttress* of Middle Cathedral Rock (V 5.8 A3), and later established an elegant route up the *East Buttress* (IV 5.9 A1). Besides the excellent rock of the *East Buttress,* the first-ascent team also encountered a memorable ant-infested ledge. While Harding climbed above the ledge, Jack Davis and Bob Swift endured the biting fury of the aroused insects. They were soon engaged in a fierce battle with the swarming arthropods, and many ants were sacrificed that day to the great cause of Yosemite climbing.

Harding also completed the second ascent of the Lost Arrow Chimney. On the upper part of the climb, the wiry Harding left his mark on the route by working out a new variation called the Harding Hole, which tunneled through directly to the notch.

His lighthearted antics and post-climb drinking bouts also left a mark on the Valley social scene. Harding was the ultimate free spirit, enjoying fast cars and cheap wine, and regaling his partners with poignant observations: "In rock climbing it's not really necessary to reach a summit; the game seems to amount to finding the most difficult ways of getting nowhere. Why would anybody want to get involved in such a ludicrous activity? Viewed objectively, climbing is totally absurd!" But he was still a frequent visitor to Yosemite because, in his words, "If you're going to do something silly, you may as well seek pleasant surroundings."

The summer of 1954 also saw a pudgy novice named Mark Powell arrive in the Valley. The overweight newcomer was introduced to climbing on Lower Cathedral Spire, where he climbed poorly, thrashing his way up the rock. His partner Jerry Gallwas concluded that Powell would never amount to anything in the climbing world. But after this inauspicious beginning Powell went on a strict diet and approached rock climbing with a new intensity. He would soon dramatically disprove Gallwas' prediction.

By this time climbers were beginning to get serious about a route on the sweeping northwest face of Half Dome. Campfire discussions often revolved around where the route should go and who would accomplish it. Most climbers agreed that the route should ascend the broken left side of the face to about midheight, and then traverse right for several hundred feet to a prominent flake system. This traverse looked difficult and fiercely exposed. To top it all off, the uppermost part of the route was capped by an ominous roof—the

Visor—which added even more to the uncertainty of this intimidating climb.

For the local climbers, however, the foreboding appearance of the wall was tempered by its haunting attraction. Since the time of the Ahwahneechees, Half Dome has commanded a special place in the souls of all who see it. This remarkable formation, seemingly cleaved in two by the mighty hands of the mountain gods, soars so high above the peaceful repose of Mirror Meadow that it almost appears to be a part of the sky. The Ahwahneechees believed that it embodied the spirit of the Indian maiden Tis-sa-ack, and that the black streaks upon the northwest face were her tears of sorrow as she anguished for her lost husband. At times the great rock does seem alive, as in winter when huge slabs of ice detach from the wall and explode onto the boulders below in a thundering roar. And in the evening, bathed in the ethereal light of alpenglow, the great rock appears as an immense beacon of stone which calls out to its faithful disciples. Although the northwest face seemed to have weaknesses, climbers were still humbled by it. Could this magnificent granite sculpture really be climbed?

Hoping to answer some of these troubling questions, three climbers stepped forward to make a reconnaissance of the route. In 1954, Dick Long, Jim Wilson, and George Mandatory ascended just 200 feet of the 2000-foot face. They reported that the climbing was slow, strenuous, and very difficult.

In spite of this account, a strong four-man team decided to attempt the route in 1955. The first two members were Robbins and Harding. They had initially met and climbed together at Tahquitz. "I remember that well," Robbins recalled. "We were doing a short new route; he nailed up one pitch and belayed in a sort of alcove. When I got there I found he was sitting in slings hanging off two pitons: an angle driven in low down, and a wafer-thin pin driven straight up. Just as I arrived the angle came out, leaving us both hanging from this one little piton. . . . I remember it well though, because that was just the sort of thing that none of our group would have done. We were very careful, and always had quite a lot of pitons at stances. Harding must have been made of different stuff or something." Robbins' Sentinel companions, Jerry Gallwas and Don Wilson, rounded out the team.

The climbers pushed the route 450 feet up the northwest face in three days of climbing. As on the earlier probe, progress was slow. "I spent a whole afternoon just doing one pitch," Robbins noted. Despite the pace, he and Harding were eager to continue. However, the other two members, whom Robbins described as "more balanced individuals," were not as determined. So the climbers descended, and Robbins and Harding agreed to return the next year.

This next Half Dome attempt never materialized. The most noteworthy activity during 1956 was the stellar efforts of the new Mark Powell. Since his fiasco on Lower Cathedral Spire he had lost weight, left college, and dedicated himself totally to climbing. Like John Muir, Yosemite's original climbing bum, Powell climbed intensively and put up many excellent routes. Among his first ascents were *Arrowhead Arete* (III 5.8), the *East Buttress* of Lower Cathedral Rock (IV 5.8 A3), the *Powell-Reed* route on Middle Cathedral Rock (IV 5.8 A3), and the *South Face* of North Dome (III 5.7). He

also teamed up with Robbins and Joe Fitschen on a difficult new line up the South Face of Liberty Cap (IV 5.8 A3). During a frenetic span of one and a half years, Powell established 15 new routes. On all of these ascents he pushed the free climbing to remarkable limits and boldly aided scary cracks. In addition to his ability, Powell's style of ascending hard routes without reconnaissance or rehearsal was also widely admired. In contrast to Gallwas' earlier prediction, Powell was a dominating force on the Yosemite climbing scene during the mid 1950s.

In the summer of 1957 an extraordinary series of events began to unfold. The fortuitous coincidence of the right people being in the right place at the right time was about to produce a series of stunning advances in Yosemite climbing. And the two old friends from Tahquitz, Royal Robbins and Warren Harding, would play crucial roles in this exciting new age.

Half Dome: Northwest Face

In June 1957 Robbins prepared for another attempt on Half Dome. Throughout the previous months he and his partners, Jerry Gallwas and Mike Sherrick, had been quietly preparing for this historic contest. "We thought about the climb a lot," Robbins said. "We pictured ourselves on the route again and again. We resolutely worked on our technique, strength, and stamina. I especially wanted to get back on those first 400 feet, and defeat my weakness from the previous attempt."

The climbers met in the Valley and readied their provisions and climbing gear: food for the next several days, 13½ quarts of water, 45 pitons, 25 bolts, and 1200 feet of rope. Accompanied by Wayne Merry, they carried their loads to the base of the great northwest face. Staring up at the somber gray wall, each man mentally prepared for the unknown rigors they would surely encounter.

Although Half Dome was clearly the next logical step for Robbins after Sentinel's north face, it had taken four years for him to feel ready for this attempt. The delay was due to two primeval emotions. "One was fear and the other was dread," he explained. "First of all, we feared the enormity of the wall—we were awestruck by it—and we were very aware that no one had ever ventured onto a wall so steep and so vast. And also we dreaded the contest. We dreaded what it would take to get up this rock. We dreaded having to reach so

deeply within ourselves, and maybe finding ourselves lacking."

In spite of their misgivings, the climbers started up the wall on June 24. They ascended strenuous direct-aid cracks all day before reaching a bivouac ledge at the 500-foot level. Easier climbing the following day allowed them to gain another 400 feet by early afternoon.

They were now at the point where a rightward traverse was necessary to reach the upper flake system. Robbins found some easy ledges which led up and right. Above the uppermost ledge a small crack rose for about 35 feet and then ended in a blank wall. He and Gallwas placed seven bolts on this blank section. A pendulum traverse, longer than any yet tried in Yosemite, was then

The 1957 route on the northwest face of Half Dome

needed to reach cracks 40 feet to the
right. After several tries Robbins completed the exposed pendulum, fixed a
rope across for his companions, and
then returned to their ledge just before
dark. The crucial Robbins Traverse
now opened the way to the upper part
of the route.

The next day they moved across
the traverse, carefully leaving a rope
in place. Sherrick noted that the purpose of this fixed line was to "facilitate
a retreat across the traverse if one
proved necessary." The Half Dome
team wished to avoid the fate that had
befallen four European climbers during a 1936 attempt on the Eiger's north
face. The Europeans were trying desperately to descend during a storm but
could not get back across the notorious
Hinterstoisser Traverse. All four eventually perished. Ever since this tragedy,
climbers have been wary of lengthy
traverses and have sought to keep open
their line of retreat.

After crossing the traverse, the climbers came to grips with the upper flake
system. "Some of these flakes were huge
in size," Sherrick recalled, "and either
leaned against the rock leaving a crack,
or were separated from the wall forming
a chimney." These flakes and chimneys
shot upward for about 450 feet. Much
of the climbing was strenuous free
climbing with sections of direct aid.
One particular section, consisting of a
large block sticking out of the chimney,
left a lasting impression. Robbins led
this committing 5.9 pitch by grasping
underneath the block using classic
undercling technique. He then shuf-
fled or walked along the bottom of the
block and up around its lip to a belay
stance. Shortly after this Undercling
Pitch the climbers settled down to a
cramped bivouac near the top of the
flake system.

Approaching the summit overhang near the top of
the Northwest Face

The next day, their fourth on the
wall, proved to be the toughest. "By
this time," Sherrick wrote, "lack of
sufficient water, food, and sleep, plus
the enervating hot sun rays had fa-
tigued us. With Jerry doing most of
the leading, we climbed only 300 feet."
The team moved slowly up the steep
cracks, known as the Zigzags, before
nightfall. Now just a few hundred feet
from the top, the comforting thought
of completing the route made their
uncomfortable bivouac a little more
bearable.

In the morning Gallwas continued
up to the end of the Zigzags. To his
surprise and relief, a narrow ledge shot
straight left for about 50 feet. This
amazing ledge, which they named

Thank God Ledge, allowed the climbers to escape around the left side of the horrendous summit roof. To move across this ledge required the climbers to first walk, then crawl, and then hang by their fingertips. While performing the spectacular crossing, even these experienced climbers could not fail to notice the ferocious void beneath them—a drop of nearly 5000 feet into Tenaya Canyon. This memorable section would become one of the truly classic pitches in Yosemite.

Above the ledge, a tiny crack required some tricky piton placements and four bolts. The difficulties then eased, allowing the exhausted team to reach the summit before dark. The dirty, thirsty climbers had accomplished the longest and most demanding rock climb in North America (VI 5.8 A3).

They were greeted on top by Warren Harding. He had also hoped to make the first ascent of the northwest face, accompanied by Mark Powell and Bill Feuerer. But they arrived in Yosemite to find the Robbins-Gallwas-Sherrick ascent already in progress. In spite of his disappointment, Harding graciously hiked to the summit and congratulated the successful team.

But on his return to the Valley, Harding's disappointment continued to grow. "Well, shit," he thought as he moped around the Valley. "We're here with all this gear—might as well climb something! There certainly were plenty of attractive new routes to be done, but everything else seemed to represent some sort of 'put down' compared to Half Dome. All but one, that is . . . "

El Capitan: The Nose

Standing at the western gateway to Yosemite Valley, El Capitan is the park's most imposing cliff. John Muir described it as "unrivaled in height and breadth and flawless strength." Magnificently sculptured from El Capitan and Taft granite, the immense size of the cliff was hard to comprehend. If, as Muir suggested, Yosemite Valley was the inner sanctum of the Sierra— the holy of holys—then El Capitan was surely the range's most sacred altar.

Allen Steck's 1953 route on the East Buttress, at the far right-hand margin of the cliff, was still the only line up the rock. But the towering south buttress— The Nose of El Capitan—rose in a single menacing sweep 3000 feet from the forest floor to the summit. The huge cliff appeared to be guarded by an endless array of formidable obstacles: numerous roofs, blank rock, disconnected cracks, and an unrelenting angle. Being 1000 feet longer than Half Dome's northwest face, the south buttress of El Capitan had always been beyond the scope of climbers. "We didn't think it was worth looking at," Steck said. "We were just intimidated by it! We never thought of even going up to test it!" But for Harding, an ascent of The Nose was the only possible response to Robbins' Half Dome climb. Accompanied by Mark Powell and Bill Feuerer, Harding formulated an audacious plan to ascend El Capitan.

Since "The Captain" was so big and so sheer, it seemed that progress would be painfully slow. Much of the route looked to require tedious direct aid, and the ascent would probably take many days. As a result, the climbers decided to adopt a new strategy. They would ascend the rock in phases and establish a series of camps. Each camp would be connected to the others by fixed ropes. The climbers would periodically return to the ground on the

Warren Harding (left) and Mark Powell on The Nose

aid, and about as difficult as can be imagined."

They established Camp One on Sickle Ledge and continued on. After completing two wild pendulums to the right, they spent the next four days methodically moving up a prominent crack system. But the crack was so wide that only four of their pitons could span its width. These special pitons were forged from the legs of an old stove which they had scrounged from the Berkeley city dump. To ascend Stove-leg Crack required the leader to leap-frog gear by placing the four special pitons in a row, descending from the highest piton to remove the lower three, and then continuing above by renail-ing these three pitons. This nerve-wracking and scary procedure had to be repeated many times. After reaching the 1000-foot level, the climbers finally succumbed to fatigue and battered equipment. They returned to the ground, leaving their ropes in place.

Back on the Valley floor they were confronted with an unforeseen prob-lem. "It seemed that our climbing presented quite a spectacle," Harding recalled, "and had attracted a crowd of tourists which created a traffic jam at the road-junction near the base. The park rangers were understandably distressed and we had to agree to stay off the rock during the tourist season, between Memorial Day and Labor Day. This meant that we would be climbing with shorter days and less certain weather. Difficulties of the El Capitan ascent were not confined to the rock!" In order to replace some worn ropes, the rangers allowed Harding and Feuerer, accompanied by Wally Reed and Allen Steck, to make a short foray back up the rock about a week later. The climbers replaced their ropes,

fixed ropes to replenish supplies. This "siege climbing" method would be a sig-nificant departure from the style used on ascents such as Lost Arrow Chim-ney, the Steck-Salathe on Sentinel Rock, and the Northwest Face of Half Dome, where climbers reached the sum-mit in a single push. But even Harding himself could never have imagined how long the project would eventually last.

On July 4, 1957, just six days after Robbins' success on Half Dome, Har-ding began nailing up El Capitan. He had no intention of reaching the summit on this first attempt. The immediate goal was El Cap Towers, a large series of ledges about halfway up the face. After three days the team reached Sickle Ledge at the 500-foot level. Harding described the climbing as "almost entirely 6th class, direct

reached Dolt Tower at the 1200-foot level, and then came down.

Then in September a number of setbacks occurred. First, Powell suffered a serious ankle injury on an easy climb. Then the weather took a turn for the worse, varying from unpleasant to atrocious. Little progress was made during the autumn and winter. In the spring of 1958 the climbers returned to El Cap and ascended their ropes to Dolt Tower. Feuerer, who was known as the Dolt for his memorable blunders, introduced the two-wheeled Dolt Cart at this point. It was designed to ease the job of hauling supplies up the rock, but it always seemed to flip over and make the hauling even worse.

During May the team climbed three pitches above Dolt Tower to the fine ledge atop El Cap Towers. They then followed an unprotected chimney to the top of Texas Flake, and went to work on a series of bolts which allowed access to the tiny perch atop Boot Flake. From there, the leader was lowered about 60 feet on the rope, and then he began a spectacular double-pendulum to the left. It was the longest and most committing pendulum that Valley climbers had ever tried. Known as the King Swing, this wild traverse brought the climbers to a crack system leading higher. Several pitches above, threading carefully through some loose sections of diorite, they established Camp Four on comfortable ledges.

Although pleased to have good ledges to work from, the climbers silently worried about a huge overhang called the Great Roof which loomed above their heads. They also had to endure nightly invasions of rats that raided their food supplies and chewed their equipment. These amazing rodents somehow managed to scurry up and down the cliff's

Mark Powell working on the bolt ladder leading from Texas Flake to Book Flake

vertical cracks. In the ensuing days, the climbers pushed the route higher, to the 2000-foot level and then returned to the ground.

But tensions associated with this lengthy endeavor, which had been silently brewing for several months, began to split the team apart. Powell was still hobbled by his injury and felt less a part of the effort, and Feuerer also became increasingly disenchanted. Both members soon left the team. Although little progress was made during the summer, Harding would not give up. "I continued with whatever 'qualified' climbers I could 'con' into this rather uncompromising venture," he recalled.

In October, Harding was back on the rock with a new team composed of Wayne Merry, George Whitmore, and

Rich Calderwood. "By this time *The Nose* had really gotten to me," Harding noted. "This thing had completely dominated my life for over a year. I was having trouble getting off from work and, what with fear that a rival party would move in and the uncertainties of the climb itself, I was rather frazzled." In addition, the chief ranger, weary of the constant commotion and traffic delays, ordered the climbers to finish the climb by Thanksgiving or abandon the project. Harding wrote that he "never understood how this was to have been enforced. But it didn't matter; we were all determined to reach the summit before winter."

On November 1 they started up the familiar fixed ropes for what they hoped would be the last time. Above their high point they attacked the long-dreaded Great Roof. This spectacular pitch, while incredibly exposed, turned out to be much easier than expected. As one day faded into the next they slowly continued on through the upper dihedral. The sweeping walls of El Capitan converged here into a stunning corner, creating the illusion of climbing inside an exquisite diamond. They discovered two excellent ledges, which would form Camp Five and Camp Six, and doggedly climbed upward.

Finally, after nine days of climbing, Harding and Merry were only 200 feet from the top. Whitmore was below at Camp Four, and Calderwood had retreated to the ground with "an attack of nerves." The two lead climbers figured they could finish the climb the following day. "We liked the thought, anyway," Harding recalled. "We were getting just a little tired of the whole thing."

As they started up the next day, encouraging shouts from friends on the rim bolstered their spirits. By 4 P.M. they reached the last obstacle on the route, but what an obstacle it was: a blank, 50-foot, overhanging wall. Determined to finally complete this drawn-out affair, Harding decided to go for the top—even if he had to climb all night. Strapping on a headlamp, he began one of the most infamous leads in Yosemite climbing history. The tale of Harding hanging in slings for 14 hours, 3000 feet above the Valley, and drilling 28 bolts in a row at night would be retold around campfires for years to come.

At six the next morning, a feeble Warren Harding staggered onto the summit of El Capitan. The ascent, which required 45 days spread over 18 months, was finally complete (VI 5.8 A3). Although he had succeeded on this overwhelming wall, Harding felt that it was not completely clear "who was the conqueror and who was conquered: I do recall that El Cap seemed to be in much better condition than I was."

Like the 1957 ascent of Half Dome, Harding's climb up The Nose would revolutionize how climbers looked at big walls. "Harding was definitely the person for El Cap," said Royal Robbins. "He was cut to the mold for that climb because he was the only one with the burning desire, the savage determination, and the inner toughness to go do it and stick with it."

Harding's ascent represented a major breakthrough in Yosemite rock climbing. The psychological barrier of El Capitan had finally been overcome. The Golden Age of Yosemite big wall climbing was now well underway.

Fairview Dome: North Face

The ascent of El Capitan was not the only significant Yosemite climb in 1958. Another important route was established in a different part of the park. This climb symbolized the opening of an outstanding new climbing area—one of the most beautiful and most enjoyable rock-climbing areas in North America. To experience this area, climbers had only to travel a short distance northeast from the Valley— to Tuolumne Meadows.

Although the Meadows were popular with hikers and mountaineers, few rock climbers had noticed Tuolumne's exceptional landscape. A myopic concentration on Yosemite Valley had caused most climbers to ignore the region's excellent rock, superb scenery, and comfortable summer weather. As a result, this outstanding vertical wonderland, in many places just moments from the main highway, still waited to be explored. The plentiful menu included clean face climbs and challenging crack systems, on some of the most spectacular granitic domes in the world.

One climber who did recognize Tuolumne's potential was Wally Reed, a top-notch climber who had participated in the first ascents of several Yosemite classics. But Reed's modesty and shyness resulted in his seldom receiving proper credit for his accomplishments. Quietly exploring the high country for climbing possibilities, he was quickly drawn to the aesthetic north face of Fairview Dome.

Rising 900 feet above the fragrant pine forest, Fairview's north face is the biggest wall in the area. Reed noticed a conspicuous crack system near the center of the face. It appeared to ascend for about 300 feet and end near a huge crescent-shaped ledge. The crack did not look too difficult, and the rock higher up looked even easier. The longest route in the region seemed to be surprisingly straightforward.

In the early summer Reed invited a young climber named Chuck Pratt to join him on Fairview. Reed had heard that this young newcomer was blessed with an incredible amount of natural talent, and was an up-and-coming star on the Yosemite climbing scene. Although Pratt had not seen the proposed route, he was excited to be considered for a first ascent. He accepted the offer without hesitation. The talented climbers, filled with anticipation, headed for Tuolumne.

As they started up the route, they found that the lower section involved some difficult climbing. Pratt described this part of the route as "predominantly sixth class, requiring careful piton work in thin and frequently bottomed cracks." Reed was repeatedly entertained as the 19-year-old Pratt, still learning the intricacies of climbing, fumbled with his aid slings. The setting sun found them 400 feet up the route. With the difficulties of the climb better understood, they descended with confidence that their next attempt would finish the route.

In August the pair returned to the climb. They progressed beyond their previous high point and reached Crescent Ledge in the evening. After passing a brisk moonlit night on the ledge, the climbers continued on. As they moved higher a myriad of sparkling knobs began to appear. These glorious protrusions, characteristic of the Cathedral Peak granodiorite, consisted of unusually large feldspar crystals. The huge protruding crystals allowed the high-angle face to be climbed with relative ease. In addition to Tuolumne's other features, these knobs would soon become fabled in the rock-climbing community.

Higher up, the difficulties of the

climb continued to decrease. A spectacular four-foot roof was easily surmounted, thanks to some hidden handholds. Then they discovered that the upper part of the dome was broken into broad ledges and ramps, permitting them to quickly gain height. Before they knew it the climbers were on the summit (III 5.8 A2). A majestic panorama of peaks and domes greeted them. It was a scene, and an experience, that neither would soon forget.

From this simple beginning, climbing activity in the high country began to blossom. The numerous cliffs and domes near Tuolumne soon received the attention and appreciation they deserved. The future would be very bright for this special part of Yosemite.

The future would also be bright for Wally Reed and Chuck Pratt. Reed quietly pioneered other quality routes in the Valley and throughout the high country. And Pratt soon mastered the vertical world to an astonishing degree. In the coming years he participated in some of Yosemite's boldest climbs and greatest adventures.

As the 1959 climbing season opened, Pratt was again at work on a major new route, this time in the Valley. He teamed up with Bob Kamps and Steve Roper to establish a difficult line, the *North Face* of Middle Cathedral Rock (V 5.9 A4). One month later, in July, Pratt accompanied Warren Harding and Glen Denny on an ascent of the *East Face* of Washington Column (V 5.9 A4). Harding again used siege tactics on this intimidating wall, placing fixed ropes from bottom to top. The route was completed after several tries. Then in September Harding, Denny, and Herb Swedlund finished a ten-pitch climb on the broad *Southwest Face* of Mt. Conness (V 5.9 A3). The route had

been attempted earlier by a group of Bay Area climbers. But that attempt ended in tragedy when Don Goodrich was hit by a huge rock on the second pitch and died. Harding's attraction for the high country would later lead him to complete another elegant route— the striking *East Face* of Keeler Needle (V 5.9 A3).

Certainly the wackiest ascent to be completed that year was one by Yosemite veterans Chuck Wilts and Mike Sherrick. Heading south from the park, their objective was to ascend one of California's most recognized landmarks—the Matterhorn at Disneyland. The Yosemite pair were invited to make the unique "first ascent" of this artificial mountain as part of the attraction's opening ceremonies. Near the top of the climb, Sherrick took a staged fall to entertain the audience, which included Richard Nixon, Vice President at the time.

One of the most innovative ascents of this period occurred on a little-known formation in Merced Canyon. Although it tended to blend in with the forest, Kat Pinnacle had attracted the attention of climbers for many years. William Kat had originally hoped to make the first ascent of the small spire in the late 1930s by using a very unusual strategy: attaching a rope to the tail of a kite, flying the kite over the summit of the pinnacle, anchoring both ends of the rope to the ground (with the middle of the rope stretching over the spire's summit), and then climbing the rope to the top of the pinnacle. Kat's grandiose scheme never succeeded. He was beaten to the summit by Dewitt Allen, Torcom Bedayan, and Robin Hansen, who attained the top in 1940 via a tyrolean traverse.

Yet the overhanging southwest corner of Kat Pinnacle remained untouched.

A series of extremely thin cracks looked like an interesting aid climb, and it was these cracks that attracted Yvon Chouinard and Tom Frost in early 1960. The two young climbers both had a talent for designing new gear to meet a specific need—Frost was a technical whiz who studied engineering at Stanford, and Chouinard knew the crucial details of metalworking. They had previously tinkered with a new type of piton, about the size of a postage stamp and having a super thin tip. The new pegs seemed perfect for the incipient seams on Kat Pinnacle.

But when they first tried the new pitons, they quickly discovered a subtle flaw in the design. "We got up to where the crack thins and started to put in these new pins," said Frost. "But on the very first swing of the hammer, they shattered into a million pieces like they were made of glass! They just disintegrated! So we cleverly deduced that they were a bit too brittle."

The pair went home and made a new batch of pitons out of chrome-moly, which resulted in a product that was still very strong but not as brittle. The innovative piton required an equally innovative name, which Chouinard would quickly provide. Frost recalled, "Yvon came up to me and said, 'Do you know what this is? This is a Realized Ultimate Reality Piton!' And I said, 'Well yeah, OK. Of course it is!' "

When they returned to Kat Pinnacle, the magic "rurps" did the trick. The pair nailed over the A4 crux and established a new level in Yosemite climbing. Like John Salathé's high-strength steel pitons and Chuck Wilts' amazing knifeblades, the diminutive rurp would open a significant new frontier in direct-aid climbing.

Soon after, Chouinard and Frost applied their new expertise in a big way. In 2½ days they pioneered an impressive route up the magnificent *West Face* of Sentinel Rock (VI 5.9 A4). This route would come to be regarded as a classic Yosemite big wall due to its clean rock and sustained difficulties. "The climbing ranged from difficult to some of the most extreme climbing that we have ever done," Chouinard recalled. "Two pitches stand out especially: one was a traverse which involved putting in pitons straight up under a 35-foot long, very thin flake; the second man had to repiton the pitch as most of the pitons had fallen out because the crack between the flake and the rock had expanded. On the other pitch, Frost made the finest lead I have ever seen up an 80-foot long, 8-inch-wide jam

Yvon Chouinard, here belayed by Royal Robbins, leads the scary Dogleg Pitch on the west face of Sentinel Rock

crack with only a wooden block for protection."

Following this climb, Chouinard shifted his focus to the Cathedral Rocks. Accompanied by Chuck Pratt and Bob Kamps, he first climbed the sinister *North Face* of Higher Cathedral Rock (V 5.9 A4), and then the *Chouinard-Pratt* route on Middle Cathedral Rock (V 5.8 A3).

He also became more serious about designing new climbing hardware, even though his finances were always limited. "Yvon only worked about two months a year," said TM Herbert. "The rest of the time he'd be off climbing. He'd clean some old woman's garage once in a while to get a few dollars, but that was about it. He'd buy old second-hand gear, and wear old shoes stuffed with paper in them because they were too big. That's the way he lived! He just existed! We thought he'd either starve to death or be a hobo for the rest of his life." But the wheels in Chouinard's mind were always turning, thinking of new climbing gear. Frost noted, "Half the time he'd go down to the beach, throw his anvil down on the sand, and make pitons until the waves got good enough to surf."

Royal Robbins also re-emerged in 1960. For the previous several years he had been serving his military obligation at the Army's Fort Bliss in Texas. He'd been able to manage only cameo appearances in the Valley when he could forge a weekend pass and hop a military transport plane to California. It was like the good old days of riding the freight trains around Southern California. Finally, freed from military service, Robbins returned to the Valley full-time and climbed with a new intensity. "My passion was climbing," he explained. "I didn't know or care where money would come from. I didn't know about old

Royal Robbins sorting gear prior to the first continuous ascent of The Nose

age, or retirement, or family. But I had this conviction that everything would fall into place if I devoted myself to the central principle of climbing."

In June 1960 Robbins put up the desperate *Arches Direct* (VI 5.9 A5) with Joe Fitschen. Robbins recalled that they were simply hoping to establish "what we thought would be an enjoyable, classic, two-day, sixth-class route." Instead he found himself battling "the most formidable direct-aid problem" he had ever encountered. On the crux pitch Robbins took several falls, one a 50-footer, during the ten-hour lead. This was for a time the hardest aid climb in the Valley.

That same summer Robbins also accomplished the most severe free climb in Yosemite. The *East Chimney* of Rixon's Pinnacle had been originally climbed by Don Goodrich and Dick McCracken four years earlier. The chimney's first pitch, consisting of a slippery, overhanging corner, had always required several points of aid to ascend. But Robbins led the pitch completely free, thus completing the first 5.10 pitch in Yosemite.

With these arduous ascents behind him, Robbins became even more interested in The Nose of El Capitan. He was keenly aware that it had yet to receive a second ascent. Chouinard and Frost had climbed the first few pitches using rurps instead of bolts, but they went no farther. Robbins decided to answer El Cap's seductive call by climbing it in a single push without fixed ropes. He invited Frost, Pratt, and Fitschen to join him.

At the time, few others would have considered such a daring attempt. "A lot of experienced climbers felt that you'd perish if you went up there self-contained," Frost recalled. "That was the mentality back then because it had never been done. And for me, I remembered all too well going to Kat Pinnacle and getting totally thrashed nailing just 90 feet! We probably drank a gallon of water, and we still felt about ready to perish from the heat and fatigue! So now, how were we going to climb a rock not 90 feet high, but 3000 feet high?!"

After much preparation, the four climbers started up El Capitan in September. They divided themselves into two two-man teams. One team did all the climbing on a given day while the other team wrestled with their considerable mass of gear and supplies: seven 150-foot climbing ropes, two 150-foot haul lines, 67 carabiners, 100 pitons, several wide "bong-bong" pitons made by Frost, and 60 quarts of water, all stuffed into four huge duffel bags. They estimated that the climb would require about ten days. This time would be much faster than Harding's first ascent. But the second-ascent team

had a huge advantage because they knew which cracks systems to follow on the route, and all the necessary bolts were already in the rock. The four climbers, however, were surprised that they were able to reach the summit even quicker than estimated, in only seven days.

This important ascent reinforced their notion that fixed ropes and siege tactics were no longer needed on El Capitan. "The day will probably come when this climb will be done in five days, perhaps less," Robbins declared. He also thought that some "younger generation" would someday climb a route on El Cap's beautiful southwest face. This towering wall, one of the most attractive in the Valley, would obviously present a great challenge. Surprisingly, the future came a lot quicker than Robbins ever imagined.

El Capitan: Salathé Wall

By September 1961 Robbins found that he and his friends were that "younger generation." The strong trio of Frost, Pratt, and Robbins prepared to embark on one of the great endeavors in Yosemite climbing. They delineated a circuitous route which seemed to link up the major weaknesses of the southwest face. The route would begin just left of The Nose and ascend prominent cracks to Mammoth Terraces, 1000 feet above the ground. From there they would rappel 150 feet down and left to Heart Ledge, and then attempt to traverse left several hundred feet before heading for the summit.

They also decided to use fixed ropes only on the lower third of the route. Robbins noted that they "wished to avoid [siege] methods if possible so as to keep the element of adventure high with at least a moderate amount of uncertainty. It was perfectly clear to us that given sufficient time, fixed ropes, bolts, and determination, any section of any rock wall could be climbed." The route was dubbed the Salathé Wall in honor of big wall pioneer John Salathé.

While Pratt left the Valley to gather some last-minute supplies, Robbins and Frost began the initial phase of the climb. A series of cracks led them up to a large blank area at the 500-foot level. Robbins kept the number of bolts on this section to only 13 through some "enterprising free climbing . . . and some nerve-wracking piton work." He found this delicate pitch to be "one of the most interesting on the route." After 3½ days they reached Mammoth Terraces, rappelled to Heart Ledge, and then descended to the ground. Their

ropes were left in place up to Heart Ledge.

On September 19, with supplies and hardware replenished, the three climbers prusiked up their ropes. From their high point they dropped the fixed ropes to the ground, thus severing their umbilical. Above them rose 2000 feet of unexplored rock. A retreat from here would be very tenuous. Never before had El Capitan been climbed in such a bold style.

Several tricky traverses were completed above Heart Ledge. Then they moved up a series of cracks to the left of a huge depression called the Heart. Much of the climbing in this section was direct aid. But one particular feature required some terrifying free climbing. A large flake (the Ear) jutted out

Royal Robbins climbing delicate friction below the Half Dollar, Salathé Wall

from the wall and seemed to block their upward progress. They spent several frustrating hours looking for some way to avoid this obstacle which Robbins described as a "frightening formation." But when no alternative could be found, they were eventually forced to climb it. "This involved using chimney technique to move 30 feet horizontally behind the flake, with the bottom of the flake yawning abruptly into space—an unnerving procedure," Robbins recalled.

Higher up they discovered the surprisingly flat surface atop El Cap Spire, one of the most spectacular ledges in the Valley. The next several days were spent pushing the route up through a vertical maze. Squeeze chimneys, thin cracks, hanging belays, and awkward pendulums appeared one after another. They had no way of knowing what the wall would confront them with—they had only each other to rely on. "In those days," Frost remarked, "we were truly frightened of these climbs!"

At about the 2500-foot level they came to a huge tiered overhang called the Roof that shot out completely perpendicular from the cliff. From the ground it had seemed unlikely that they could directly attack this daunting feature. But Frost gingerly nailed tiny seams leading up and right without hesitation, despite the wild exposure of hanging backwards above half a mile of air.

When he finally turned the Roof, Frost found himself looking up at a 200-foot, overhanging wall. A single, shallow, winding crack split the intimidating Headwall, and it was this crack that allowed the team to slowly make their way through the unrelenting terrain above. As they stood in slings, methodically placing pitons, while

Royal Robbins atop El Cap Spire

constantly being pushed out into space by the overhanging rock, the team found the Headwall to be an unforgettable place.

Robbins recalled one memorable section: "There was one point when I was hanging from two pitons on the wall. Chuck had just cleaned the pitch and was above me. They fixed the lines for me, and I got my prusik knots fixed. I was so frightened that I tied a big knot in the end of the rope as well. Finally, I let myself out on the end of the rope for about eight feet; I thought that that would be about right, so I let the rope slip through the piton. But it had been holding me in so much that I swung 20 feet out from the wall—2500 feet above the ground. I had a good

Chuck Pratt (below) and Royal Robbins survey the route above from the top of El Cap Spire

eer Emilio Comici once said, "Where the drop of water falls from the summit—that is the line I wish to climb." But the Salathé Wall has a splendor of a different type. Its beauty lies in its serpentine path—an elegant and challenging route up a magnificent rock wall, established without siege tactics, and with just 13 bolts. The rock is of outstanding quality, and a wide variety of climbing techniques are required throughout the 35 pitches: crack climbing, face climbing, chimneys, roofs, off-widths, sling belays, and overhanging aid. The route is continually challenging and the scenery is always magnificent.

These are among the reasons that the Salathé Wall, over 30 years after its first ascent, is still today often called the greatest rock climb in the world.

Although the ascent of the Salathé Wall was a milestone in big wall climbing, 1961 also witnessed another important development in free climbing. Less than a month after struggling up El Capitan, Chuck Pratt became entranced by two formidable, 400-foot cracks on the western flank of Elephant Rock. The awkward, overhanging cracks looked as difficult as any he had yet climbed. But looks would be deceiving—they were harder! After several attempts Pratt succeeded in leading the route he called *Crack of Doom*. It was Yosemite's second 5.10 route. "Chuck was the gifted one," said Robbins. "He was the best climber of our generation. He climbed so gracefully that even when he fell, he looked graceful."

Meanwhile, Warren Harding was completing an improbable route on the unclimbed *West Face* of the Leaning Tower (V 5.5 A4). His partner Allen Macdonald described the West Face as bulging "sickeningly out into space,

rope and everything, but I was so afraid that I could barely suppress a shout of terror!"

On the afternoon of September 24 they had just one pitch to go. The obvious crack above them turned out to be one of the toughest problems on the route. Yet Pratt flowed through the tight, bottomless slot and the 5.9 crack above with his characteristic grace. Finally, after six days on the wall, and what Robbins described as "the most rewarding climbing we had ever done," the three men stood atop the *Salathé Wall* (VI 5.9 A4).

In relation to other climbing routes throughout the world, the Salathé Wall has a special allure. Some routes are attractive because they follow a direct path to the summit. Italian mountain-

overhanging the entire distance to the summit in one grand sweep." The extreme angle of the climb was indeed unbelievable, reaching 115 degrees in some places. Like his ascent of The Nose, Harding resorted to siege tactics and fixed ropes. And like the 125 bolts he drilled on El Cap, 110 bolts were put in on the Tower. Several attempts spread over about ten months were needed to reach the top.

This dramatic new route did not receive universal praise in the climbing community. Many felt that the earlier ascent of the Salathé Wall proved that huge walls could be climbed without siege techniques. But the general consensus never bothered Harding, since he held a "slightly irreverent attitude toward the rock climbing establishment." And he never worried about fitting in with the resident climbers. "Harding was different," noted Doug Robinson. "He had a Corvette, and while the leisure class was truffling in its boulder pile, he was holding down a job, making love to women in skirts, and driving in on weekends to work on his climbs." Harding had always been a free spirit, and once remarked that "the Leaning Tower was a face that I'd long wanted to do (as was The Nose on El Cap). So in my oversimplified manner, I just went ahead—whatever it took."

Feelings against siege climbing intensified after the 1962 siege of El Capitan's Dihedral Wall. Ed Cooper and Jim Baldwin, two climbers from the Pacific Northwest, took 38 days to complete the route, and used 1900 feet of fixed rope. Although Valley local Glen Denny also participated in the ascent, the climb was seen as a step backward in terms of style and adventure. And it didn't help that Cooper and Baldwin were from the Pacific Northwest. For

Chuck Pratt on the overhanging Headwall

as Steve Roper noted, "The Northwest had a reputation for producing highly conservative mountaineer types, people who climbed dreary volcanoes and rotten crags, people who actually believed in taking the 'Ten Essentials' with them. We could just see Cooper up on the wall plodding along gamely with his compass and flashlight and hard hat. (Harding's list of ten would probably have included wine and perhaps a copy of *Playboy*)."

A growing number of Valley climbers believed that aesthetic new lines, especially on El Capitan, should only be climbed in good style, without a lengthy siege. Royal Robbins explained, "We were annoyed that an outsider would come in, after we thought we put siege climbing to sleep, and forced this route up El Cap which we felt should have been done in the right style." *What* was climbed now became less important than *how* it was climbed.

Yvon Chouinard was also among those who felt this way. He was extremely busy in 1962, establishing three new routes in good style. These climbs remain some of the most popular in the Valley. He first put up the classic *Direct North Buttress* of Middle Cathedral Rock (V 5.8 A3) with Steve Roper. While bivouacked on the route, the climbers were awakened about midnight by heavy rainfall. "By dawn our down jackets and our spirits were waterlogged," Chouinard reported. Yet they managed to complete the climb, and eagerly returned to camp to see how much their soaked jackets weighed. Each coat weighed in at 7.5 pounds. A new record!

Then in August Chouinard and TM Herbert established the *Chouinard-Herbert* route on Sentinel Rock (V 5.8 A3), followed by the *North Face* of Quarter Dome (V 5.8 A3). Chouinard and Roper then hoped to cap their season by completing the prestigious second ascent (and first continuous ascent) of the Salathe Wall. But a badly worn haul bag, and the overwhelming nature of the wall, put an end to their attempt at Heart Ledge. "I was quite scared," Roper later admitted. "It's hard to imagine in 1962 how intimidating that wall was. First of all, physically overpowering, and second, the respect we had for Robbins—only Robbins had climbed this thing. Who were we to pretend we were in that league!" Robbins and Frost eventually made the first continuous ascent of the route later that year in four and a half days.

Roper returned to El Capitan in 1963, pushing a new route in the company of big-league climber Layton Kor. The hard-driving Kor was already well known for his many impressive ascents in Colorado and the Southwest, and he would soon be off to the infamous Eiger Direct. "He was just full of positive energy," said Jim Bridwell. "He was always going! He'd grab anybody to do a route, including me. Kor was a climbing animal. You'd think he was on speed the way he raced up one route after another! And he could tell the stupidest jokes, but you'd still be laughing your head off because of the way he told them, and the energy he had." Tom Frost recalled a typical Kor climbing trip: "He'd come storming into the Valley, do about five big walls in a row,

Climber on the Dihedral Wall

exhaust all of his climbing partners, and then leave. He didn't need any rest days. He didn't stop climbing until he ran out of partners!" Pat Ament once described Kor as "a rebel with a bit of a temper, supremely talented, fueled by sheer force, set off from other climbers by a light—an illumination or charisma—and by profound competence. . . . He loved to go out on a limb, to be cleansed and dirtied by the deep shade and undiscerning power of his singular, high asylums."

In 1963 Kor was applying his boundless energies to El Cap's *West Buttress*. During April he and Eric Beck climbed the first 700 feet of the route. He returned the next month with Roper to finish the climb in a three-day effort (VI 5.9 A3).

Royal Robbins was also blazing important new ground in 1963. He first soloed the West Face of the Leaning Tower in four stormy days. This was the first time a major Yosemite wall had been soloed. "It was a spontaneous thing," he explained. "The weather was bad at the time but I still wanted to climb something. I was aware that the Tower only had one ascent, so I thought why not? And approaching it alone, on a climb that you can't escape from by rappelling off, and people can't rescue you from above—that piqued my imagination. I had a vision that I could do it. And when you have those visions, you have to respond."

The ascent was a huge step forward, and a fitting testimony to Robbins' confidence and skill. But to those around him, Robbins was never lacking for confidence. Dave Rearick recalled the time that Robbins descended the northeast slabs on Half Dome without using the cables or a rope: "My heart was in my throat! . . . His fall line at certain points would have taken him off the

The Leaning Tower

south wall. There was no sitting or skidding along on his rump. I felt very nervous watching him. The rock that the earliest climbers had once thought unclimbable was being walked down. That was all Robbins. He had the confidence!"

In June Robbins became embroiled in one of Yosemite's earliest climbing controversies after his ascent of the *Direct Northwest Face* of Half Dome (VI 5.9 A5) with Dick McCracken. The controversy stemmed from the fact that Robbins and McCracken completed this route, which Ed Cooper and Galen Rowell had initially started. Cooper and Rowell initially climbed several pitches up the rock, placed a series of bolts across a blank section, and then descended leaving fixed ropes in place. Days later after Rowell completed a final exam at UC Berkeley, he and Cooper returned to find Robbins and McCracken high on the route. Rowell explained, "They went up in stormy weather during a brief period when Cooper and I had descended with a clear intent to complete the climb that was well known throughout the small climbing community. They made the first ascent in five continuous days, using the bolts I had placed for direct aid, and justifying their appropriation of the climb as a single, ground-up effort in better style, without the umbilical cord of the ropes we fixed on the lower face. This was one of the seminal events that led Warren Harding to coin the phrase 'Valley Christians' for climbers who put down others and plotted vindictive strategies to further their own agendas as true believers in a single, right way to climb rock walls."

Rowell was further incensed by the whole incident after he saw the disheartening effect that it had on Cooper. Rowell mourned that "Cooper was so devastated, that he gave up climbing for life on the spot and took an office job in Manhattan."

These series of events clearly showed that Yosemite climbing was no longer the simple, carefree pastime that had once been shared among a supportive group of close friends. A growing sense of competition began to surface, and would continue to surface increasingly in the future. Elegant routes in the Valley were now viewed as precious commodities, to be reaped only by those who showed themselves "worthy" of such rewards.

Despite the hard feelings created in June, Yosemite climbers also traveled extensively to exotic locations that summer. This continued a tradition begun years before. As early as 1954, a group of Valley climbers had left the familiar confines of the Sierra for the mighty Himalaya. Allen Steck, Fritz Lippmann, and William Dunmire went to Nepal that year, drawn by the strikingly beautiful peak Makalu (27,825 feet), the fifth highest mountain in the world. Dunmire joked that they were so eager and excited, they would gladly use equipment discarded by other climbers and even "live on oatmeal." Although the enthusiastic team did not reach the summit, they still enjoyed a marvelous adventure. Several years later, George Whitmore went to South America and soloed Tulparaju (16,752 feet) and climbed the North Peak of Huantsan (20,056 feet).

Yvon Chouinard was only too happy to continue the trend, establishing many new routes throughout the Teton Range and the Canadian Rockies. Royal Robbins had earlier caught the travel bug, pioneering a superb line in the Alps (the *American Direct* on the Petit Dru) with Gary Hemming. In 1963 he ventured to Canada's Cirque of the Unclimbables with Layton Kor, Jim McCarthy, and Dick McCracken to ascend the *Southeast Face* of Proboscis. He later returned to the French Alps with John Harlin, climbing another extremely sustained route on the Petit Dru.

Tom Frost was also busy in France, climbing the Aiguille du Fou and Mont Blanc's Hidden Pillar of Freney. Frost was also part of an international expedition to the Himalayan peak Kantega (22,340 feet), and would later climb Chacraraju, Palcaraju, and Huandoy Sur in the Andes. And Will Siri and Willi Unsoeld, partners on the original ascent of El Cap Tree, were reunited on the successful 1963 American Everest Expedition, which saw Unsoeld, Jim Whittaker, Tom Hornbein, Barry Bishop, and Lute Jerstad reach the top of the world via the South Col and the West Ridge. Although trained in California, Valley climbers showed themselves to be first-rate mountaineers in the great ranges of the world.

Meanwhile in Yosemite's high country, climbers continued to establish outstanding new routes. The driving force behind many of these climbs was Bob Kamps. Kamps had previously established some impressive big routes: *Camp 4 Terror* (V 5.8 A4), the *North Face* of Higher Cathedral Rock (V 5.9 A4), the *North Face* of Middle Cathedral Rock (V 5.9 A4), and the imposing *East Face* [the Diamond] on Longs Peak (V 5.7 A4) in Colorado. He also established an enjoyable route on the beautiful *Northwest Face* of Clouds Rest (IV 5.8).

After these routes he began to push his free climbing to the limit. With Wally Reed he made the first free ascent of Fairview Dome's *Inverted Staircase* (5.10b). He would later team up with an ambitious young climber named Tom Higgins to complete other difficult lines on Fairview—such as *Always Arches* (5.10) and *Lucky Streaks* (5.10b)— as well as numerous high-country routes that still remain popular: *The Way We Were* (5.9) and *Eunuch* (5.7) on Stately Pleasure Dome, *The Coming* (5.9) and *Chartres* (5.9) on Medlicott Dome, and *Rawl Drive* (5.9) on Lembert Dome.

Like many other climbers, Higgins felt that Tuolumne's quiet atmosphere and cooler temperatures created the perfect conditions for climbing. "Chuck Pratt is perhaps the sole exception," Higgins teased. "Some climbers contend that Chuck is so fond of hot weather that he has never seen snow and knows what ice looks like only because it comes with Cokes."

Besides Kamps and Higgins, Frank Sacherer was also on the move, in both the high country and the Valley. After an ascent of *Bishop's Balcony* (II 5.5 A3), a dramatic line that directly attacked a large roof, he dispensed with direct-aid paraphernalia and concentrated on free climbing. He first climbed the excellent *West Crack* on Daff Dome (5.9), and then embarked on a relentless crusade for hard free climbs. With partners of the caliber of Kamps, Pratt, Wally Reed, Chris Fredericks, Tom Gerughty, and Jim Bridwell, he compiled a stunning resume of free ascents in 1964: the upper section of *Reed's Pinnacle Direct* (5.10a), a one-day ascent of *Lost Arrow Chimney* (5.10a), the *Right Side of the Hourglass* (5.10a), the *Ahab* route on Moby Dick (5.10b), *Sacherer Cracker* on the Slack (5.10a), the *Southwest Face* of Half Dome (IV 5.10b), the *Northeast Buttress* of Higher Cathedral Rock (IV 5.10a), plus the *Sacherer-Fredericks* route (IV 5.10c) and *North Buttress* (V 5.10a) of Middle Cathedral Rock. The latter route was especially significant because few other routes at the time had as much 5.10 climbing on them as the North Buttress did. Although Robbins and Pratt introduced 5.10 to Yosemite, Sacherer consolidated and cemented the standard.

He and Eric Beck later shook up the locals by making an impressive one-day ascent of Sentinel's West Face. "Frank frequently accomplished what others thought impossible," recalled Jim Bridwell. "He had free-climbed routes that the best climbers of the day said couldn't be done free. He had climbed in a day routes they said could not be climbed in a day. In a word, Frank Sacherer was a visionary. The driving force of climbing in the 1960s, he did more to advance free climbing as we know it today than any other single person in America at that time."

Sacherer's drive and his amazing control in difficult circumstances were the envy of many climbers. Yvon Chouinard noted that Sacherer "had a unique technique that virtually eliminated even the tight situations. He always climbed on the verge of falling over backwards . . . and rarely bothered to stop and place protection."

"He was somewhat tormented and austere," added Bridwell, "almost like an ascetic. I remember one time I was in camp eating a bowl of oatmeal, and he came up to me and said, 'Did you go climbing today?' I said no. And he replied sternly, 'Well, then you shouldn't eat!' That was typical Sacherer. He was just totally crazed and possessed!"

Two major new walls were also completed in 1964. Both required new levels of commitment and tenacity. And both would catapult Americans into the forefront of the rock climbing world.

Mt. Watkins: South Face

Of the many striking formations at the eastern end of Yosemite Valley, the main big wall activity had usually focused on Half Dome. Although several impressive routes were established on Washington Column, it was the northwest face of Half Dome that still seemed to offer the biggest and most obvious challenge to climbers. But Warren Harding, always on the lookout for grand new projects, became increasingly interested in the south face of Mt. Watkins.

Named for the renowned landscape photographer Carleton Watkins, the broad summit of the mountain was rounded and unimpressive. However the south face soared 2800 feet above Tenaya Creek. The lowermost part of the face was broken into large ledges and ramps, while the upper section was clean, sheer, and ominous. This huge wall was completely unexplored. Harding had to try it.

Armed with a photo of the south face, Harding asked Chuck Pratt to join him. "In a moment of spontaneous rashness I heartily agreed," recalled Pratt, "and we enthusiastically shook hands, confident that the fate of Mt. Watkins had been sealed." Yvon Chouinard was also invited along, and the three climbers soon assembled their gear and set off.

On the approach to the route they met two young women, who inquired if Yosemite climbers really did scrape and chafe their hands on bare rock to allow them to ascend the Valley's walls. Pratt and the others "assured them that the preposterous myth was true." When Harding then described how they would live exclusively on beer and wine, "we left the incredulous young ladies wondering about the sanity and good judgment of Yosemite climbers. And so the legends grow."

Upon reaching the south face, the three climbers easily scrambled up the broken lower section. At the top of a large, tree-covered ledge, an 80-foot headwall presented the first obstacle. To avoid this blank section Chouinard completed a series of pendulums and reached a prominent dihedral system.

But even this early in the ascent it became apparent that the difficulties would not be limited to the climbing—the weather would also play a significant role. "It was the middle of July and temperatures in the Valley were consistently in the high 90s," Pratt recalled. "We had allowed ourselves one and a half quarts of water per day per person—the standard quantity for a sustained Yosemite climb. Still, we were not prepared for the intense, enervating heat in which we had found ourselves sweltering for

Looking up the South Face of Mt. Watkins

an entire day. Those mountaineers who scorn Yosemite and its lack of Alpine climbing would find an interesting education by spending a few days on a long Valley climb in midsummer. Cold temperatures and icy winds are not the only adverse kinds of weather."

Struggling against both the climb and the heat, the climbers continued up. "The climbing was both strenuous and difficult," Pratt described, "as we resorted more and more to thin horizontal pitons and knife-blades driven into the shallow, rotten cracks. However, our biggest problem continued to be the heat. We were relieved only occasionally from the unbearable temperatures by a slight breeze. Although we tried to refrain from drinking water during the day so as to have at least a full quart each to sip at night, we were all constantly digging into the climbing packs for water bottles. Even the hauling, which should have been a simple task, became a major problem. Yvon, who was hauling that day, exhausted himself on every pitch, becoming increasingly tired as the day wore on." That evening they discovered some huge ledges which they named the Sheraton-Watkins. They climbed a short distance higher, left a rope in place, and then settled down for the night at the "Sheraton."

On the third day a strenuous and committing traverse carried them into the center of the face. Although Harding had often been criticized in the past for his use of fixed ropes and siege tactics, on this ascent he and his partners were committed to a single push for the summit. The consequence of this sporty approach was that if anything went wrong, they were in big trouble because retreat became more and more difficult. "It was here that we began

to literally walk out on a limb," Pratt noted. "We could see the broken ramps leading across the face for several hundred feet. Once we left the dihedral, retreat would become increasingly more difficult. Not only would the route have to be possible, but we would have to consistently make the correct decision as to which route to follow." All day the drained climbers moved resolutely across the wall, repeatedly using rurps and knife-blades in the tiny cracks. Their progress was painfully slow. Still 700 feet from the top, their four-day supply of food and water was quickly running out.

By the afternoon of the fourth day they were in serious trouble. Pratt described the scene: "Warren had nearly fainted several times from the heat, Yvon was speechless with fatigue, and I was curled up in a semi-stupor trying to utilize a small patch of shade beneath an overhanging boulder. In an effort to provide more shade we stretched a bivouac hammock over our heads, but it provided little protection. For the first time we considered the possibility of retreating, but even that would require another day on the wall. It seemed that those very qualities which had made the climb so appealing might now prove to be our undoing." They managed to climb a little higher before collapsing for the night on some small ledges. By this time Chouinard had lost so much weight that he could lower his pants without undoing any buttons.

As the fifth day began, Chouinard and Pratt forced themselves upward. Harding, although suffering from intense thirst like the others, refused to take any water so the two lead climbers would have enough. Pratt called this sacrifice "a display of courage and discipline that I had rarely seen equaled." They continued higher through awkward jam-cracks, rotten chimneys, blank walls, and tiny rurp seams, while the relentless sun beat down on them.

Finally in the fading light of sunset, Chouinard completed the final pitch to the summit. In spite of the suffocating heat, lack of water, and constant uncertainty, the weary climbers completed the demanding route in impeccable style (VI 5.8 A4).

The rigors of the ascent had required every bit of their strength and determination. It would be a fitting highlight to any climbing season. But in a few short months, Pratt and Chouinard would

Yvon Chouinard ascends a fixed line far out in space on the North America Wall

again be hanging from another intimidating Yosemite wall. After sticking out their necks on Mt. Watkins, they would give new meaning to the phrase, "Out of the frying pan and into the fire!"

El Capitan: North America Wall

By the Fall of 1963 the southwestern side of El Capitan contained four great rock-climbing routes. All were demanding, multiday climbs on superb rock. In contrast, no routes had yet penetrated the somber dark rock on the southeast side. Given the wall's menacing appearance this was hardly surprising. To begin with, a large intrusion of loose diorite, forming a crude resemblance to North America, dominated the wall. Any route to the summit would surely encounter a considerable amount of dangerous, unstable rock. Huge roofs also punctuated the wall in several places, seeming to block any upward progress. Between these daunting roofs, several blank sections indicated that long, committing traverses would probably be needed. But what would a climber traverse to? The route was not at all obvious, and seemed to be characterized by discontinuous crack systems. As if these factors weren't enough of a challenge, the entire upper half of the wall was also overhanging. Retreat from high on the route would be virtually impossible, because if they tried to rappel, they would be left dangling in mid-air away from the rock. As a result, climbers were not exactly lining up to try the North America Wall.

But a huge, untouched wall on El Capitan was finally more than Royal Robbins could resist. "By this time things had gone so far that I was getting greedy," Robbins admitted. "I was anxious to get a certain wall before someone else did." So in October of 1963 he and Glen Denny made several probes of the route, reaching a high point of 600 feet. Robbins found the third pitch to be particularly difficult and sustained, consisting of a long A5 run of nested, tied-off pins.

In May 1964 Tom Frost joined the project and the team climbed 1200 feet up the wall to Big Sur Ledge. Having verified that the first half of the route was possible, they rappelled to the ground without leaving fixed ropes. Their next attempt in the autumn would be an all-out push for the summit. Robbins noted that they "wished

Royal Robbins searching for a way up the North America Wall

to do the North America Wall in as classical a style as possible. Siege climbing makes success certain, thus depriving alpinism of one of its most important elements: adventure!"

By October 1964 Robbins and Frost were back in the Valley. "We half expected, and half hoped, others would do the climb before we returned," said Robbins. "But when Tom and I arrived back in Yosemite the wall stood somber and still virgin—waiting." They decided that the formidable wall required a strong four-man team, so Chuck Pratt was invited to join. He had recuperated sufficiently from Mt. Watkins and felt ready for El Cap. When Glen Denny was unable to come, Yvon Chouinard took his place. Four of the strongest climbers ever to come out of Yosemite now confronted the most feared big wall in the country. Robbins summed up the emotions of the group: "A large part of our individual selves did not want to attempt this face. But another part was lured on by the challenge of the greatest unclimbed rock wall in North America."

As the Valley baked under the blazing sun of Indian summer, the four climbers began the historic ascent. They spent four days retracing the route to Big Sur Ledge. On this attempt Chouinard had the pleasure of leading the notorious third pitch. Even this early in the climb, Chouinard had a healthy dose of fear about their route. "The reason it was so scary," he recalled, "was that there was probably only one other climber in the United States capable of rescuing us, and that was Layton Kor and he was in Colorado. Other than that, the four of us on that climb were essentially the only four capable of doing it . . . . You were completely on your own! You're going for a line that looked devious at best, capped

Tom Frost

Royal Robbins (below) and Chuck Pratt on the traverse into the Black Dihedral

by 30-foot overhangs! So it was pretty scary!"

From Big Sur, Frost began a long traverse to the left in a rather unusual way. He first climbed up and to the left for a short distance and placed a bolt. His companions then lowered him 60 feet on the rope until he was about level with them, but 30 feet away. "With a separate rope to his waist we pulled him toward us," Robbins recalled. "When we had him tight as a stretched rubber band we let go . . . " and he went flying across the wall. After accumulating some extended air time, Frost reached a small flake and placed another bolt. He left a rope in place and returned to Big Sur for the night.

Robbins was very happy to have

Frost along on the climb. He noted, "Tom has a large reservoir of that most important ingredient in alpinism: spirit. And despite his record in championship sailboat racing, and his almost unrivaled list of great rock climbs, Tom is brazenly modest. This modesty, combined with talent and cheerfulness, make him an excellent climbing companion."

Robbins and Pratt completed the intricate traverse the next day. Then they started nailing up the loose, overhanging Black Dihedral. They had now crossed the point of no return. The overhanging rock precluded any thought of retreat—because if they tried to rappel down, they would be left hanging in mid-air away from the face, unable to reach the rock. From now on, the only

Tom Frost on the unique Slingshot Traverse

way out was up. Even their bivouacs were not lacking in intensity, as they spent the night dangling from precarious perches like the Black Cave. "Suspended over space, we hung one above the other, like laundry between tenement flats," Robbins described. "We were astonished at the tremendous exposure!"

In the morning Pratt climbed out of the cave through a horrendous roof, which Robbins called "the most spectacular lead in American climbing." Even the followers were impressed, and more than a little scared of this pitch. Frost remembered, "After Chuck and Royal left, Yvon and I looked at each other with considerable worry because now it was our turn! The dreaded moment had arrived! We heard this voice from above

yell, 'Come on up. The prusik line is anchored.' And I shouted up, 'Oh yeah? How well is it anchored?' Man, we were scared!"

But the difficulties did not let up. They struggled higher through loose rock and awkward cracks, fighting to overcome a fierce storm and their own inner anxieties. "We climbed onward, searching, always searching," Robbins recalled. "Searching for handholds and footholds, for piton cracks and the right piton. And searching ourselves for the necessary human qualities to make this climb possible. Searching for adventure, searching for ourselves, searching for situations which would call forth our total resources."

Although the climbers were now just a few hundred feet from the top, the demanding route would not allow them to relax. Robbins described one particular pitch in this way: "I moved upward on rurps, knifeblades, and the tips of angles, slipping on the moss-covered rock, while ice water ran down my arms and legs. At the top of the arch a sling through a hole in the flake and then a skyhook got me five feet higher. Standing for 20 minutes in short slings I drilled a hole and placed a bolt, a poor one for it chipped away the rotten diorite. It was our 38th and last bolt . . . One of the hardest leads in my experience, it was just another pitch on this wall." Even these hardened wallmasters were being pushed to a new level. Robbins admitted that "a climb with such unrelenting difficulties was a new experience to us."

By the ninth day, the difficulties of the route had worn them down. Near the summit Frost was emotionally spent, and suggested that Robbins lead a crucial pitch. "Royal thought that I was being generous by giving him a pitch that he wanted," said Frost. "But the truth of the matter was that I'd had enough. This climb was serious!"

That afternoon the climbers finally reached the top. Their combined talents had established what was then the most difficult and most committing rock climb in the world (VI 5.8 A5).

A fresh blanket of snow greeted them on the rim. As they savored the view of myriad white-capped summits, the Range of Light seemed to take on a new allure. They quietly shook hands and exchanged congratulations. And inwardly, they all knew that they'd been

The memorable hanging bivouac in the Black Cave: Tom Frost (top), Royal Robbins (middle), Yvon Chouinard (bottom)

changed—for they had acquired some of El Cap's strength and boldness. "No longer would we ever be afraid of spending so many days on a climb," Chouinard recalled, "whether it was a Yosemite wall or a long Alaskan ridge." The lessons they had learned, though extremely hard-won, would prove to be invaluable as they continued to push themselves in Yosemite's vertical world.

El Capitan: Muir Wall

The tremendous accomplishment of the North America Wall appeared to be a difficult feat to top. Yet in the early summer of 1965, Yvon Chouinard was preparing to do just that. He decided to up the ante in a dramatic new way. He would attempt a new route on El Capitan in a single push with just a two-man team, instead of the usual three or four. Fixed ropes, siege tactics, and previous reconnaissance would not be used. This bold plan would increase the work and the uncertainly that each man faced, while decreasing their margin of safety. But that was what made the concept such an interesting challenge.

"Probably the basis for this type of climbing was established by the naturalist John Muir," Chouinard explained. "He used to roam the Sierra for weeks, eating only bread and whatever he could pick off the land, sleeping under boulders in only his old army coat, and rejoicing with the summer storms. He chose to accept nature as it was without trying to force himself onto the mountains and to live with them, to adjust himself to the rigors of this sort of life."

Chouinard's partner in this grand scheme was TM Herbert—an individual who personified the word "unique." "TM defies description," said Tom Frost. "He could laugh you off any climb, any time, anywhere! If we were out bouldering and TM started in, we

(From left) Tom Frost, Royal Robbins, Chuck Pratt, Yvon Chouinard atop the North America Wall

would all just fall to the ground and collapse in a heap from laughing so hard."

"His purpose was always to bring out the absolute hilarity of any situation," added Royal Robbins. "He'd get into these ridiculous tales—like the story of Bladder Man who pees on everyone he meets, or some tale about drunken butterflies advancing across the pampas." Although Herbert was renowned for his quick wit and loony antics, he was a first-rate climber who always seemed to be up to any challenge. And a new route on El Capitan would definitely present just such a challenge.

The two climbers scrutinized their proposed line of ascent, located on the southwest face between The Nose and the upper Salathé Wall. "If there was ever anyone who has an eye for elegant routes on aesthetic walls it is Chouinard," noted Robbins. "A poetic soul, Chouinard rather disdains the analytical mind, for he hates to see beautiful

things ripped and torn." On one occasion Robbins and Chouinard became engrossed in a deep philosophical discussion about celestial astronomy. "For a while Yvon joined me in celestial speculation," Robbins recalled. "Then he shrugged his shoulders and turned to discussing drugs, hippies, and the love generation. That's him. He likes to keep his feet on the ground."

For this daring attempt, Chouinard and Herbert estimated the equipment they would need "down to the last piton and cup of water." In tribute to the outstanding climbing style and many contributions of John Muir, the route would be known as the *Muir Wall*.

The two men started up the rock in the early morning of June 14. They first climbed the deep chimney called Moby Dick and then began nailing a long series of left-facing corners. Four days of mixed free and aid climbing took them above Mammoth Terraces and up the right side of the Heart. An afternoon downpour on the fourth day forced an end to the day's progress. They huddled together through the night, trying to ward off the storm's intense cold and driving rain. Even the renowned Herbert, Yosemite's hilarious king of comedy, wasn't laughing now. "TM had a particularly bad night," Chouinard recalled, "shivering so violently that he could hardly speak. When he did, he sounded almost delirious. We were despondent and for the moment had lost the vision, and our courage."

The next morning their spirits returned. The rain abated somewhat so they continued on. In order to reach the great upper dihedral they were forced to traverse toward the right across a blank section. Herbert painstakingly placed eleven bolts here. Chouinard then climbed another pitch before dark, reaching some broken ledges at the 1900-foot level. They settled down for another wet, uncomfortable night.

As the sun rose on their sixth day, the weary climbers were confronted with what Chouinard described as an appalling sight. Above them towered 1000 feet of awkward, overhanging rock capped by a 30-foot roof. By now they had only two days worth of food and water left, and only nine bolts. The most critical decision of the climb was now at hand. Should they retreat? Did they still have the resources to complete the route? "Here was the line that had to be crossed," Chouinard explained. "The cost of failure can be dear, but the values to be gained from a success can be so marvelous as often to change a person's whole life." They resolved to continue upward and finish the climb.

The demanding pitches above occupied their whole existence. Extreme corners, overhangs, jam-cracks, and chimneys forced their weary bodies to a higher level of performance. And their minds, freed from society's distractions, became more attuned to the intricacies of their granite environment. "We now felt completely at home," Chouinard recalled. "Bivouacking in hammocks was completely natural. Nothing felt strange about our vertical world. With more receptive senses we now appreciated everything around us. Each individual crystal in the granite stood out in bold relief. The varied shapes of the clouds never ceased to attract our attention. For the first time we noticed tiny bugs that were all over the walls, so tiny they were

Is TM really scared or just clowning around? Only his hairdresser knows for sure

barely noticeable. . . . How could one ever be bored with so many good things to see and feel! This unity with our joyous surroundings, this ultra penetrating perception gave us a feeling of contentment that we had not had for years."

On the eighth day they consumed the last of their food and water. Four bolts were left, and 400 feet remained. They slowly worked upward through the day amid yet another rainstorm. The cracks were relentless in difficulty, requiring all the tricks in their climbing repertoire. Progress was agonizingly slow, but still they continued with singular determination. "TM is normally a fairly conservative climber," Chouinard noted, "but now he was climbing brilliantly. He attacked the most difficult pitch of the climb, an overhanging series of loose flakes, with absolute confidence; he placed pitons behind the gigantic loose blocks that could break off at any moment, never hesitating and never doubting his ability."

Finally, after sunset the climbers pulled up over the summit overhang. Their waiting friends happily immersed them in a feast of roast chicken, fresh fruit, beer, and champagne.

Chouinard and Herbert cut it very close on the *Muir Wall* (VI 5.9 A4). They relied only on themselves, and performed at an extraordinary level with a minimum of food and water. Like John Muir, they adapted themselves to the requirements of the natural environment. This bold approach placed a premium on inner strength and determination. Chouinard later summarized the attraction of their approach: "This purer form of climbing takes more of a complete effort, more personal adjustment, and involves more risk, but being more idealistic, the rewards are greater."

Although Yosemite climbers enjoyed considerable success on big walls during the 1960s, outstanding free climbs were also being established. In 1965 Frank Sacherer was again roaring up long routes, eliminating direct aid from all he surveyed. Perhaps the highlights of his season were completing the first free ascent of two excellent routes on Middle Cathedral Rock—the *East Buttress* (5.10c) and the *Direct North Buttress* (5.10b). Both of these routes remain among the finest free climbs in the country. Jim Bridwell, Eric Beck, and Chris Fredericks were also active, putting up the enjoyable Snake Dike on Half Dome's southwestern flank. Although the route's hardest move was 5.7, most of the climbing consisted of "exciting 5.4," owing to the paucity of protection bolts between belay stances.

As the summer months began to wane, Chuck Pratt teamed up with

Free-climbing the crux 5.10c section on the East Buttress of Middle Cathedral Rock

Fredericks and climbed the strenuous *Entrance Exam* (5.9) at Arch Rock. Pratt then led the fearful, hard to protect *Twilight Zone* (5.10d) at the Cookie Cliff. This latter route again showed Pratt to be one of the Valley's best all-around climbers.

Through the years Pratt had been consistently successful on hard aid problems, intimidating big walls, and desperate free climbs. "Just about every aspect of climbing appealed to me," he later remarked. "I enjoyed a short, difficult challenge as well as spending many days on a wall. I tried to do both." Many climbers came to respect what Robbins had called Pratt's uncommon talents. "Chuck Pratt turned difficult rock into art," noted Pat Ament. "Patient, with a good sense of humor, he climbed because he loved to. There was no hidden agenda. He valued the solitude and the friendship and the experience. As with Royal, Pratt's love for Yosemite went deep into the trees and into the mystical experience of such wonders. . . . On the most difficult crack climbs, with no protection and looking at a death fall, or on the most spectacular lead in American climbing, he was imperturbable."

Admiring friends would swap tales about how a slightly intoxicated Pratt, wearing clunky army boots, was still able to pull off ridiculously hard boulder problems even on wet rock at night. His lighthearted description of the first ascent of Ribbon Falls' *East Portal* (V 5.9 A4), with Allen Steck, Dick Long, and John Evans, is typical of his humor: "The first day Long and Evans did the clinging and hanging, while Steck and I managed the hauling and tangling. As if to show contempt for the difficulties, we deliberately made the ascent as hard as possible. We began by throwing rocks at our new nylon rope.

After several tries, Evans finally succeeded in striking and cutting the rope about 30 feet from its lower end with a large, sharp rock. Then, by traversing to the right, Evans was able to avoid the clean and secure rock above him in favor of some filthy and rotten granite which led to a vertical jungle all but hidden by mud. Finally, as we settled down for a bivouac 600 feet up, we decided that too much food and water had been brought so we sacrificed some. Two-thirds of the food, and over half the water, together with some bivouac gear, all went singing down the face, neatly held together by a duffel bag."

Far from being an embarrassment, this comedy-of-errors ascent simply added to Pratt's unique persona. Warren Harding noted that Pratt was still able to excel despite some personal characteristics "which have driven him to squander much valuable climbing time in such dubious activities as hanging around the nurses' dormitories in Yosemite and guzzling copious quantities of cheap wine."

By now, a number of trends were firmly established in the minds of Valley locals. Siege climbing, fixed ropes, and excessive bolting were to be avoided at all costs. The ideal was to ascend a challenging route in a single push from the ground up. Climbers would talk for hours about the great ascents that had already taken place in the Valley, and discuss where the future of Yosemite climbing would go. And the usual place where these discussions were held, and the place that climbers called home, was the dusty campground of Camp 4.

Doug Robinson described Camp 4 (currently known as Sunnyside Campground) as "the most trampled and dusty, probably the noisiest, and certainly the least habitable of all Yosemite's campgrounds. . . . Yet the Yosemite climbers will stay nowhere else. It was near the Curry cafeteria, where the price of leftovers was right if you were quick enough, and the fireplace lounge was handy for sitting out storms. A pretty easy lowride, really, for the few who had gathered there in the early days of big wall climbing."

"During the Golden Age of Yosemite climbing, all a climber needed were a few leftovers, one shirt, one tattered pair of pants, and a little knowledge of the freight lines," noted Pat Ament. "With bare billfolds, a few of us had some of the best summers of our lives."

Although some may have harbored secret fantasies of cranking desperate routes all day and then retiring to the plush Ahwahnee Hotel, it was always Camp 4 to which they returned each night. Bizarre meals, unwashed dishes, strewn climbing gear, and late-night parties were the norm. Whether by chance or by design, Camp 4 was "the climbers' campground," Robinson noted, "the focus of a force field of tradition and emotion."

Climbers enjoyed the fact that Camp 4 received the early morning sunlight sooner than many other campgrounds, and that the place had excellent bouldering. So it was a comfortable spot to hang out, compare notes on various Yosemite routes, swap stories about other climbing areas, and suggest new schemes to bum their way through another summer. "Back then," recalled Robinson, "most of the climbers hanging out in the Valley were beatniks—bums who had probably studied physics someplace but had decided that it would be more fun to hang out in a certain boulder-strewn camp in Yosemite, talk philosophy, and drink a little wine. Climbing was the only thing that made sense of our lives and we ended up happy, living like mountain hobos in this paradise of stone."

In Camp 4, communing among the dirt and the boulders, they found acceptance and a feeling of community. "At that time, the only inhabitants of Camp 4 were climbers, tourists with pets, and the bears," said Tom Frost. "Spartacus was the main bear. Pratt in particular was always waging war with him. But since he was slightly smarter that Spartacus, Chuck usually won. That was the scene in Camp 4: climb, fight the bears, and climb some more. We all felt that life couldn't be any better than that. We didn't possess anything, but we felt rich!"

Many of them had shared identical experiences—not only the elation and the torment on the Valley's great walls, but also the hardship of dropping out of college, enduring the scorn of outraged parents, and being dumped by impatient girlfriends. (Nearly all climbers at this time were men). But these shared experiences simply molded them into a close-knit group. They knew that their grubby attire was not appreciated in the Curry cafeteria. They knew that their late-night parties were often an irritant to tourists and rangers. They knew they were at the bottom of Yosemite's social ladder. But the disdain which they often felt from the outside world simply increased their commitment to the Camp 4 lifestyle. They didn't fit in, and they didn't want to fit in. These misfits were different and they liked it that way. "It wasn't like tourists were saying, 'Hey, those climbers are doing great things,'" said Royal Robbins. "Mostly, they were saying, 'What are those fools doing?' That suited us fine. We didn't want any more than that. We were happy with people thinking we were crazy."

Lively philosophical debates, often interspersed with sessions of bouldering, commonly went on with no apparent end. Discussions might center around the Vietnam War, the civil-rights movement, or the female attributes of various waitresses and maids at the Ahwahnee Hotel.

One particular topic that often surfaced was speed climbing. Climbers were becoming more and more interested in seeing how fast they could ascend certain routes. Steve Roper was particularly adept at climbing fast. He had earlier made the first one-day ascent of the Lost Arrow Chimney with Yvon Chouinard. That ascent was noteworthy not only for the pair's rapid pace, but also for their discovery of the decomposed remains of a climber who had previously fallen to his death. After this macabre ascent, Roper and Frank Sacherer climbed the Steck-Salathé route on Sentinel Rock in an impressive time of eight hours.

Succumbing to a feeling of friendly competition, Royal Robbins decided to try to beat that record. He convinced Tom Frost to join him. Frost recalled, "I was just getting back from a normal two-day ascent of Sentinel and was walking into camp. Royal said, 'Tom, we've gotta go up and do Sentinel!' I was tired and dirty, hadn't even had a chance to sit down and rest yet, and still had my rucksack on my back. But I said, 'Well, OK. I know the way.'"

So two days after Roper and Sacherer came down, Robbins and Frost went up and completed the route in an astounding 3 hours and 15 minutes. "When we got to the top, I pulled out the watch and we were astonished," said Frost. "We didn't have any idea we were climbing so fast. And we weren't even tired! I mean, you can't get tired when you're only climbing for three hours! So we walked back to the Valley, had a nice lunch, and thought "Well, what'll we do now?"

Without saying a word, they had made their point.

All of these rapid ascents were even more exceptional because of the limitations of their equipment; comfortable seat harnesses, mechanical ascenders, and detailed climbing topos were simply unavailable at this time. But climbers of the day compensated for the lack of modern amenities with determination and skill.

Not only was speed climbing in vogue, but speed driving was also popular among some of the locals. For a few climbers, the most dangerous part of an ascent was surviving the drive. Jim Bridwell, in particular, had a reputation for hair-raising journeys along the roads of Yosemite. "Everyone always got into my car with a few reservations," he remarked. Eventually, an informal contest developed among some climbers to see how fast one could drive along a section of Highway 140 just west of the park entrance. "It was a loose, casual arrangement," recalled Bridwell. "Whenever one of us went to the Valley we logged our time on that stretch of road and relayed the results to our peers when we next saw them. . . . The best times were often turned in by Frank Sacherer. He drove an old VW beetle, which he would fling into a turn so fast that the weighted rear end began to slide. Using a delicate touch on wheel and throttle he'd keep the ungainly vehicle just on the point of spinning out. I was in Camp 4 one weekend when he arrived with the news that he'd covered the 27 miles in just 27 minutes, at that time a record. Sacherer was pretty casual and laconic about it. However, his passengers, slack jawed and dazed, were simply speechless. I guessed they would be making alternative travel arrangements in the future."

With speed still in mind, Roper and

Jeff Foott turned to the great Northwest Face of Half Dome in 1966, climbing that highly respected route in a single day (16 hours). This was the first one-day ascent of a Grade VI rock climb in Yosemite. During this period, Roper ascended many of the Valley's classic routes. "I specialized in second ascents," he said. "I guess I was scared of first ascents. I'd read an article in the journal [about a particular climb] and I'd just have to go up and do it. Maybe I was the only guy who could read!"

Also active at this time was climbing bum Eric Beck, who completed the first solo ascent of the Northwest Face of Half Dome. This impressive accomplishment required just 2¹/₂ days.

Another notable event was the arrival in the Valley of five British climbers, including the renowned Don Whillans. Of the climbers from outside California who had previously come to Yosemite, only Layton Kor had been able to keep up with the locals. Most climbers had been intimidated and humbled by the towering walls, parallel-sided cracks, and smooth rock. Tales had emerged that the Valley was home to a race of superhuman, suntanned, blond giants. So the smug resident climbers quietly waited for the new visitors to also get spat off the cliffs. But the British group displayed exceptional skill, climbing such respected routes as the Northwest Face of Half Dome, the Steck-Salathé on Sentinel, the Crack of Despair, and the Crack of Doom. Chuck Pratt expressed the view of many locals when he declared that "the era of supremacy of Yosemite climbers has ended."

Over the next several years, an eclectic mix of talented young climbers and familiar old veterans would continue to establish new routes. Royal Robbins established the *Nutcracker* (III 5.8) in 1967, and many still regard this as one of the best short climbs in the Valley. The name of the route came from the artificial chocks, or "nuts," that Robbins used instead of pitons. These British inventions helped to eliminate the growing damage being done to cracks by repeated placement and removal of pitons. The Nutcracker was the first major US climb done entirely with chocks.

Robbins' reason for embracing the use of chocks was simple. "We were driven by a John Muir ethic of preservation, of naturalness, of leaving the rock the way we found it," he explained. "Using chocks accomplished two things at the same time: not only could we save the rock by preventing piton damage, but we could also elevate climbing to a higher level because using chocks required more skill and imagination."

Robbins was an early advocate for the use of nuts. "The time has come to climb clean," he pleaded, "because it is a finer and higher form of endeavor, because it is aesthetically satisfying, because it develops our climbing skill and craft, and most persuasively because the preservation of our routes demands it." He enthusiastically noted that on the 600-foot Nutcracker "pitons are unnecessary. It can reasonably be climbed with nuts and natural runners alone."

Soon after, he emphasized the utility of nuts even more by using them extensively on the first ascent of El Capitan's *West Face* (VI 5.9 A4). Robbins and TM Herbert placed only one bolt during the entire ascent. "I loved using chocks," Robbins remarked, "because it made the game harder and more interesting. The bottom line is that you must have adventure in it. You must have uncertainty and challenge. If you eliminate the adventure, you've got nothing!"

In terms of free climbing, the most noteworthy ascent of 1967 was Jim Bridwell's free ascent of the Stoveleg Cracks on The Nose of El Capitan. These formidable cracks had always been the realm of slow, tedious aid work with big angles and bongs. But Bridwell, inspired by the vision of Frank Sacherer, began to look at big walls from the standpoint of pure free climbing. And from such a standpoint, an exciting new world was completely untouched. Freeing the Stovelegs would be a first step into this alluring new realm.

So with their ropes fixed as far as Sickle Ledge, Bridwell remarked that he and Jim Stanton "charged the wall in classic Yosemite fashion—after a leisurely breakfast." After this appropriately casual start, Bridwell climbed through the 5.10 difficulties by early afternoon. For the resident climbers, who were becoming increasingly interested in long free climbs, this was a major achievement.

Bridwell complemented his free climbing with two difficult new wall routes: the *East Face* of Higher Cathedral Rock (VI 5.9 A4) and *South Central* on Washington Column (V 5.10 A3). Meanwhile, Layton Kor, Jim Madsen, and Kim Schmitz ascended the difficult *Great Slab* on Washington Column (VI 5.9 A5). Madsen and Schmitz also posted rapid ascents of both the Dihedral Wall and The Nose, climbing each route in 2½ days. Such masterful climbing prompted Robbins to remark that "attitudes toward El Capitan will never be the same."

The following year, 1968, was marked by unusual turmoil and dismay. Events around the world seemed to defy explanation: Martin Luther King and Robert Kennedy were assassinated, protests against the Vietnam War became louder and more violent,

Yvon Chouinard on El Capitan

an Air Force B-52 carrying four nuclear bombs was lost over Greenland, the US intelligence ship *Pueblo* was captured by the North Koreans, and the North Vietnamese launched their bloody Tet offensive.

In Yosemite, climbers were also forced to confront drama and tragedy. The first shock came when Jim Madsen was killed. The disaster occurred in October, when he hiked to the top of El Capitan to check on some friends; they were waiting out a storm high on the Dihedral Wall. As Madsen rappelled down toward them, the rope somehow slipped out of his rappel device and he fell 3000 feet to his death.

A few weeks later another tragedy appeared imminent, this time on Half

Dome. Warren Harding and Galen Rowell were being pounded by a violent storm on the monolithic south face. Pinned down by the weather, their strength drained by wet clothes and freezing temperatures, the climbers found themselves in a life or death struggle. Suspended in wet hammocks for two days, tormented by snow and sleet, Rowell finally made a desperate attempt to rappel the route, despite the icy conditions. "I thought it was our only hope," he later explained. "I did not want to hang in one place and freeze to death, as I thought we might after another night in the storm. Dying without an effort to escape seemed a most unforgivable thing."

But after he descended only 80 feet, the ice-covered rock and frozen rope seemed to prevent any progress either down or back up. He tried returning to his hammock, but the mechanical ascenders were jammed with ice. The cold began to overtake him as he was hit by a constant stream of small avalanches. "My hands felt like two boards," he recalled. "I often felt like blacking out and I had to make conscious efforts not to faint. Warren stood in slings at the pothole helplessly; there was nothing he could do. He couldn't help pull me up in these conditions any more than I could climb the rope hand-over-hand. . . . My body revolted. It wanted to give up. My mind forced it to painfully and slowly move upwards . . ."

Two hours after beginning the attempt, Rowell clawed his way back to his drenched bivouac, colder and weaker than when he began. Fortunately, their spirits received a critical boost as their water-soaked walkie-talkie crackled with a message that help was on the way. Several hours later they caught sight of a helicopter flying toward them. The helicopter made several landings on the summit of the dome, ferrying loads of men and equipment for a rescue.

Finally after sunset, the climbers caught sight of a solitary man being lowered from above. Rowell had this description of their rescuer: "He was wearing a full down parka with a hood, carrying a walkie-talkie, a large pack, and had a headlamp strapped to his forehead. From now on if I ever envision a guardian angel it will be in this form." He talked to the man for several minutes. Although Rowell didn't recognize him, "something about the voice, the mannerisms, and the self-assuredness seemed familiar." Rowell finally realized that their "guardian angel" was Royal Robbins. They all ascended the rope and found dry clothes and supplies on the summit. With the danger now passed, the group relaxed and enjoyed a warm dinner and a superb view. To the relief of everyone, a second tragedy was averted.

Amidst these dire situations, 1968 also saw a milestone in Yosemite climbing. Not surprisingly, it emerged from the vision of Royal Robbins. He had already made either the first or the second ascent of all the major routes on El Capitan, except for the Muir Wall. And Robbins was not one to settle for exceptions. Not only was he always searching for a new adventure and a new challenge, he also valued his spot atop Yosemite's unofficial pecking order.

So in an incredibly bold move, Robbins made a ten-day solo ascent of the formidable Muir Wall. TM Herbert vividly recalled hearing the news: "I just happened to be walking around the Valley and I ran into Liz [Robbins].

'Hi Liz. Where's Royal?'
'He's up on the Muir Wall.'
'He's making the second ascent?
That's great! Who's he with?'
'No one. He's up there alone.'

"I was stunned! Yvon and I thought we were big, bad-ass dudes by putting up the route. And afterwards, we were trying to think if there was any human being who could ever climb our route. And we figured, no, there was no man alive who could ever do it, and here's Robbins up there alone!"

Robbins later explained, "For me, at that time, Muir was just the next obvious step. In order to feel that I had achieved something comparable to our original Half Dome route, I had to solo it."

This ascent made a huge impact on the Yosemite climbing scene, clearly showing that Robbins was an innovator—and a true master of the game. "Most of the big breakthroughs came from Royal," noted Herbert. "I felt that I could probably keep up with most of the other climbers, but I knew I would never equal Royal. Going up on a wall with him was almost like cheating. If anything went wrong, you'd just give him the lead!"

Pat Ament agreed, noting that Robbins had "an undeniable flair—and the legends are not the man, only the roaring edges of his sea, while somewhere farther out, far away, there is great calm. . . . In truth he is a bit shy, neither humble nor self-adoring. Philosophical, brilliant, defensive, cutthroat, he is one of the unique ones."

As the decade slowly crept to a close, the two old buddies from Tahquitz were still busy forging new routes. Warren Harding climbed the *Lost Arrow Direct* (V 5.8 A3) with Pat Callis, and two demanding lines with Galen Rowell: the *Southwest Face* of Liberty Cap (VI 5.8 A4), and the *Firefall Face* on Glacier Point (V 5.8 A4). One particular pitch on the Firefall Face was so complex and devious that Harding took three hours just to follow it. Meanwhile Robbins and Glen Denny put up *The Prow* on Washington Column (V 5.9 A4), which remains today one of the Column's finest routes.

Then in the waning months of 1969, in the aftermath of the Apollo 11 moon landing and the Woodstock megaconcert, Robbins put up the intimidating *Tis-sa-ack* on Half Dome (VI 5.9 A4) with Don Peterson. This fearsome route, which Robbins described as "an ordeal," required eight days to complete. The climb was unusually severe and taxing, even for Robbins. Two blank sections high on the route required long, memorable bolt ladders to traverse. Robbins confessed, "The ladder I placed below the summit is certainly the worst anywhere. I hope those who make the next ascent (God pity them!) will be indulgent of the poor workmanship up there. It was the job of a desperate man. . . . I was so far gone that anything went. I just wanted to get up!"

It was fitting that Royal Robbins should complete a demanding new Half Dome route at the end of the Golden Age. His 1957 ascent of the Northwest Face had opened the era, and Tis-sa-ack would be the closing chapter. The Age had come full circle.

In the short span of 12 years, Yosemite climbers advanced from youthful mountaineers to the best rock climbers in the world. They were a rag-tag assortment of serious thinkers and whimsical jokers, but the routes they established would come to be revered in the climbing community. Drawing strength and inspiration from their predecessors, these climbers were able to accomplish routes of unbelievable length, severity, and elegance. But even as they pushed ahead, they had a clear sense of where Yosemite's climbing heritage had come from. Personal challenge and adventure were what drew them to the sport, and the familiar Valley walls always seemed to offer something new.

With each bold step forward—from the ascent of the Northwest Face, to The Nose, the Salathé Wall, the North America Wall, the Muir Wall—their techniques and philosophies revolutionized the sport. The methods and attitudes developed in the Valley would soon have a major effect on how climbers applied their skills.

Yvon Chouinard in particular envisioned how the advances made during this era would profoundly influence the climbing world. He summed up his prescience with this poetic prophesy: "Yosemite Valley will, in the near future, be the training ground for a new generation of super-alpinists who will venture forth to the high mountains of the world to do the most aesthetic and difficult walls on the face of the earth."

The coming decade would verify that his vision was right on target.

6

PUSHING THE LIMITS

The general concept of climbing in Yosemite is centered on the mystique of big walls. . . . In more recent years an ever-growing vanguard of imaginative and progressive young climbers have been fostering a fast-moving renaissance of Yosemite free climbing. Redefined techniques, strength training, equipment improvement, and purification of ethics have led to amazing new routes.

JIM BRIDWELL

As a new decade began in 1970, a haunting sense of change seemed to hang in the air. The release of Paul McCartney's solo album in April signaled the end of The Beatles and the psychedelic '60s. The breakup of this prolific band, and the feeling of change this created, seemed to set the tone for the coming decade.

The Yosemite climbing scene was not immune to this atmosphere of change. For one thing, the once-terrifying reputation of El Capitan began to seem a bit overblown. During the spring of 1970, two out-of-state climbers quietly came to the Valley and without fanfare established the impressive *Heart Route* (VI 5.9 A4) on El Cap's southwest face. The ascent by Chuck Kroger and Scott Davis required eight days and just 27 bolts. "Chouinard, Herbert, and Robbins had already shown that fine alpine climbing style is possible on El Cap's big walls," Kroger noted. "So with nothing left to prove, we simply planned to have a good time."

The pair originally planned on doing a new route on the southeast face, immediately right of The Nose. But they arrived in the Valley to find another team's gear on the rock. Kroger noted that the other party consisted of "two local barbarians." He described these unique creatures as "big hairy guys who live in the Valley and run around in funny-looking tennis shoes, and play on impossibly hard short free climbs and boulder moves. . . . The big boss barbarian (let's call him Jim) made it pretty clear that his stuff was already on the route and that we'd be pretty dead pretty fast if we tried to steal his route from him and his partner (we'll call him Kim), who has a bit of a killer instinct. Not wishing to contribute to the problem Chouinard mentions of 'an aura of unfriendliness and competition,' and

The Triple Direct ascends the left side of El Capitan, including portions of the Salathé Wall, the Muir Wall, and The Nose

especially not wishing to be torn limb from limb by barbarians, we immediately changed plans."

Instead of competing with "Jim" Bridwell and "Kim" Schmitz, they settled on a line between the Dihedral and the Muir walls. The route boldly attacked a huge depression called the Heart, and was memorable right from the start. "The first pitch was only A3," Kroger recalled, "but the belay was A3 too. It was nice to be with someone as competent as Scott. He carefully divided the load between six pitons. Only one of them popped out as I jumared."

Difficult nailing and awkward free climbing were their constant companions for the days that followed. But they took it all in stride and kept their sense of humor. Near the top of the route, they humorously named one particular section the "A5 Traverse." Kroger confessed that "it was really A2, but every other big El Cap climb has an 'A5 Traverse', so we figured that we needed one too."

Although the weary climbers later described their arduous ascent as "just like being dead for a week," it was an outstanding achievement. Indeed, the locals were shocked that so-called "outsiders" had established such an elegant route. Many still remembered the lengthy siege of the Dihedral Wall in 1962, and believed that few out-of-state climbers could ascend a new El Cap route by sporting means without fixed ropes. But now they saw another example of the point first made by the successful foreign ascents of 1966—that times were changing, and that California held no monopoly on excellent climbers.

The year 1970 also marked a significant changing of the guard in Yosemite. The renowned and aging visionaries of the past decade were steadily being replaced by an increasing number of talented young climbers. This passing of the torch could perhaps be symbolized by the May ascent of *Vain Hope* (V 5.7 A3) in the Ribbon Falls area. The climbing team consisted of Royal Robbins, Jim Bridwell, and Kim Schmitz. Robbins was the living legend of Yosemite's Golden Age, while Bridwell, known to his friends as The Bird, epitomized the daring new breed who would soon shatter the old standards. "Guys like Robbins and Kor were the heritage that we inherited," said Billy Westbay, another talented young climber. "But Bridwell was the crossover between the Golden Age and us. He knew what Robbins and those guys had done, and he had this really incredible vision of what more could be done." Robbins himself added, "Jim's a bit of a madman. He has this volcanic energy and personality—very passionate and driven!"

Although they were of different eras, the climbers worked well together in establishing this new route. But climbing with Robbins left a definite impression on Bridwell. "I thought it'd be fun doing the route with three people," he said, "because you'd have somebody to talk to at the belays. But when Royal and I were at a belay, he would just stoically stare off across the Valley and never say a word. It'd be one thing if we were in Nepal where there was really something to look at. But that was him. He had kind of an imposing personality—kind of aristocratic, above reproach."

One of Robbins' long-time partners, Tom Frost, added these comments on the Robbins persona: "Climbing with Royal was different. You knew what the assignment was and you did it. There wasn't a lot of chatter. Royal's not the gabbiest guy in the world, and I'm kind of quiet too, so we could go for days without saying much. We just enjoyed each other, and the environment, and the extreme privilege of being in those places. But it was also very organized. Like at a bivy, Royal would get the salami and cheese and slice off precise one-inch pieces of each for dinner. It wasn't like he'd say, 'Hey Tom, let's have a party! How about an inch and a half of salami?!' It was all precision. But without question, some of the very best times in my life have been up on those climbs with him. He was my hero!"

Bridwell and Robbins were also busy with other projects during May. At Arch Rock, Bridwell teamed up with Mark Klemens to climb *New Dimensions* (5.11 A1), the first Yosemite route to be graded 5.11. The severe new line followed overhanging hand-jams and flared chimneys for four pitches. The route went almost completely free except for the last pitch. "I was one move from the top," Bridwell lamented. "All I had to do was match hands on this one hold. But I balked because I knew my protection lower down was worthless. So I reached over to an easy 5.7 crack on tension and then went up."

While free climbing limits were being expanded, Robbins decided to push the boundaries of big wall climbing. With his customary vision and daring, he made a solo first ascent of a new route on the elegant western side of Sentinel Rock. His new route, called *In Cold Blood* (V 5.8 A4), marked the first time that a major Yosemite wall had been soloed on a first ascent. But for Robbins, it was just a new way to challenge himself.

His inspiration for soloing stemmed from the visionary climbing of the Italian alpinist Walter Bonatti. Over six agonizing days in 1955, Bonatti made a solo first ascent of the awesome Southwest Pillar of the Petit Dru. At the time, this terrifying 2000-foot needle of frigid ice and granite was the most difficult climb ever accomplished in the French Alps. Despite the Dru's notorious reputation, the loss of most of his food and fuel, and accidentally slicing off the tip of one finger with his piton hammer, Bonatti stuck with the climb and achieved one of mountaineering's greatest prizes. "Bonatti's superb feat stands as a great example to us all," Robbins observed. "He should be emulated. His achievements are neither technological nor technical tricks, but are achievements of the human spirit, and that goes deepest."

Like Bonatti, Robbins also felt that solo ascents had their own special allure. "The thing about a solo climb is that it is all yours," he remarked. "It is also a way of exploring oneself. A solo climb is like a big mirror. One is looking at oneself all the way up. If it is a way of showing off, of proving something, it is also a test—a way of finding out what one is made of."

Robbins then went back to the northwest face of Half Dome and put up Arcturus (VI 5.7 A4) with Dick Dorworth. The process of nailing away at another Half Dome route was certainly nothing new for Robbins. But several aspects of the climb were not easily forgotten.

First, there was the intense July heat. Robbins noted that "the heat made us dizzy. It had an unreal quality. What seemed unreal was the idea of our climbing in it. More logical to bask like lizards on the sandy shore of the Merced. Alas for the voice of reason. Climbers are madmen. So we shook off our stupor and started up." Then a second hazard materialized. "From the top parapets, unknown soldiers were attempting to repel our assault by hurling stones," fretted Robbins. "For three days we received rockfall from hikers tossing

The breathtaking traverse along Thank God Ledge

ABOVE. Warren Harding

FACING PAGE. The second pitch of Reed's Pinnacle Direct

Climber wrestling with the wide jams on Twilight Zone

Wheat Thin

ABOVE. Lynn Hill

FACING PAGE. Peter Croft on the Alien variation (5.12b) of the Rostrum

Steve Schneider on Circus Circus (5.13c), Tuolumne Meadows

Warren Harding in his Bat tent on the South Face of Half Dome

granite from the summit. Some of these projectiles were blockbusters and cut the air with a terrifying, sucking roar, doing unpleasant things to the imagination. Fortunately, the energy of those manning the ramparts exceeded their skill, and we emerged from the bombardment unscathed, physically. The ascent had its Eiger-like qualities." And worst of all, Robbins almost had the dubious honor of setting the record for a speed descent of Half Dome. He described the situation this way: "I was mucking around in the darkness trying to get the haul bag up to a better ledge and using two jumars to protect myself while climbing around on broken ledges, and thinking I should only use one jumar—it's so much simpler—when the jumar holding my weight came off. There I was hanging by the other, wondering once again if I have been lucky or smart to still be alive after 20 years of climbing." In spite of these distractions they completed the climb, marking the fifth new route established by Robbins on Half Dome.

Meanwhile, Warren Harding was still working on his first route on the Dome. With the tenacity he was famous for, he returned for a sixth time to the south side of the rock, joined once again by Galen Rowell. From their previous attempts dating back to 1965, Harding had developed an extensive array of new aid techniques and equipment. He had dubbed these new approaches BAT, meaning Basically Absurd Technology. Included were such things as Bat hooks, which consisted of Chouinard cliff-hangers filed to a sharp point. The new hooks could fit into shallow drilled holes to allow easier progress across blank sections of rock. Rowell noted that the gadgets were used "much to Yvon's consternation." New hammocks, called Bat tents, fully enclosed and able to hang from a single point, were also developed. And Harding himself emerged as the nefarious Batso, a self-proclaimed "raffish-looking little fellow, with a proclivity for thinking up questionable mountain-climbing equipment."

In contrast to their epic rescue on Half Dome in 1968, Harding and Rowell successfully completed the 2000-foot *South Face* route without incident in six days. But once again Harding's use of the drill raised the ire of some climbers. Over 180 holes were drilled for both hook placements and bolts. For some of the locals, this represented an unnatural line forced up a blank wall.

The controversy simmered throughout the summer as climbers debated where the limits of bolting should lie. It was in fact not an easy question to answer. Some routes, like the West Face and the Salathé Wall on El Cap, were clearly beyond ridiculing because so few bolts were used. The Nose required 125 bolts, but virtually no one condemned Harding for that. However, his Leaning Tower route needed 110 bolts, and there were those who thought this excessive. Yet Robbins, who also drilled 110 bolts on Tis-sa-ack, was not subject to the same criticism. Clearly there was a murky area that defied universal agreement. Were 100 bolts the limit? Were 150 acceptable but 151 too many?

The point was also raised whether there should even be a hard and fast boundary. Many climbers were originally drawn to the sport because of its refreshing lack of rules, and the sense of freedom that it conferred. Was this new Half Dome route simply the wave of the future? Or was it an aberration, a blight on the Yosemite climbing scene? Although the debate seemed intense, it was only a prelude to the fury that later erupted. And once again, Warren Harding found himself right in the middle of it.

El Capitan: Wall Of The Early Morning Light

Of the many colorful characters who have left their mark on Yosemite climbing, few have had more of an impact than Warren Harding. His routes were hailed as inspired and courageous, as well as ridiculous and silly. On one hand, The Nose of El Capitan became the standard by which all other big walls were compared. Even today it is still revered as one of the classic rock climbs of the world. Likewise the South Face of Mt. Watkins clearly showed that big, challenging routes could be done in impeccable style, in a single push, without fixed ropes or excessive drilling. Yet climbs like the West Face of the Leaning Tower and the South Face of Half Dome were criticized as bolt-heavy stunts. Many climbers had trouble believing that such widely differing routes were the work of a single person. But Harding always defied simple labels.

He prided himself on being a free thinker, answering only to himself. While others became caught up in deep ethical debates, Harding thumbed his nose at the establishment and quietly went off to do whatever climbs he wanted in whatever style he wanted. In terms of the whole ethics and bolting debate, he simply stated, "I really don't give a damn. If all or most other climbers feel a need for the comfort and shelter of structured thinking—if there are those who feel a need to establish these principles and lead the masses to a better 1984-ish life—fine with me. I still feel inclined to do my own thinking. As long as the V.C. ("Valley Christians": Harding's term for climbers intolerant of any climbing style but their own)

Warren Harding in the great arch on the South Face of Half Dome

don't get their own secret police and employ Spanish Inquisition methods, I won't worry about being imprisoned, stretched on a rack, forced to confess my sins, and then burned at the stake as a heretic. Rather, to the self-appointed climbing gurus, I say: Bugger off, baby, bugger off!"

So he continued to follow his own star and not take the whole thing too seriously. To counter what he perceived as the excessive altruism of the Sierra Club and the American Alpine Club, Harding established the Lower Sierra Eating, Drinking, and Farcing Society. "In the years of its existence," he explained, "its accomplishments have been few and of little or no importance: three climbing expeditions to Daff Dome (with steadily diminishing degrees of success), two issues of a wretched magazine called Descent (which features obscure humor, lies, gossip, weak pornography, general 'yellow journalism'—nothing of any value), and summer sessions of a climbing school of dubious character called Downward Bound." He went on to note that the purpose of Downward Bound was to "provide assistance in exploring the depths of sloth, gluttony, boozing, cowardice, avarice, and other fun things!"

Yet the whimsical Harding was always on the lookout for challenging new climbs. During a forced convalescence when he was nursing a badly broken leg, he decided to hobble around the Valley with two of his best friends—Glen Denny and a jug of wine. The goal that day was to locate the ultimate Yosemite climb. "In due time," he recalled, "and well into the jug of wine, we gravitated to El Cap Meadow. Surely it must be somewhere on El Capitan."

As they sat in the meadow enjoying the sunshine and their booze, they both

Climber at work on the blank traverse midway up the Wall of the Early Morning Light

began studying the clean sweep of rock between The Nose and the North America Wall. They noticed that overhanging, right-leaning cracks seemed to lead upward for about 1500 feet to an enormous blank area. Above this, a huge dihedral shot straight up to some wild-looking summit overhangs. The line looked bold, direct, and very committing. Their search was over. This was it—"The Big Motha Climb!"

Other climbers such as Yvon Chouinard, Chuck Pratt, Jim Bridwell, and Kim Schmitz had also considered a new route on this part of El Capitan. But their attempts would follow a prominent corner system up the right side of El Cap Towers. Harding felt such a line should be part of a completely separate route, independent of his proposed climb. So he focused on the direct line that he and Denny had spotted, even though it would mean bolting across a 300-foot blank section. And since the first light of morning struck the top of their route, only one name would do— the Wall of the Early Morning Light.

In mid-July Harding went to work. He took some telephoto shots of the wall and had these enlarged to form a photographic strip map. He also began organizing the formidable mass of gear that would be required. Since Denny was unable to join him, his partner in the project was Dean Caldwell, a climber he had previously met in the Mountain Room Bar. "I hit it off in fine fashion with Dean," Harding recalled. "We seemed to have much in common, including a penchant for rather excessive eating, drinking, and sloth. Even more exciting, Dean was some sort of minor fugitive following a scrape in Yosemite Lodge—very glamorous!"

As the days crept on into September, their project suddenly took on increased urgency. Harding happened to run into Jim Bridwell, who informed him that Royal Robbins was supposedly coming to the Valley to attempt this particular route. "This worried me," Harding confessed. "Of all the hot-shot climbers in the Valley, R.R. was the only one we felt had what it would take to get up the wall. The others who'd tried it were certainly brilliant climbers, but they lacked the perseverance to get through the big blank areas—or they were handicapped by ethical inhibitions. Royal, though a frequent moralizer, had put up one hell of a route on Half Dome (Tis-sa-ack) that required quite a few bolts. There was no doubt in my mind that R.R. could do this climb. So we had to get our ass in gear!"

They hurriedly started putting together the gear and supplies they would need, and then began ferrying loads to the base of the wall. This was no small task, considering their supplies were stuffed into five giant haul bags that had a combined weight of over 300 pounds. They tried to maintain some secrecy about their plans. However, the mountain of gear accumulating at the base of the route, and the unbelieving looks they got from climbers passing by, indicated just how conspicuous they were.

Throughout this phase they were still concerned about Robbins' beating them to the route. "We lived in fear of the dreaded R.R. appearing to take over the climb," said Harding. "Worse, we were in danger of becoming 'over trained.' All summer we'd trained hard—eating, drinking, loafing. Now as we waited out some bad weather, the excitement of the impending climb precipitated almost constant partying. Dave Hanna had lined up some sort of business relationship with Christian Brothers winery. It seemed C.B. might be interested in some action photos for advertising. How exciting! Connections with a major winery! Now we're getting somewhere!!"

When the weather appeared to clear, Harding and Caldwell climbed the first two pitches and then descended, leaving two ropes in place. The next day they hauled their baggage up to a tiny ledge at the top of the first pitch. Then with their characteristic flair, they decided it was time to party. "We uncorked the wine," recalled Harding, "Cabernet Sauvignon (it photographs better than white wine). We poured and photographed, and had a few glasses. Soon the wine expanded our minds a bit. We got the idea of putting Dean on the fixed rope running up the next pitch, which was overhanging and leaning to the right. This was great fun: Dean swinging gaily back and forth, 200 feet above the ground, delicately sipping from a crystal wine glass."

Even in their altered state they managed to rappel back to the Valley floor that evening to gather some last-minute supplies. Then finally on October 23, with excitement oozing from every pore, they awoke promptly at the crack of noon and started up the wall for good.

The climbing was difficult right from the beginning. Over the next seven days they nailed upward at a rate of only 150 feet per day. Yet even at this glacial pace, several incidents kept their attention level high. At a point about 750 feet up the wall, Caldwell was suddenly attacked by a shrieking horde of birds while jumaring the rope. Harding could only watch with amazement from the belay as Caldwell simultaneously jumared, removed pitons, and fended off a maelstrom of sharp beaks. Then Harding took a 40-foot fall while leading a tricky A4 crack.

His diligent belayer, who happened to be reading the comics from an old Sunday newspaper, still managed to keep Harding from flying too far.

In the days that followed they continued up the crack system until it faded. Then they started drilling horizontally across the dreaded blank area. "Bolting vertically is tedious and strenuous enough," Harding lamented, "but bolting sideways is the utter shits: awkward as hell and takes damn near twice as long. . . . Lean over to the left, tap-tap. Five or ten minutes later you have another rivet placed. Clip in and move about two feet. Eight or ten rivets, then a bolt. Shit, this could give a guy a backache! . . . Oh well, whatever it takes."

After two days of drilling they crossed the blank area and reached the huge dihedral forming the upper part of the route. But then another storm blew in, bringing heavy rain for the next three days. At first they weren't worried about the weather, feeling confident that their new Bat tents would keep them dry. Unfortunately, the new hammocks were still no match for the weather. So they languished and shivered in wet sleeping bags while the storm dragged on. "We were acutely aware that we were in one helluva tight spot," Harding recalled. "The big question seemed to be: Would we be able to continue climbing after the storm was over? Simply surviving is one thing. Being strong enough to continue extremely difficult climbing for perhaps another week is quite another matter. By now we'd been on the wall for 13 days and were only about halfway up. . . . I began to feel that maybe I wasn't going to make it, the same feeling I'd had in 1968 when Galen and I were pinned down on Half Dome—a deep, dreadful feeling that death is not far away."

However, the rain finally ended, permitting them to escape their soggy cocoons. Rejuvenated by dry clothing and warm sunshine, they doggedly continued upward. Yet the climbing in this section remained exceedingly hard. They averaged only about 100 feet of progress per day for the next several days. But their biggest worry was even more serious—their bottle of brandy was almost empty!

More days of nailing, drilling, and hooking brought them to a wonderfully spacious ledge they called Wine Tower. Reaching this point, only 800 feet from the top, provided a huge boost to their morale. Although they had been on the wall over 20 days, and their food supply was almost gone, the climbers prepared a mini-feast of goodies they had set aside for this very occasion: salami, cheese, French bread, and Cabernet Sauvignon (Christian Brothers, of course).

Feeling upbeat and relaxed, they were surprised to hear a voice shouting up from the base of the cliff asking if a rescue was needed. Harding angrily shouted his refusal while Caldwell furiously wrote a note stating flatly that a rescue was unneeded, unwanted, and would not be accepted. The note was attached to a small stone and then dropped off the cliff. They hoped this was the end of it, but then noticed ropes being lowered from the rim and a solitary person rappelling toward them. Another explosion of shouts, curses, and obscene gestures ensued, until the confused rescuer gave up and returned to the rim.

When their blood pressures returned to normal, the climbers settled down on Wine Tower and began enjoying their feast. Harding explained, "Later, somewhat in the grip of Demon Wine, we fell to discussing in rather bold terms what might be happening at this very moment had we been unable to convince the Park Service that it should—damn well better!—call off its rescue. It was not difficult to visualize a gallant team of Camp 4's best rappelling onto our ledge in the moonlight, staring in amazement at the 'desperate' climbers quietly engaged in a nice little party. Dialogue:

'Good evening. What can we do for you?'
'We've come to rescue you!'
'Really? Come now—get hold of yourselves.
Have some wine.' "

On into the night they laughed and joked about the absurdity of the whole thing.

As the days continued to pass they eventually reached a small ledge only 60 feet from the top. Tomorrow would be it. They really were going to make it!

At this point Harding began to consider what they had been through. "God," he thought, "we'd been on this wall almost a month now. When we had started up back in October, leaves on the big oak trees in the meadow a half-mile below were still green. As the days and weeks passed, we'd watched them turn a brilliant gold and slowly fade. Now they'd almost all fallen. It seemed that I'd never done anything but climb —hammer, drill, haul—on this damn wall. Now that it was drawing to a close, I felt a little sad."

In the morning Harding organized his rack for the triumphant final lead. Although nailing through the remaining overhangs was still difficult, he made quick work of it. But as he reached his hand over the very top and clambered onto the summit, Harding almost fell off in utter surprise. After being isolated from civilization for 27 days, he was shocked to see a small army of friends, photographers, and newspaper reporters waiting impatiently on the summit. Caldwell soon joined him on top and the two climbers happily surrendered to the carnival atmosphere of eating, drinking, and hugging. "Only thing missing was a mariachi band!" joked Harding.

But the completion of the climb (VI 5.7 A4) was simply the opening salvo of a tumultuous controversy that immediately exploded. To begin with, many climbers in Yosemite were appalled at the 330 bolts and rivets drilled in the rock. TM Herbert declared, "I have seen fine free and aid climbers pushing themselves to their limit using runners, nuts, pitons, and a rare bolt for protection. Many of my companions have risked nasty falls, even their lives, trying first ascents without placing a single bolt. In the 2000 feet of the West Face of El Capitan, Robbins and I kept the bolts down to just one!"

Like most climbers, Herbert regarded El Capitan as something special—the supreme jewel in Yosemite's magnificent granite crown. "This mountain of rock has given me the finest climbing experiences of my life," he mourned. He thought Harding's route was horribly contrived, and that the 27-day effort was just a case of glorified flagpole-sitting that had demeaned the splendor of El Capitan.

The locals were further incensed by the extensive media coverage of the whole affair. Harding and Caldwell made TV appearances on the Merv Griffin Show, the Steve Allen Show, and Wide World of Sports. The media hailed their climb as a major achievement, and this only served to rub salt in the wounds of those who despised the route.

As the weeks passed, emotions on both sides continued to rise ever higher. There began to be an increasing clamor among critics to go up and deliberately chop all the bolts from the route. This would "erase" the route from Yosemite, and maybe prevent other climbers from establishing similar routes.

One of the strongest advocates for chopping the route was Royal Robbins. "I'm not totally against bolts," he explained. "I've used enough of them myself. I'm just against anything that encourages pure technology. . . . Here was a route with 330 bolts. It had been forced up what we felt to be a very unnatural line, sandwiched between other routes, merely to get another route on El Capitan and bring credit to the people who climbed it. We felt that this could be done anywhere; instead of 330 bolts, the next might involve 600 bolts, or even double that. We thought it was an outrage, and that if a distinction between what is acceptable and what is not acceptable had to be made, then this was the time to make it."

Robbins spent several weeks considering what to do. "I remember going to see Schmitz and Bridwell to talk the whole thing over," he recalled. "I was keen on doing the second ascent and seeing what the route was like, so I suggested that I should do this and leave the third ascent and the problem of erasing the route to them. But they said that if I did this, it would give the route currency, and they wouldn't subsequently take the drastic step of erasing it. In other words, to repeat the route once without erasing it would be a form of approval. So that way they put me in a spot." After considering all the twists and tangles of the debate, he finally resolved to erase the route. Accompanied by Don Lauria, he set off for Yosemite in January 1971.

When they reached the Valley and

Royal Robbins near the top of the Wall of the Early Morning Light during the second ascent

started climbing, Lauria led the first pitch. As Robbins began to follow, out came a cold metal chisel. With forceful swings of his hammer he methodically chopped every bolt he found. The severed ends of the bolts dropped delicately to the talus below with a frail, tinging sound. The pitch was soon erased.

At the belay, Robbins asked Lauria if he still felt right about what they were doing. "Hell yes," Lauria replied. "I didn't like the way Harding and Caldwell did the route. I didn't like the publicity." Lauria later noted one additional reason for continuing that was even more important: "Royal had assured me that if we descended without accomplishing complete erasure, TM Herbert would personally castrate both of us."

But at the end of the first day, Robbins became very uneasy with the whole thing. The four pitches they had climbed turned out to be surprisingly good. The cracks were demanding and challenging. And in contrast to the rumors, there was not a bolt every two feet. In fact, Robbins found the route to have first-rate climbing. So should they continue erasing the route?

"That night I lay awake in my hammock thinking about it," he explained, "and I finally decided that I no longer felt right about destroying the route.

My inner feelings weren't going along with it, and I'd be crossing myself if I kept on doing it. So the right thing at that point seemed to be to stop the bolt chopping and just concentrate on climbing the route. At this stage I also thought about what the hell people were going to think. We'd started out doing something and now, through weakness or whatever, we'd changed our minds. Everyone was going to think that we'd started something we didn't have the strength to continue. So I was faced with this existential problem which I could see quite clearly: should I act for the sake of consistency, which would certainly bring me harsh criticism, or should I stop something I now felt was wrong—and by doing so look like a fool? I decided I had to stop, because if my actions were going to be motivated solely by consideration of what people would think, I was finished anyway. So I talked to Don in the morning, and that's what we did."

They dispensed with the chisel and simply climbed upward. The higher they got, the more they were impressed with the route. "We found some of the hardest nailing I have ever done," Robbins said with amazement. "There was one good lead after another. Both Caldwell and Harding must have been climbing at a really inspired level."

After six days on the wall they reached the summit, thus completing the second ascent of the route, and the first winter ascent of El Capitan. In the aftermath of their ascent the whole controversy became even more complex. Some were offended by the bolt chopping, believing that it was a personal attack on Harding. But Harding's reply was simple: "I don't give a rat's ass what Royal did with the route, or what he thought he accomplished by whatever it was he did. I guess my only interest

in the matter would be the possibility of some clinical insight into the rather murky channels of R.R.'s mind. . . . I could only assume that it was more of the evangelistic work that R.R. seems to feel called upon to indulge in."

Robbins had originally believed that although others were talking about erasing the route, only he would have the nerve to actually take such drastic action. Now he had to defend that action, and the fact that he didn't even finish the job. "We acted on a theory," he later said, "and it seems clear now that we would have been better not doing it that way. But it looked right at the time, and the iron was hot, so we took the risk that we might turn out to be doing the wrong thing. But everyone makes mistakes. I'm happy to admit that this was one."

The Wall of the Early Morning Light, sometimes referred to as the Dawn Wall, is today remembered as Yosemite's most controversial climb. A multitude of factors—the number of bolts, the lengthy 27-day ascent, the media hype, the vicious rumors, the confusing rescue offer, the bolt chopping, and the beliefs of those involved—all contribute to the tangled web of this memorable ascent. But in the end, the route remains as a fitting testimony to the convictions and the tenacity of Warren Harding.

With this in mind, Royal Robbins offered these words of summary: "Although this climb may not have been done exactly to our taste, and although we might have fretful little criticisms that envy always produces, we can better spend our energy in ways other than ripping and tearing, or denigrating the accomplishments of others. . . . I admire Harding because he is a great exponent of individualism, which I think is one of the most important features of climbing. It's one of the things I came into climbing for. . . . He has always been a loner, and in these days of conformity, of the death of individualism, of joiners and organizations, of group assertion, it is refreshing to see the crusty, intense, eccentric individualism of a Harding. Good to have a man around who doesn't give a damn what the establishment thinks. As our sport becomes rapidly more institutionalized, Harding stands out as a magnificent maverick."

With the approach of summer in 1971, another unique character began to exert a powerful influence on the direction of Yosemite climbing. Jim Bridwell had first come to the Valley as a wide-eyed teenager nine years before. During that time he had repeated many of Yosemite's classic routes, both free climbs and big walls. He also established new lines such as the *East Face* of Higher Cathedral Rock (VI 5.9 A4) and a new variation up El Capitan. Known as the *Triple Direct*, this latter route included parts of three different routes: the first 10 pitches of the Salathé Wall, then 7 pitches of the Muir Wall above Mammoth Terraces, and finally the upper 13 pitches of The Nose above Camp Four ledge. With this wealth of experience behind him, he now stepped to the forefront of the Yosemite climbing scene.

Bridwell's initial project that summer was another new route on El Capitan. He and Kim Schmitz chose a line to the left of the Dihedral Wall. The route ascended a chillingly blank slab for 900 feet before connecting with steep cracks higher up. The route was so demanding, and the weather so uncooperative, that numerous attempts were made over several years. But for Bridwell, an additional hurdle to overcome was the bizarre behavior of his partner. He later remarked, "I probably had a harder time getting up a route with Schmitz than with anybody else. He'd be up there on the wall and you'd think he was dying because he'd make these horrendous moans, and it'd be from something stupid like his harness was too tight or his feet hurt. But listening to those screams and moans all the time, your psyche would just be destroyed!"

The pair went on to complete the route, which they called *Aquarian Wall* (VI 5.9 A4) in June. It was another in a long line of new routes that Bridwell would establish on the Big Stone.

He was also very interested in challenging free climbs. With partners such as Mark Klemens, Charley Jones, Jim Pettigrew, Jim Orey, and Peter Haan, Bridwell put up some of the Valley's best free routes that summer of 1971.

The focus of his energy was the Cookie Cliff, a delightful little crag in lower Merced Canyon. The cliff is blessed with an amazing wealth of superb cracks, and it was these features which drew Bridwell like a magnet. *Outer Limits* (5.10c) and *Catchy* (5.10d) followed obvious crack systems, while *Butterfingers* (5.11a) climbed a devilishly thin seam at the top of the Nabisco Wall.

A huge flake in the middle of the cliff also looked interesting. It seemed to offer excellent potential for underclings and liebacks, but looked dangerously fragile. Bridwell feared that pounding pitons behind the flake for protection could cause it to break off, much to the detriment of both leader and belayer. So he and Peter Haan went to the top of the cliff and rappelled down to the flake, drilling bolts for protection. "We did it to preserve the flake," Bridwell explained. "We weren't sure how strong the thing was. Nobody made a big deal about it. Maybe because nobody knew about it ahead of time. We just went up and did it."

The drilling of bolts on rappel, or rap-bolting, would later create a bitter rift among climbers, not only in Yosemite but around the world. Some climbers would demand that all bolts should be placed while actually leading the climb. These traditional, or trad, climbers wanted to keep the element of adventure and uncertainty at a high level. Others would counter that bolts were bolts, and that routes established by rap-bolting were usually safer and more enjoyable. In this case, Bridwell's route *Wheat Thin* (5.10c) was accepted without any uproar because the rap-bolting was done to preserve the delicate flake.

Bridwell's free-climbing partners were also active on their own. Klemens climbed an ominously wide crack to produce *Cream* (5.11a), while Barry Bates put his renowned strength to good use on such classic routes as *Lunatic Fringe* (5.10c), *Vanishing Point* (5.10d), and the *Center of Independence Pinnacle* (5.10d).

In reference to Bates, Bridwell later remarked, "That guy is just too strong! I hated climbing with Barry—he'd hang in the middle of these desperate liebacks and casually put in a pin. The rest of us could barely follow the thing, and here he was just hanging there. He's sickeningly strong!" Although extremely modest and unassuming, Bates was a master of difficult routes and took his climbing very seriously. Steve Wunsch, one of his frequent partners, once remarked, "The thing I remember most about Bates was his intense drive that would get him above and beyond where he expected to be—so far out that he would have died if he fell. . . . The

quintessential Bates was intense, meticulous, and perfectionist on every type of climbing. But on occasion, he would break loose with yelling or obscenities, or calling for his mother."

One of the season's highlights was Peter Haan's solo ascent of the Salathé Wall. What made the climb even more remarkable was Haan's lack of experience on big walls—he was basically a free climber and had never even completed a multiday route before. He admitted, "This climb, which I had secretly, boyishly thought of for five years, was in complete disjunction with my experience." But Haan didn't let a trivial detail like lack of experience stand in his way, especially since he had two burning reasons for attempting the route: "I was in better shape than ever, prepared for intense climbing," he noted. "And for me, it was inevitable that I would have to attempt, for better or for worse, a resolution of the desire I had to develop friendship of solid character within thorny Camp 4, and thus ratify climbing as a sufficiently rich lifestyle. And it was in the cards that in searching for respect, understanding, and meaning there that I would attempt first a rejection of the arena and then maybe its reconciliation. The Salathé Wall done solo would catch it off guard, both kick it in the teeth and then bring that motley crew's respect, primitive as it might be. But also I, even more unrealistically, hoped for their love."

Haan definitely made an impression among Camp 4's residents, finishing the route in six days. In so doing, he joined Royal Robbins (who soloed the Muir Wall) and Tom Bauman (who soloed The Nose) as the only climbers to ascend El Cap completely on their own.

In a different region of the park, Warren Harding and Galen Rowell were back on another virgin rock wall, this time in Hetch Hetchy Valley. Rowell was one of the few climbers to recognize the untapped potential of this magnificent area. He had previously climbed *Wapama Rock* (V 5.9 A3) with Joe Faint, and *Hetch Hetchy Dome* (VI 5.10 A3) with Chris Jones. Now he and Harding focused their attention on the north face of Kolana Rock, an elegant formation which rose directly above the placid waters of the reservoir. They succeeded on the 12-pitch route (V 5.9 A3), although it was no picnic for Harding. "This was the first climbing I'd done since El Cap," he confessed, "and I was in lousy shape. My leg ached, and my feet hurt like hell. I could barely make the backpack in! Can it be that serious drinking and general debauchery are not the way to train for a strenuous rock climb?!"

The following summer was a banner year for strenuous new routes. As usual, El Capitan was the stage for these developments. And the two leading performers of 1972 were Jim Dunn and Charlie Porter.

Dunn achieved a major coup by completing a solo first ascent of El Cap. His route *Cosmos* (VI 5.8 A4) was located between the Dihedral and the Salathé walls. He initially started up the rock with Gordon Smaill. However, at the 800-foot level Smaill was injured in a fall. The pair retreated leaving several ropes fixed.

But Dunn was not about to let the project die. "I don't like to be sidetracked," he later said. "When I have to do other things I just get bummed!" So he returned to El Capitan and started up alone. After several days of mind-numbing toil, and dealing with the constant anxiety of being alone and exposed on this colossal wall, he began to crack. "I was talking to my equipment," he recalled, "and actually apologizing to El Cap for underestimating it, and getting in over my head."

Yet two factors convinced him to stay on the wall. First, there was his inner hunger to finish this challenging route in good style. But even more important, the rock was overhanging and too steep to rappel off. He was trapped. The only way out was up. So he stayed in the game and completed the route in five days. Years later, after making the second ascent, Jack Roberts called the route "an aesthetic creation of a possessed man!"

Dunn's solo first ascent was a highly coveted prize. Many climbers had dreamed of establishing such a route, one-on-one with El Capitan. Jim Bridwell remarked, "That climb was way ahead of its time—one of the all-time impressive efforts in Yosemite!" Royal Robbins added, "This stunning achievement is further evidence of the fact that the young climbers have not lost contact with the quintessence of the sport."

In fact Robbins himself just barely missed adding this very prize to his already replete climbing resume. He made a strong attempt to solo a new line on the cliff's southeast face, immediately right of El Cap Tree. In the spring, well before Dunn went up on Cosmos, Robbins spent seven days battling the formidable difficulties of the face. "The southeast face is quite different from the southwest," he said, "one significant difference being that things are generally worse than they look. . . . I was surprised to find that the route overhung continuously for 900 feet. At the 700-foot level, I was 40 feet out from the base of the cliff." At this point he had already used almost half of the 100 bolts he had brought. "The upper part appeared to demand at least another 100 bolts," he lamented, "and

I was not prepared, either morally or practically, to place that many." With the whole painful fiasco of the Dawn Wall still fresh in his mind, Robbins could not justify doing a route which required drilling his way up the rock. So for one of the few times in his life, he simply gave up and descended. It was his last major climbing effort in Yosemite Valley.

Then Charlie Porter stepped to center stage. He first repeated Robbins' formidable route Tis-sa-ack on Half Dome, achieving the sought-after second ascent. Later he soloed a new route called *New Dawn* (VI 5.9 A4) on El Capitan. This route completed the line first attempted by Chouinard, Bridwell, and others up the right side of El Cap Towers. The nine-day ascent was done in impeccable style—a remarkable achievement considering that Porter dropped his haul bag low on the route, nearly fell off a ledge trying to save it, and spent the majority of the climb existing on starvation rations while sleeping in slings without a sleeping bag.

This type of adventurous misadventure somehow seemed to fuel Porter's energies. He loved the atmosphere and challenge of Yosemite's great walls, and the great stone sentinel of El Capitan became his mecca. "In 1969, the emphasis had been on big walls and being a well-rounded climber," he recalled, "but by '72 the focus had switched to one- or two-pitch free climbs, mostly cracks. For me it was quite nice because there was a wide open field, lots of great wall routes to do and not many people wanted to go out and put in the work." When some of his friends tried to interest him in short free routes, Porter's response was simple: "I'd just get all my pitons and wander off to do something else."

In the fall he and Gary Bocarde wandered off to try another new route on El Cap. The climbers had previously spotted a magnificently sculptured, overhanging bulge of granite to the left of the Muir Wall. There appeared to be a series of tiny thin cracks leading through this beautiful vertical frontier. But once they started climbing, the pair were shocked at just how thin the cracks turned out to be. "Small pitons, small nuts, and rurps were the main tools while climbing," Bocarde noted. "The 21st pitch was the most insane pitch on the climb, and Charlie, the Mad Rurper, led it. He climbed mainly on rurps for the entire 150-foot lead, with a few knifeblades and copperheads placed for security. He used so many rurps on the lower portion of the pitch that he had to retrieve some of them so he could finish the pitch. And we'd brought over 40 rurps! I had very little trouble hand-cleaning most of what he put in. . . . Charlie is definitely *the* rurp expert!"

This Porter masterpiece, which came to be known as the *Shield* (VI 5.9 A4), is still regarded as one of the most aesthetic aid lines up El Capitan. And the 21st pitch, where Porter placed an unheard of 35 rurps in a row, became legendary in Yosemite. Royal Robbins exclaimed, "Porter is a connoisseur of the rurp. He knows more about the rurp and how to use it than anyone has ever known. He has gotten inside the rurp and is looking out."

Yet even this route could not quench Porter's big wall thirst. So in November 1972 he set his sights on El Cap's southeast face. Undaunted by the fact that few climbers were still in the Valley and he couldn't find a partner, he went up on the wall alone and established *Zodiac* (VI 5.9 A4). This 16-pitch route linked a series of ramps and crack systems up a relentlessly overhanging

Climbers on Zodiac

wall. Like the Shield, it remains one of the most popular and satisfying aid lines on El Capitan.

In the years to come, Porter would add an astonishing number of new routes to El Cap with a variety of different partners: *Tangerine Trip* (VI 5.9 A4), *Mescalito* (VI 5.9 A5), *Horse Chute* (VI 5.9 A4), *Excalibur* (VI 5.10 A4), and *Grape Race* (VI 5.9 A5). The eight routes he established on Yosemite's biggest cliff far surpassed the productivity and creative energy of any other climber. Porter created more demanding routes in better style than anyone ever thought possible. And since he always strived to be a well-rounded climber, Porter would continue to push the limits of possibility on challenging routes around the world, including an audacious 36-hour solo of the ultraclassic *Cassin Ridge* on Denali (20,320 feet), the first ascent of Canada's superb ice climb *Polar Circus*, and a solo first ascent of a 40-pitch big wall route on Baffin Island's Mt. Asgard. He was one of the first climbers to fulfill the prophecy of Yvon Chouinard—to "venture forth to the high mountains of the world and do the most aesthetic and difficult walls on the face of the earth." And he fulfilled it in a big way. But he never lost touch with the haunting allure and the innocence of the climbing game. "For me, climbing was a very personal thing, and it still is," he said. "It's a neat game with no written rules, a game of one-upmanship. It has a bit of a mystical aura about it."

Although Porter's exploits made him a legendary figure in Yosemite and around the world, he remained easygoing beneath his bushy beard and bright eyes. Mark Chapman once remarked, "My first impressions of many of my early idols were disappointing. More often than not, these people came across as a little too full of themselves, a little too competitive, and a little too quick to judge others while turning a blind eye to their own shortcomings. This, however, was not the case with Charlie. His character left a bigger impression on me than the sum of his climbing accomplishments."

While Porter concentrated on Yosemite's big walls, the free-climbing renaissance which he ignored continued to gather momentum and prominence. More than ever before, climbers sought to push themselves on thinner cracks, steeper cliffs, and blanker slabs. This intense search for more challenging routes pushed the standards of the day to amazing new levels.

Without question the most important factor in this free revolution was the attitudes of the climbers themselves. With a vision remarkably similar to that of the young Sierra mountaineers of the 1930s, climbers of the early 1970s looked at the immense walls of the Valley with a new perception. Instead of seeing routes that required many days of tedious aid work, they envisioned making fast, free ascents dressed in T-shirts and shorts.

These attitude changes were accompanied by some equally profound changes in equipment. The introduction of gymnastic chalk gave fingertips increased friction to pull on ever smaller handholds, and the magic liquid called tincture of benzoin toughened fingers and hands for the skin-tearing abuse of modern free climbing. Advances in footwear were even more important. The clunky kletterschuhe of yesteryear went the way of the Model T as it was forever replaced by tight, responsive climbing shoes with flexible rubber soles. The blue and gray E.B. shoe became the standard for serious climbers and dominated the crags for over a decade. And for climbing protection, Yvon Chouinard made a major impact with the introduction of artificial chocks, including 6-sided chocks called Hexentrics, and wedge-shaped chocks called Stoppers. This movement away from pitons and toward clean climbing honored the earlier vision of Royal Robbins to preserve the rock with non-destructive protection.

In the early summer of 1973, Yosemite free climbing received a huge boost with the arrival of Henry Barber. This husky loner from the East Coast had slowly nurtured his climbing skills for several years under the conservative tutelage of the Appalachian Mountain Club. However, he didn't exactly fit the image of a bold trendsetter who would single-handedly advance free climbing around the world. "I was a nerd," he admitted frankly, "a complete and total nerd. As a matter of fact, people still think I'm a nerd when it comes to traditional ethics, styles, and new ideas." But although he may not have been part of the "in" crowd, Barber had a burning desire to excel at climbing. "I wanted to get good because I've never really been good at anything in my life," he explained. "I saw something that I

The latest rage in climbing footwear

found naturally easy, something I could excel at, and I wanted to be the best."

Barber's accomplishments that summer convinced many people that he was indeed in a class by himself. One of his first goals was an ascent of the Steck-Salathé route on Sentinel Rock. A close friend of his had been killed on the route the previous year and Barber wanted to do the climb as a tribute. When he couldn't find a partner in Camp 4, Barber went to the north face alone and soloed the route unroped (although he did carry a 20-foot nylon sling to protect 5.9 face climbing on the upper part of the route). The shadowy face that had originally required five days of agonizing toil was blitzed by Barber in an amazing 2 hours and 45 minutes.

News of this stunning ascent spread like wildfire. What made the achievement even more masterful was the fact that Barber had never even tried the route before—his ascent was completely unrehearsed, yet he flashed it in a bold and uncompromising style. "More than anyone else, Henry was the stylistic leader of the new generation," said Royal Robbins. "He was doing things that were unquestionably a step above anything that had been done before. Soloing Sentinel, in record time, on his first time up, that was simply visionary—an inspirational achievement!"

But Barber himself, although generally pleased with the climb, still felt somewhat unfulfilled. "Somehow the route deserved better," he stated. "A party would have enjoyed it and savored it more. It was sort of indecent lowering a great mountain to that level."

Barber and a partner then raced up The Nose in two days, climbing the route almost completely without pitons. Yet again something was missing. "I would have enjoyed it more if I could've sat down, goofed around, and laid in the sun," he remarked. "That's the sort of thing that makes Yosemite routes enjoyable."

In search of a more satisfying experience, he concentrated on shorter routes. *Ahab* (5.10b), a smooth two-pitch climb along the base of El Cap, was just what he needed. And with his characteristic confidence he soloed it without a rope. "Ahab was really enjoyable to solo because it was just a rock climb," he explained, "overhanging hand-jams and a little bit of slab climbing. I felt free. I wasn't being cheated and I wasn't cheating anybody else. Moving freely up this supposedly very hard rock climb was a really enjoyable experience. It was one of the finest climbs I ever did."

Barber also displayed extraordinary energy and endurance by stacking several difficult ascents back-to-back in a single day. Climbers had previously been content to do a single route like *New Dimensions* (5.11a) and then head for the bar to slam a few beers. But Barber thought nothing of cruising up several of the toughest routes at the Cookie Cliff in the same day, with little rest in between.

Besides repeating established routes, Barber also added a significant new line of his own. He chose an often-tried thin crack at the Cookie Cliff. Steve Wunsch had been working on the route for some time, yet had never managed to climb past the committing crux moves. After one span of attempts covering 11 days, Wunsch took a break and suggested that Barber give it a try. Soon after, Barber teamed up with George Meyers to do exactly that. Barber climbed up to inspect the difficulties, returned to the belay, and then sailed through the moves with apparent ease. "So much of that climb was attitude," Meyers noted, "and Henry had the attitude!

He's an intense guy, and couldn't be intimidated too easily."

This new route, called *Butterballs* (5.11c), along with Barber's speed ascents and solos, were a major jolt to the local climbers. In terms of free climbing, Barber was simply in a different league than everybody else. In fact he was so gifted that others became jealous of his accomplishments. Jim Bridwell, who started referring to Barber as "Hot Henry," explained the situation this way: "Henry came to the Valley all steamed up and in good shape. The climbers in Yosemite at the time were kind of lolly-gagging around, so Henry went off and bagged some real gems. And that pissed some people off. I remember one time he and Wunsch were hitchhiking back to the Valley from some climb, and Steve says to Henry:

'Hey, why don't you go hide down there in the bushes. We'll have a better chance of getting picked up if people don't see you.'

"That shows you how popular Henry was in the Valley. But it wasn't Henry's fault. It was the locals' fault because they were snoozing."

Barber himself echoed these sentiments: "Everyone sits around talking about the stuff that should be done, but there is only so much time before someone wants the good line. This is especially true in Yosemite, because the climbs are really beautiful lines. They were bound to get plucked."

Now that Barber had given the local climbing scene a swift kick in the pants, he left in a whirlwind to conquer new crags. During the remainder of 1973, new routes began to appear with increasing frequency. Jim Bridwell spearheaded the trend with routes such as *Hot Line* (5.10c A1) on Elephant Rock, *Central Pillar of Frenzy* (5.10d) on Middle Cathedral Rock, and the sustained *Right Side of the Folly* (5.10d). Steve Wunsch and Mark Chapman finished the line previously started by Bridwell, Mark Klemens, and Jim Pettigrew to establish *La Escuela* (5.11a), the first route in the Valley to have two 5.11 pitches. In addition, Kevin Worrall and George Meyers made the first free ascent of the intimidating corner of the *Bircheff-Williams* route on Middle Cathedral Rock (5.11b). In addition to the stunning crack systems on Middle Cathedral, Worrall and Meyers also explored the cliff's blank faces. Their efforts in 1973 produced a series of classic and very bold routes such as *Quicksilver* (5.9), *Freewheelin'* (5.10b), and *Stoner's Highway* (5.10c).

It seemed like free climbing and clean climbing (without pitons) were here to stay. This latter trend was especially accented by the no-pitons ascents of El Capitan and Half Dome. Yvon Chouinard, describing his chocks-only climb of The Nose with Bruce Carson, explained simply that "Chocking up aid routes has two things to offer climbers. First, with the increased use of nuts, we no longer have to make a choice between fixed pin and piton erosion on commonly climbed routes like The Nose. But more important to me is the added challenge offered by silent aid climbing. By leaving the hammer at home, the nut aficionado can regain the uncertainty and adventure of the first ascentionists." Galen Rowell felt similarly about his no-pitons ascent of Half Dome's Northwest Face with Doug Robinson and Dennis Hennek. He noted that this time they were "committed to an adventure." Both climbs clearly demonstrated the utility and the purity of chocks.

But if ever there was one region of Yosemite that was synonymous with free climbing and clean climbing, it

would have to be that magical wonderland of exquisite domes and spectacular vistas around Tuolumne Meadows. The routes that continued to be established here made a powerful impression on the Yosemite climbing scene. Each new route seemed to open more eyes to the grandeur of this enticing high-country treasure.

The pace of route development, however, often seemed as slow as the Ice Age glaciers that had sculpted the land. For example, 15 years had passed since Wally Reed and Chuck Pratt had completed Tuolumne's first major route, the *North Face* of Fairview Dome (III 5.9). And over three decades had elapsed since Chuck Wilts and Spencer Austin put up the excellent *Southeast Buttress* of Cathedral Peak (III 5.6). Yet a handful of dedicated individuals would soon develop Tuolumne climbing to an extraordinary degree. Nowhere was this trend more evident than on the region's biggest cliff, Fairview Dome.

Fairview Dome: Fairest Of All

"Tuolumne is a spiritual place. The blue skies, pine-scented air, and mountain splendor create a temple for all who visit. Many are the climbers who've been inspired on the golden granite domes that decorate the region. Their prayers are recorded in white puffs of chalk, a sea of knobs, and the unique traditions of those who make their annual pilgrimage."

With these words, Alan Nelson summarized the feelings of many climbers. He was among a growing number of people who began to appreciate the unique gifts that Tuolumne has to offer. A place that had once been overlooked was fast becoming a hallowed climbing sanctuary. Nelson would proclaim, "Pity the poor fools who bravely battle blistering heat, tourist hordes,

The north and west faces of Fairview Dome

and thieves in that sweltering seasonal hell of Yosemite Valley, in a vain search for masochistic glory on great granite walls. Little do they realize the proximity of paradise." Climbers became inspired to spend more and more time exploring the superb rock of the high country, and their efforts were always rewarded.

Most climbers were content to just sample the routes that had already been established. But Bob Kamps, one of the most gifted of the Tuolumne locals, envisioned much more. The easygoing Kamps spent years happily roaming the Meadows. Whether on a bright summer afternoon or a cloudy autumn morning, on a glacially-polished slab or a typical knobby dome, Kamps was irresistibly drawn to the high country. Season after season the modest, wiry school teacher could be found in Tuolumne. The list

of routes that he pioneered, either as a first ascent or as a first free ascent, can only be called prolific. He climbed with amazing grace and control, and his footwork, often with feet splayed duck-like on minuscule nubbins, became legendary among those fortunate enough to share a rope with him.

A young climber named Tom Higgins was one of those lucky ones. Right from the beginning, the impressionable youth fell under the captivating spell of Kamps' personality and Tuolumne's majesty. As a Tuolumne veteran, Kamps patiently taught his young apprentice the ins and outs of the local scene—things like which type of climbing protection worked best, the pattern of afternoon thunderstorms, how to prevent pilfering bears from swiping one's food, and methods for sneaking into the nearby showers for free. With Kamps providing the wisdom gleaned from years of experience, and Higgins adding a steady stream of youthful enthusiasm, the pair made a formidable team.

One of their favorite formations was Fairview Dome. They were especially drawn to the soaring west face of this graceful monolith. They made several determined attempts at a new route on the west face, reaching a high point four pitches up. But each time they were stymied by an utterly blank 85-degree headwall. Higgins lamented, "As unlikely as this seems for Tuolumne, the wall would simply not go free. We had already used four bolts to protect 5.9 and 5.10 climbing immediately below. Would four or five aid bolts now be appropriate? We pondered the situation and finally decided to go down." Their belief that Tuolumne should remain a bastion of free climbing was so strong that they were willing to give up a route rather than do it with aid. This simple philosophy would set a powerful precedent in the high country. The ethic and tradition that developed were basic—do a route from the ground up, and do it without aid, or don't do it at all.

For years after Kamps' and Higgins' initial attempt the west face remained virgin, quietly waiting. Then in September 1973 Higgins was eager for another try. By now Kamps had moved on and was not spending as much time in the Meadows. So Higgins convinced Mike Irwin to join him on Fairview.

The first several pitches passed routinely. But time seemed to be racing by as they climbed. After trading leads on the lower part of the route, Higgins reached the high point of his previous attempt with Kamps, directly below a series of huge roofs. "After my several visits to the vicinity of these roofs, I have realized that they are strangely beautiful but not even barely climbable," he explained. "If any route is

to be accomplished here it must jog right under the roofs, attain a dihedral, then a bowl, and finally the top."

As the fading sun dropped closer to the horizon, Higgins traversed right for a full pitch beneath the ominous roofs. The next pitch looked easy so he casually started up, hoping the summit would soon be theirs. "Suddenly," he recalled, "the wall steepens again. Angry with myself for not anticipating a possible bivouac, I try to force the route directly upward. The climbing seems hard, ridiculously hard. Is it me? Next I traverse right seeking easier rock. I'm working across 5.8 rock, first 40, then 50, then 60 feet from my last

Fairview Dome

protection. . . . I find myself verging on tears! The sun can't be down! I can't be stuck 60 feet out! We can't be without water or food or even the lightest parkas! But it is all true, like the senseless and improbable fates linked together to down the hapless souls described in the AAC Accident Reports."

In the gathering darkness Higgins dropped the bolt drill but still managed to reach a huge ledge called the U-shaped Bowl, only a short distance from the summit. But darkness prevented them from going any further. So like it or not, they settled in for an unplanned night on Fairview.

Surprisingly, the huge bowl was littered with dead wood. They briefly comforted themselves with visions of a hefty bonfire roaring throughout the night. But besides lacking food, water, and warm clothes, they were also without matches. For two hours they tried to start a fire by pounding the rock with their hammer, hoping that sparks would set their toilet paper aflame. Their efforts proved fruitless. So they huddled together for warmth under their ropes, stuffed their feet into the rucksack, and resigned themselves to a long cold night beneath the stars. Higgins stated, "I can't believe that Mike is still patient with me, as well as calm and happy. Supposedly an experienced climber, I've landed both of us dry, cold, empty, and matchless in a tinderbox on Fairview Dome." Higgins couldn't help feeling that "an appropriate punishment is about to ensue."

However, the autumn night turned out to be hauntingly serene. They talked, laughed, dozed, and rubbed each other's backs to control their shivering. In their hurried climbing earlier in the day there was no time to stop and consider the magnificence of their surroundings. Now that fate had forced a halt, they became more in touch with this special place, and with their own emotions. "The heavens are at once beautiful and vacant of a word for us," Higgins recalled. "Under the time-face of the heavens, we find the pace of all things unaltered by our struggle, and are awed and frightened by the prospect. We know now how infinitesimal is our climb under this starry night, the ascent meaning whatever it will to us and us alone. Like broken bodies, we slump onto one another and let the universe take care of itself."

In the first light of morning they resumed their ascent and soon reached the summit. "We are happy with ourselves," Higgins explained, "with having withstood the cold of the night. We hadn't been sullen or angry. Instead of inventing a solution to our predicament of yesterday, perhaps groping to the top by moonlight, we had sat down and watched the entire sky turn black, the stars slowly appear, arrange their patterns, move when we thought they wouldn't, and then release the dawn. We had stopped ourselves long enough to find that the earth ignores yet contains our small destinies, and can be kind."

At first glance, the completion of this route, *Fairest Of All* (5.10c), may not appear to be exceptional. It was not the most difficult climb accomplished in Yosemite, nor was it the longest or the most committing. It did not require the development of any clever new technology, nor involve the participation of any world-famous climbers. Yet in its own way, the route was a triumph—for it made an unequivocal statement regarding the ethics of Tuolumne. Kamps and Higgins chose to pass up the route rather than climb it in a way that would compromise their style. Only when Higgins felt he was worthy of the route did he go back and finish it with Irwin.

This respect for the rock, and respect for his own ideals, gave Higgins a satisfaction that would always stay with him. Looking back on this climb, and on the many seasons spent in the high country, he would say, "The years I've spent climbing in Tuolumne were pure nourishment to me. The Meadows always made the regular flat world bearable, and the flat world made the Meadows a sanctuary."

In addition to his love for Tuolumne, Higgins would always treasure the special feelings he had for his mentor Kamps. The loving spirit of the affable school teacher seemed to permeate the high country, guiding the path of his young recruit. In an open letter written to Kamps years later, Higgins expressed these emotions: "Well, man, as if you didn't know it, you were like a father to me for those summers, modeling a conniving, effortless style, clever protection, and witty love for those soaring virgin walls. So I'll say thanks, and thanks also to Tuolumne for holding us like a mother, between deep blue and granite folds in the warmth of the Meadows sun."

The route Fairest Of All made an eloquent proclamation regarding the importance of ethics, and the current state of Yosemite climbing. And remarkably, that same month another climbing team would demonstrate a similar love and respect for Yosemite rock, this time on the park's grandest wall. And for the first time, people in El Cap Meadow would look up toward El Capitan and ask not "Who are those guys up there?" but rather "Who are those GALS up there?!"

El Capitan: A Woman's Place . . .

The accomplishments of women climbers have historically been given a back seat to those of their male counterparts.

Mountaineering was an activity dominated by men, and strong masculine overtones had always permeated the sport. Climbers liked to believe that it was their fortitude and determination that enabled them to "conquer" the savage peaks. So women, who may have appeared petite and somewhat frail, were commonly either excluded from participating or relegated to second-class status on an ascent.

Still, a few women could be found in the mountains. The obstacles that they overcame were not limited to problems of strength, endurance, or climbing difficulty. More often than not, they also had to surmount the daunting barriers of prejudice and bias.

With increasing frequency, women began to attempt and succeed on notable peaks around the world. Nineteenth-century women took inspiration from the accomplishment of Frenchwoman Marie Paradis, the spry 18-year-old who became the first woman to climb Mont Blanc (15,771 feet), the highest peak in the Alps, in 1808. Still, over half a century would pass before Britain's Lucy Walker reached another milestone by ascending the Hornli Ridge on the Matterhorn (14,782 feet) in 1871. Because of the prevailing attitudes of the day, the pace of women's climbing was agonizingly slow. Yet this pace kept moving relentlessly forward, gathering both speed and momentum.

In the 1930s women climbers began to really make their presence fully known. Miriam Underhill, who has been called America's greatest woman climber, began a bold trend of all-female ascents of the classic routes in the Alps. In short order she led ascents of the Monch (12,980 feet) and the Jungfrau (13,642 feet), followed by the Matterhorn. She also climbed extensively throughout North America, including the High Sierra and Tahquitz Rock.

Her accomplishments were even more impressive considering the primitive equipment that climbers used at the time. "Ropes were 90-foot and 130-foot 7/16 inch manila, the best yachting line available," she explained. "We compensated for its lack of strength with dynamic belays. Steel carabiners were imported from Germany. . . . We sewed leather patches onto pants and shirts to protect us from the friction of body rappels. For footgear in the high mountains we had men's work shoes or old leather ski boots nailed with tricounis. For rock climbing we wore tennis shoes or crepe-soled basketball shoes. With this gear, the better climbers of the time put up routes judged very difficult to this day. In recent years a male climber remarked, 'Imagine climbing the Mechanic's Route [at Tahquitz] in tennis shoes!' I said, 'I don't have to imagine it. I did it!' "

Other climbers active at the time were Helen LeConte, Marjory Farquhar, and Ruth Mendenhall. These women started quietly succeeding on a host of impressive routes throughout the High Sierra, such as the South Face of Mt. Maclure (12,880 feet), the East Face of Mt. Tyndall (14,018 feet), the Swiss Arete on Mt. Sill (14,153 feet), and the East Face of Mt. Whitney (14,494 feet). In the years to come, these adventurous pioneers were followed by such climbers as Ellen Wilts and Irene Ortenburger, who participated in new routes on Matthes Crest (10,918 feet), Ken Minaret (11,760 feet), and The Thumb (13,665 feet).

Given this rich but little-known history of women's mountaineering, the stage was clearly set for someone to break into that male-dominated fortress of macho climbing—Yosemite Valley.

Liz Robbins began the trend back in 1967 when she climbed the Northwest Face of Half Dome with her legendary husband Royal. She thus became the first woman to ascend a Grade VI route in Yosemite. But a myriad of routes still awaited a woman's ascent. "I recall a pervading fear of the early Yosemite climbers," said Doug Robinson, "that someday a gymnast would arrive on the scene and show us all for the frauds that we were. And one day *she* did." Unlikely as it may have seemed, Bev Johnson was that long-awaited someone.

Lean, athletic, and petite, Bev Johnson had a school-girl look and a charming demeanor. But underneath her pleasant exterior lurked a determined rock climber. She would soon demonstrate beyond any doubt that she had what it takes to succeed on the Valley's biggest walls.

Like any other aspiring big wall climber, Johnson first tested herself on several of the Valley's less formidable routes. She made an impressive solo of Washington Column's South Face before climbing her first El Cap route, The Nose, with Dan Asay.

But her dream was an all-female ascent of El Cap, something that had never been done before. So in 1973 she cajoled Sibylle Hectell, a talented climber who had previously completed ascents of the Leaning Tower and Half Dome, into joining her on El Capitan. However, the unassuming Hectell had some serious misgivings. "At the time I was dubious about this," she recalled, "being a relative novice at climbing and also a busy student. But Bev had her plans firmly in mind and needed only an accomplice."

As if the difficulties of the climb weren't enough, both climbers were also aware of an additional factor. "We both lived in Camp 4," Hectell explained, "and we knew that a failure of the first women's attempt on El Cap would be a fiasco we could never live down. With this firmly in mind, we took equipment for every possible contingency: extra water, rainflies, storm gear, and an extra hammer in the bottom of the haul bag. No wonder the damn thing weighed over a hundred pounds!"

They chose the Triple Direct as the route to attempt. As they were making final preparations, some unusual circumstances dictated a hasty exit from Camp 4. "Bev had lived in Squaw Valley for the previous winter and had two boyfriends," Hectell recalled, "one of whom was usually on the East Coast and the second in Mammoth. By an unfortunate coincidence, they both arrived in the Valley simultaneously. I had the opposite problem. I was madly infatuated with Walter Rosenthal, whose tent I had been inhabiting. Walter decided that he would solo the Dihedral Wall and had no time for female distractions. He replaced me with a large rack of hardware and bivy food, spread about the tent floor, and explained that he needed to concentrate on his impending solo. I decided that if he wouldn't see me because he was climbing El Cap, then I'd show him and go climb it myself. Bev and I started on the Triple Direct the same day that Walter started up the Dihedral."

The lower pitches passed routinely until Johnson and Hectell were above Mammoth Terraces. At that point, Johnson became confused as to which way to go. "Bev tried going straight up," Hectell described, "then up and left, and then started yelling for Charlie Porter at the top of her lungs. I was rather surprised until she explained that Charlie's van was right down below, that Charlie had just done the

Shield, and that he could tell us which way to go. Charlie heard us but we could never hear him. Luckily, the one remaining direction, up and right, got us back on route."

The pair continued up the Muir Wall part of the route. At the bolt ladder that TM Herbert had drilled years before, Hectell left behind the huge corner system they'd been following and began a spectacular traverse to the right. Wind blasting at her face, 2000 feet off the deck, she felt an indescribable rush of exhilaration. It was one of the most memorable pitches she had ever led. Unfortunately, it was about to become a little too memorable.

"Suddenly the bolts ended!" she exclaimed. "Mystified, I looked up for cracks, pin holes, anything. Was I supposed to hook across this?

'Bev, the bolts end! I don't have any hooks!'
'PENDULUM!'
Oh, of course, pendulum. 'I've never done a pendulum before!!'
'It's easy. I'll lower you. Just run back and forth. But be careful nailing at the end, that's an expanding flake.'"

Hectell was sure she was about to meet her doom. Yet she gathered her resolve, launched herself out into space, and ended up enjoying the wild maneuver. They soon reached Camp Four ledge on The Nose and continued up past the Great Roof toward Camp Five, which they reached in the dark. With three days of hard climbing behind them, the broken ledges of Camp Five were a most welcome sight.

As the moon began to rise over the rim of the Valley, the weary climbers ate a cold dinner and reveled in their magnificent position. Faint flashes of light occasionally twinkled from Middle Cathedral Rock, directly across the Valley from them, as other climbers settled in for the night on their own bivy ledges. The two women felt so alive, and so proud of themselves. They really were succeeding. And best of all, they were doing it all on their own.

The next day they tried to reach the top but didn't quite make it. Darkness caught them several hundred feet below the summit, without any suitable ledge to sleep on. Surprisingly, amidst all the other gear they were carrying, they didn't have any hammocks. So they were forced to spend an uncomfortable night in their slings, anchored to a vertical wall, 3000 feet in the air. But instead of complaining, both climbers made the best of it.

In the morning they packed the haul bag for the last time and climbed the final pitches to the top. With little fanfare they clambered onto the summit, a welcome patch of horizontal ground, and enjoyed what climbers before them had always enjoyed: the incredible view as the Valley basked at their feet, an eastern horizon punctuated with jagged peaks clawing the sky, and a quiet embrace shared between friends who know one another in a way no one else ever could.

Tired and dirty, but completely satisfied, the two climbers packed their gear and started the long trudge back down into the Valley. Yet they were not the same two people who had started up the rock just days before. The granite crucible of El Capitan had taught them many things—most importantly, it had taught them about themselves. On the brutally exposed mirror of El Cap, a person's imperfections are mercilessly laid bare. Up on the wall they had no one else to rely on but each other. But that was all they needed. The pair showed that they were not just good women climbers but good climbers. When things started to go wrong, as they invariably do on a big wall, John-

son and Hectell simply took it all in stride and kept on going. And if El Cap had taught them anything, it was to trust in themselves and reach for their dreams.

Both Johnson and Hectell would soon return to El Capitan. The very next month Johnson teamed up with Charlie Porter on the first ascent of *Grape Race* (VI 5.9 A5), and Hectell would later join Dave Evans on an ascent of The Nose.

Their accomplishments provided fitting testimony to the potential of women in the sport of rock climbing. Other climbers, such as Lucy Walker and Miriam Underhill, had opened the door of possibility. But Johnson and Hectell stepped through that door in grand style, accepting both the allure and the risks associated with climbing.

In the coming years, women would achieve an outstanding level of success in the mountains. The following year a women's expedition from Japan placed three climbers on the summit of the Himalayan giant Manaslu (26,760 feet), the first 8000-meter peak to be climbed by women. And the following season would see a diminutive 36-year-old Japanese wife and mother, Junko Tabei, become the first woman to climb Mt. Everest (29,028 feet), the Roof of the World.

For these talented climbers, the mountains offered something very special—something that could not be found in any other place. Longtime climber Julie Brugger expressed the thoughts of many climbers, both male and female, with these words: "I don't know where my life will lead me, but I know there will always be mountains in it. There is simply a sense of well-being, that all is right with the world, that I get from being there and that I don't want to live without. . . . For each summit reached offers a glimpse of all the others there are to climb."

As Yosemite greeted another spring in May 1974, a motley collection of teenage climbers prepared to make their mark on the Valley. Hailing mainly from Southern California, they confidently called themselves the Stonemasters, a name they chose after a basement session of smoking marijuana. Besides a hefty sense of humor, the only requirement for membership in the group was an ascent of *Valhalla*, which at the time was the only 5.11 route at Tahquitz Rock.

For several years the Stonemasters had diligently done their homework, relentlessly honing their free-climbing skills, because they had one goal in mind. "We were hell-bent on demolishing the standards," said John Long, the most powerful and imposing member of the group.

In fact they had already begun to do just that, beginning with an impressive free ascent of the *Vampire* at Tahquitz. First climbed in 1959 by Royal Robbins and Dave Rearick, the Vampire boasted several wild pitches of hideous exposure and A4 nailing up the cliff's monolithic west face. But Long, Mike Graham, and Rick Accomazzo free climbed the thin cracks and wicked liebacks to establish a bold 5.11 testpiece.

The experience had a tremendous impact on all of them, especially Long. "The Vampire was the most pivotal climb I have done," he stated. "Free climbing was in its infancy, and with this ascent we realized we could author a dramatic change in the sport." Shortly thereafter, Long took a giant step in this direction, making the first free ascent of the horrendous *Paisano Overhang* at Tahquitz. To climb the vicious, four-inch-wide crack, Long used the novel technique of wearing thick welder's gloves over his already big hands. This route was likely the country's first 5.12 route.

Then the Stonemasters set their sights on Yosemite. Among the group, Long in particular had already sampled what the Valley had to offer, and he had an insatiable appetite for more. Known to his friends as Largo, he had progressed immeasurably since his early, humbling experiences in Yosemite.

A few years previously, a boyish, 17-year-old Long had then been climbing for only six months. Yet he enthusiastically accepted an invitation by Will Tyree to attempt a free climb of the *Direct North Buttress* of Middle Cathedral Rock (V 5.10c). At the time, the DNB had the reputation as one of the longest, hardest, and finest free climbs in America. But on the crux third pitch, Long was terrified of the exposure and the difficulty. He momentarily questioned if he had what it took to really be a climber. Yet he wouldn't allow himself to give up. "Even as terrified as I was, I didn't want to go back home," he admitted. "I'd worn my bright blue Robbins boots to school just so I could field questions about them and admit I was a rock climber. I'd studied guidebooks on the toilet. Yet unless I unclipped from that anchor and started liebacking, I knew it had all been charades—but I couldn't unclip! Then stubborn conviction kicked in—I was a rock climber, goddamit! Maybe not a bold one, but I wanted to be one, worse than anything else in the world. So although my knees were clacking like wood blocks, I unclipped and started up the flake."

He'd taken a similar blow to his ego, and experienced a similar turning point, as he thrashed his way up the *Left Side of Reed's Pinnacle* (5.10b). Jim Bridwell had offered to lead the cocky teen up the distressingly wide crack that formed the route. "John was outspoken, to say the least," Bridwell recalled, "but only because he could usually back up his words with action."

However, this typically smooth Yosemite crack required good technique and not just brute strength, so the muscular Long was again humbled. As a wily old Yosemite veteran, Bridwell cruised through the difficulties without hesitation. Long was impressed with how easily Bridwell climbed. But Long was hardly surprised at The Bird's prowess, for he'd heard reverent myths that the honed Bridwell was strong enough to tear three New York city phone books in half, and routinely did sets of 100 pull-ups.

When Bridwell reached the top of the first pitch, his precocious partner started up. Bridwell described it this way: "John attacked the crack with force. His muscles bulged and his veins popped. He neared the polished six-inch-wide vertical crux section with little left but courage. Lactic acid crescendoed as panic replaced what little technique he had. He tried to slump onto the rope for a cheater's rest but I was having none of it, and paid out slack. If he made it up, I wanted him to know he had done it on his own. His face flushed with effort, his once-powerful arms quivered, but his heart wouldn't quit until the synapse collapsed. Just then I took pity, and divulged the secret rest hold he hadn't seen behind his back. John's hand shot into it like a chameleon's tongue. Saved! Air flooded into his lungs in great vacuum-cleaner rushes. After a short rest he swam his way to the top and my congratulations."

Since these early learning experiences, Long had become a major force in free climbing. He took inspiration

The Stonemasters hanging out in the Valley

from stories he'd heard about Frank Sacherer, Yosemite's infamous fanatic of free climbing. "Sacherer was never torn between aid and free climbing," Long noted. "He either free climbed or wouldn't bother. This view, still prevalent today, probably seemed rather extreme in Sacherer's era, when the summit meant so much more than the means by which it was attained. My personal convictions were roughly the same. Free climbing certainly seemed the more authentic and fitting method."

An avalanche of new routes were established that year, and Long was one of the leaders. He first teamed up with Rich Harrison and old pal Rick Accomazzo to climb *Greasy But Groovy* (5.10d), an extremely sustained face route beneath the Royal Arches. He also mastered the delicate slab moves of the *Calf* (5.11c) on Glacier Point Apron, making the first free ascent. Other climbers who played prominent roles in new Valley free routes, besides the ubiquitous Jim Bridwell, were Jim Donini, Mark Chapman, Kevin Worrall, Steve Wunsch, George Meyers, John Bachar, and Ron Kauk.

Meanwhile in the high country, it was Vern Clevenger who began to make an impact. Burnin' Vernon, who was once voted Most Likely To Die by his fellow climbers, put up several demanding routes on Fairview Dome during this period. *Piece de Resistance* (5.11c), *Mr. Kamps* (5.11b), and *Heart Of Stone* (5.12a) were among his finest efforts. All of these routes had challenging runouts and outstanding individual moves.

However, Clevenger was dogged by questions about the ethics he had used on some of his routes. At least one of the bolts on the crux pitch of Piece de Resistance had been drilled on aid, which was against the tradition of Tuolumne. Bob Kamps and Tom Higgins

had tried this section previously, but had retreated when it appeared that aid would be necessary. Higgins remarked, "Our climbing styles were founded on the belief that one should leave the impossible for another time, or for others who might someday free-climb it. If aid bolts were necessary, turn back. Leave it for later. For others. Or, for never!"

It was the same philosophy that Higgins had used on Fairest Of All. In fact, he believed so strongly in this Tuolumne tradition that he once chopped the bolts from the Lembert Dome route *Handjive* (5.11a) because the protection was preplaced on rappel. But an uneasy feeling of uncertainty hung in the air. Some wondered whether Tuolumne's traditions were out of date. Was Clevenger actually a pioneer of a new Tuolumne style?

The following summer "Hot Henry" Barber returned to the Valley, brimming with his characteristic energy. He first climbed another thin crack at the Cookie Cliff (*Hardd*, 5.11b), and then ventured to the Cascade Falls area and established *Fish Crack*, the first 5.12 in the Valley. Then, as on his barnstorming visit in 1973, he vanished into the night, leaving the locals shaking their heads in amazement once again.

But the Stonemasters did more than just admire Barber's exploits. They set out to surpass them. Throughout 1975 the fearsome foursome of Bridwell, Long, John Bachar, and Ron Kauk continually expanded the limits of modern free climbing in Yosemite. In May a mass Stonemaster assault of the lower Salathé Wall produced *Free Blast* (5.11b). The group climbed and partied their way up the first ten pitches of the route, and then rappelled back to the ground. In the process they established a lengthy free route with over half of the pitches being 5.10 or harder.

Long, Bachar and Kauk then turned to the old East Face route on Washington Column. Warren Harding had spent ten days bashing his way up the oppressive, overhanging route back in 1959. But the three young rock jocks had other ideas—namely, to climb the route fast and free.

Once on the rock they were astonished by the whole experience: the classic beauty of the line, how well the cracks lent themselves to free climbing, and how quickly they were able to move. They sped up a series of jewel-like dihedrals, completely immersed in the difficulties of the climb. And in fact the difficulties were substantial. "The continuous difficulty we had covered was then unheard of," Long explained. "Eight of the fourteen leads were 5.10 or harder, and several were harder still."

After one and a half days of finger-wrenching effort, and some of the most enjoyable climbing they'd ever done, the trio emerged on top of the Column. Since free climbing the East Face was a totally different experience from aid climbing, they renamed the route *Astro Man* (V 5.11d). It remains to this day one of the most sustained and sought-after free climbs in North America.

Long and Kauk then set out to grab another prize, the first free ascent of the Chouinard-Herbert route on Sentinel Rock. With 15 pitches of varied climbing up Sentinel's textured north face, and a 5.11c roof to surmount near the top, the route offered an obvious challenge. But the rock was water soaked in several crucial spots and the pair were forced to aid climb through a short section. Pleased with the attempt, but disappointed with the aid, Long later went back with Pete Livesey and freed the crux roof. Another of Yosemite's classic big walls fell to the determination and talent of modern free climbers.

The next step in this fast and free

movement was obvious. El Capitan, "The Captain," had instilled terror in the hearts of earlier climbers. Now there were rumblings of an all-out attempt to climb The Nose with as little aid as possible, and as quickly as possible—maybe even in a single day. Could such an impetuous feat really be done? Jim Bridwell had to find out.

El Capitan: The Nose In A Day

Throughout the last ten years, Bridwell had been quietly hatching an audacious scheme to climb The Nose in one day. But he couldn't claim credit for the original idea. That had emerged from a tireless visionary of free climbing whom Bridwell described in this way: "There was a man, but more so, there was a spirit in the form of Frank Sacherer. Had anyone but Sacherer said 'I want to do The Nose in a day' the response from any Camp 4 regular would have been incredulous laughter." But the Valley locals, and Bridwell in particular, had repeatedly seen what Sacherer could do. Because Sacherer thought it was possible, the seed was planted in Bridwell's mind.

Back in 1967 Bridwell had taken an important first step by free climbing the Stoveleg Cracks, which Sacherer believed held the key to a fast one-day ascent. Now eight years later, Bridwell was feeling fit and motivated, and was surrounded by a plethora of talented partners. So the time seemed right to make a determined attempt. But in the end it was an unforeseen circumstance—a certain magazine photograph—that finally spurred Bridwell into action.

The extraordinary plan, like so many others of Yosemite's grand projects, was meticulously formulated in the Valley's renowned nerve center for cultural appreciation and higher thinking: the Mountain Room Bar. One day Bridwell happened to see a photo of an ascent of the Eiger's North Face by a European climbing team. The climbers were striking a pompous, high-class pose in front of the Eiger wearing color-coordinated, immaculately clean climbing outfits. The text of the magazine lavished gooey praise on the climbing team.

John Long vividly recalled how Bridwell "looked annoyed, his index finger drumming the photo. Then he shoved the magazine aside. We would set the record straight, Bridwell promised. And on a class cliff, not some 'heap.' And so it happened that, over a couple of beers, the plan came together to try and climb The Nose in one day."

Bridwell decided that a team of three would best fit the objective, so he invited his long-time friend Billy Westbay to join himself and Long. Bridwell described their strategy for climbing the 34 pitches like this: "I would lead two of the four pitches below Sickle Ledge, with John and Billy taking one each. Above Sickle, John would lead as far as Boot Flake, as his big hands were most appropriate for the predominantly large cracks through this section. Billy drew the middle part of the route which was both aid and free climbing. An excellent climber from Colorado, he was used to switching from aid to free and vice versa. I had the anchor leg from Camp Five to the top."

The night before the attempt they ate a hearty dinner, had a few beers in the bar, then settled into a friend's dorm room for a brief rest. Yet their nerves were still in high gear. "We'd made no secret about our plan," Long noted, "and over the previous few days dozens of climbers approached us to wish us luck. Did we need any gear? Did we need a ride to the base? Did we want someone to meet us on top? Mike White, a Valley regular, summed it

up when he told me to 'do us proud.' We had all of Camp 4 to account to if we failed."

When the alarm went off at 2 A.M. they leaped out of bed, consumed a huge batch of omelets, and then dressed in outlandish getups of wild shirts and brightly colored pants—a not so subtle jab at the stuffy attire worn by the European climbers in the Eiger photo. "As a joke we decided to represent the non-traditional Yosemite avant garde," Bridwell said.

Suitably fed and dressed, the climbers headed for their rendezvous with the Big Stone. Each of them was totally hyped up for the attempt. Long in particular was bursting at the seams. "I felt like I was going to hoist the flag at Iwo Jima," he joked.

In the tranquil darkness at 4 A.M., they started charging up the first four pitches. Bridwell had previously worked out a system that had the leader climbing on one rope and trailing a second rope. Once the leader anchored the lines at the top of a pitch, the second climber would jumar up one rope and remove gear from the rock, while the third climber jumared up the other rope. The plan worked to perfection and they soon reached Sickle Ledge.

From there Long took over. He climbed upward a short distance and then tackled the spectacular pendulum which led to the Stovelegs. "You lower down about 60 feet," he described, "then start swinging back and forth. Now at speed you go for it, feet kicking hard, digging right, and hurdle a corner. You feel the momentum ebbing so you dive, yes dive! If you've chanced it right, you plop a hand into a perfect jam just as your legs start to swing back. You kip your torso, kick your boot in, and you're on line. The laser-cut fracture shoots up the prow for 350 feet of primarily perfect hand-jamming, each pitch ending in stark hanging belays."

Long raced upward like a man possessed, making insane runouts on 5.10 terrain. "I kept climbing recklessly fast," he recalled, "and Jim and Billy kept gassing up the lines so quickly that they gained the belays sucking wind. Then one would hand me the rack and Bridwell would ask what I was waiting for." They were all amazed at the rate of their progress. "Pitches rolled by like dollars on a New York taxi meter," Bridwell said wryly. "John flew up the Stovelegs with the certainty of the Yosemite veteran that he was, reaching the top of Dolt Tower by 6:15."

As they clambered onto Dolt Tower they awakened two climbers bivouacked there. The slumbering pair, mere mortals not expecting any company, were quite startled by the three newcomers. "Bleary-eyed, one asked where our haul bag was," Bridwell recalled. "I responded by pointing to a small rucksack on my back. His expression became quizzical as he looked at our bizarre style of dress. In our purple and pink doubleknit pants, worn with paisley and African print shirts, we presented a questionable apparition to any eyes, sleepfilled or otherwise."

Long continued upward at breakneck speed. "It seemed only minutes before John was clipping the bolts toward Boot Flake, four pitches higher," said Bridwell. "This was his 13th lead, not including the 4th-class pitch up the Sickle."

However, as Long climbed a 5.10c crack toward the top of the Boot, the furious pace he'd been keeping began to catch up with him. Forty feet above his last protection, and looking at a possible 80-foot fall, his massive arms started to writhe with paralyzing cramps. "I felt as if I had an anvil in my pants, pulling

me off," he exclaimed. "The fall looked to be a large and painful one, directly onto about where Amarillo would be on Texas Flake. I dangled off an ever-creeping left jam and desperately tried to shake out. No good. Panting, I jerkily down-climbed a few moves, slotted in a borderline nut, and hung on it long enough to jiggle the cramp out. Partially recovered, I frigged up to the top of the Boot, clipped off the cabled five-bolt anchor, and kissed the rock. My part was done. It wasn't quite 8 A.M."

At this point Westbay took over the sharp end of the rope, leading through the devious cracks and loose diorite below the Great Roof. Feeding off the electrifying vigor which they all were feeling, he climbed upward at a truly inspired level. "The total commitment by each of us brought the energy level to an unbelievable pitch," he recalled. "Time seemed almost suspended for us. Our rhythmic upward motions were the ticks on our clock."

By early afternoon the climbers reach the multi-layered ledges of Camp Five. Now it was time for The Bird to take over. His years of big wall experience paid off handsomely as he engineered the fastest and most efficient path through the final pitches. "We were 2500 feet up the wall now," Long described, "into the really prime stuff. Here the exposure is so enormous, and your perception so distorted, that the horizontal world becomes incomprehensible. You're a granite astronaut, dangling in a kind of space/time warp. And if there is any place where you will understand why men and women climb mountains, it is here in these breezy dihedrals, high in the sky."

Despite numbing fatigue, lack of sleep, a jammed rope, and dropped gear, Bridwell doggedly plodded upward toward the summit. A few key words of encouragement from Long were especially memorable: "Hurry man, we gotta make it down before the bar closes!"

The pitches continued to fly by until suddenly they reached the final belay station, directly below the overhanging headwall where Harding had drilled his epic bolt ladder. "Since Harding's day, some madman has re-engineered the last belay so that it hangs at the very brink of the headwall," Long noted, "a mind-boggling nest where all 34 pitches spill down beneath your boots. It's a master stroke, that hanging belay, for it gives climbers a moment of pause at one of the most spectacular spots in all of American climbing. Cars creep along the road three-quarters of a mile below, broad forests appear as brushed green carpets, and for one immortal moment, you feel like a giant in a world of ants."

It was a surprisingly subdued, anti-climactic juncture as the three drained climbers scrambled onto the summit. No fanfare, no news reporters, no victory feasts. In fact the enormity of their accomplishment simply didn't sink in. "During those first few instants on top, curious reactions are the rule," Long remarked. "I've heard of climbers hugging boulders, punching partners, and weeping openly—some from relief, some sad that it's over. I have seen climbers babbling incoherently, and I once saw a middle-aged Swiss team simply shake hands, abandon their gear, and stroll off for the Falls trail, their climbing careers at once made and finished right there. For us, I only remember coiling ropes and booking for the East Ledges descent route, everyone cussing at not having brought a pair of tennis shoes."

After several rappels and much scrambling they reached the high-

(From left) Billy Westbay, Jim Bridwell, and John Long after the first one-day ascent of The Nose

way as darkness fell, 17 hours after leaving the Valley floor. Never had El Capitan been climbed in such a rapid, masterful way. Despite a fatigue that pierced every inch of their bodies, and the screaming pain of their aching feet, they took a moment to look up at the Big Stone—and at last they began to realize the significance of what they had just done. "If you want to know something of the world's age, look up at El Capitan in the moonlight," Long later said. "My feet suddenly felt fine, and for a long beat we three just stood fast and gaped up at it; and the majesty of the cliff, and what it meant to us to have climbed it in one day, finally struck home."

With the ascents of Free Blast, Astro Man, and The Nose in a day, Yosemite climbers established themselves as the leading edge of American free climbing. They reigned supreme on fiendish finger cracks, polished slab routes, and long multipitch climbs.

But even more than over Yosemite's soaring walls, they continued to have sole dominion over that unsavory dumping ground for social misfits, better known as Camp 4. Like the penniless pagans of Yosemite's Golden Age, the current locals had very special feelings for the place. "Throughout the '70s, Camp 4 was emblematic for all that was illegitimate, including everyone who lived there," explained John Long. "Entire summers would pass without seeing a single ranger. They had better things to do than prowl through a ghetto of bohemians who made a career out of climbing rocks and wasting time. The place had been written off as some sort of leper colony. If you had a rack and a little nerve and no immediate future, you belonged. . . . It was crazy and cutloose, everything was done on the fly, and damn, did we feel vital and alive!"

"Camp 4 was a community in every sense of the word," added Kevin Worrall. "There were neighbors, love affairs, slums, parties, gymnasiums, loonies, territorial disputes, degeneration, and inspiration, all within its boundaries."

"One way or another, we all felt like outcasts," said Billy Westbay. "In some ways we were really cynical, but we were also very hopeful about what the future could bring. Climbing in those days was our life! But more than anything else it was like a brotherhood. We all just fed off each other, and that allowed us to achieve more than if we were on our own—we were able to discover more of what we could really do. We all exceeded what was thought to be possible, especially because we could dream big dreams. The boundaries just kept breaking down. It was magical!"

But a certain amount of competition could also be found subtly lurking beneath the surface. This competition was usually healthy, acting as an incentive for climbers to push themselves more. But it was still something which could clearly be felt. "Yosemite at that time was an intense, competitive scene," recalled George Meyers. "I remember Bridwell once said to me, 'If you're here to have a good time, you're here for the wrong reason!' And in a way that described what was going on. If you didn't take your climbing seriously enough to be out there trying to knock off challenging routes and work your way through the grades, then you were wasting your time."

Outsiders especially could sometimes feel alienated. Some newcomers detested the competition and left the Valley with a bitter taste in their mouths, swearing never to return. Others adjusted and even thrived under the scrutiny of the locals.

John Long was one of those who found a home in Camp 4. He returned to the place season after season, becoming an eloquent historian of all the wacky, disjointed aspects of camp life:

REGARDING THE PEOPLE *There was Mark Chapman, with his poet's soul, simian strength, and a voice like Frank Sinatra's. And Eric Shoen (aka mellow Brutus), who was strong enough to rip your head off at the waist but never would, because he got weepy over stray dogs and kids on crutches. There was Dale Bard—one part anorectic brat, two parts dynamite, and three parts climbing fanatic. Despite a strict diet of wild honey, hot chocolate, and Snickers bars, Dale was so lean and whey-faced you wanted to ask about his embalmer.*

One of the most unique characters in Yosemite at this time was John Yablonski, better known as Yabo. The chain-smoking, fast-climbing Yabo was famous for having survived so many near-death experiences. His most infamous fall occurred when he was trying to make a ropeless ascent of *Short Circuit* (5.11d), an overhanging crack in Merced Canyon. At the very top of the crack, 35 feet in the air, he suddenly popped off and went hurtling toward the ground—and a bone-crushing impact. But a slim tree branch somehow lodged itself under his armpits, and Yabo was lowered gently to the ground without a scratch. His exploits seemed to become more colossal and death-defying as time went on.

But foremost among the inhabitants of Camp 4 was Bridwell himself. John Long described him this way:

Jim Bridwell was the de facto lord of Camp 4 and everyone in it. He had a vulpine smile and a gymnast's frame, and was the biggest name in American climbing. . . . He was just enough older than us that he seemed to know everything. (He claimed to have known the Unknown Soldier, and who shot him). In a manner, a rope ran from Jim back to the very beginnings of the sport—for he'd climbed with Kor, who had climbed with Robbins, who had climbed with Wilts, who had climbed with Mendenhall, who had climbed with Clyde, and for all I knew, the only thing separating me from Edward Whymper and the first

ascent of the Matterhorn was the chance to rope up with The Bird.

REGARDING MEALS *Ninety percent of our money went to buying food, the other ten percent to liquor. We would eat till we felt ready to explode, rest for a bit, and then eat some more. . . . A favorite stunt was to frequent barbecues and picnics put on by various religious groups who swarmed into the park for weekend retreats. Acting pious and playing along was our ticket to the chow. So we'd all turn out in our finest gym trunks and T-shirts, smiling through a tortuous homily and crooning along with the righteous, the whole time licking our chops and growing increasingly restless until we could finally break for the vittles. I have no idea how The Bird learned about these affairs but he did, and so frequently that Dale Bard claimed a tourist couldn't so much as roast a couple marshmallows without The Bird catching wind of it.*

ON EXTRACURRICULAR ACTIVITIES *Our craving to get laid cannot be overstated. Furthermore, sex, and plenty of it, was an indispensable aspect of our training routine. According to The Bird, perilous climbs demanded steadiness and a Zen-like acuity impossible to achieve when freighted with 'urgent fluids.' They encumbered the 'terrestrial body' and distracted the 'astral body.' The fluids had to go. But the Yosemite climber worked the field at a disadvantage—90 cents away from having a buck, ragged as a roach, eating holes out of doughnuts, and trying to woo Helen of Troy. That we might end up with someone a little less was to be expected; that we ended up with anyone at all was a miracle. There was little to recommend us—no money, no threads, no future, no goals beyond lines on the rock. But we had a lot of passion for that much, and it saw most of us through the storm.*

In order to attract some nocturnal companionship, male climbers displayed their characteristic energy and creativity. Like some misplaced mating ritual from a modern urban jungle, many locals decorated their "nests" with the finest accouterments that their destitute existence would allow. Tents were painstakingly festooned with such exotic accessories as bead curtains, satin sheets, erotic photos and mirrors attached to the inside walls, and best of all, actual mattresses which were appropriated from the Curry Company.

Not surprisingly, Lord Bridwell had the best setup in camp—a large carpeted tent, tastefully decorated with drapes and bookshelves, and the requisite Curry mattress. "One way or another," he explained, "we created quite a home away from home among the rocks, dust, and pine trees." But

even The Bird's roost was lacking in one critical accessory—electricity.

So Bridwell and Werner Braun concocted a daring plan, dubbed Operation Edison, to correct this glaring deficiency. They would first "acquire" a large power cable from the Park Service maintenance yard. Then they would secretly run the cable from a light-bulb outlet in the Camp 4 restroom, through an underground drainage culvert, and finally to their camp site. The result? All the free light and loud music they could ever want.

The plan worked to perfection. The precious cable was clandestinely obtained and hooked up, and Braun was made to slither through the wet, slimy, claustrophobic storm drain with the other end. They now had the only site in Yosemite National Park with free, unlimited electricity. Bridwell re-

The sorcerer and his apprentice: Jim Bridwell (left) and John Long

Camp 4

marked, "For the remainder of that summer we bathed in the amplified sounds of our favorite bands, and in the enthusiastic approval of our friends and neighbors. Not only had we scored a social success, but we had done so at the expense of the hated Park Service."

Yet their campground concertos came to an abrupt end when the light bulb in the restroom eventually burned out. An all-too-diligent custodian discovered the hookup and began following the path of the buried cable. Step by step he yanked the cable out of the ground, like some probing prison guard unearthing an escape mechanism. He even went so far as to crawl through the wretched culvert to retrieve Government property, which he successfully did. For Bridwell and Company it was now back to primitive battery-powered stereos to meet

their musical needs. But if nothing else, the whole affair still made a good campfire story.

In addition to their schemes for acquiring food, attracting women, and fully equipping their camp sites, the male locals also needed some way to replenish their perpetually empty wallets. Ironically, one of the best ways to make money was a method begun by Bridwell in the late 1960s—working for the Park Service on rescues. Whether it was assisting an injured climber on Half Dome or finding some airhead tourist lost in the backcountry, rescues provided a welcome source of income. And being on the rescue team brought the added bonus of being able to stay for free all summer in the Camp 4 Rescue Site.

"When I rolled into the Valley in

1978, I heard stories about the Rescue Site before the bus driver could even unload my spanking-new haul bag," said Russ Walling. And indeed there was a seemingly endless string of incredible tales, some ghastly in their bloody details, others guaranteed to laugh you senseless.

George Meyers described a typical "rescue" in this way: "One time an Oregon climber broke his leg near the top of The Nose, so we went to the rim and got all set up. First we lowered down a stretcher to the victim, then we started lowering down the important stuff— six-packs of beer. Then we all just kicked back on Camp Five ledge, drinking beer and smoking dope. Even the victim was getting really loaded! Everybody had a great time. And when we got finished we got a free dinner at the Ahwahnee. Getting paid, getting loaded, and getting dinner. Can't beat that!"

Perhaps the most memorable incident ever to engulf Camp 4 occurred when a drug-laden plane crashed into Merced Lake, 16 miles east of the Valley. When word got out that the ill-fated craft was stuffed to the gills with 10-pound bales of smuggled Colombian marijuana, a stampede ensued that would have made a Klondike miner proud.

John Long recalled, "Since there was obviously enough for every rascal in Camp 4 to get quickly and shockingly rich, all The Bird's boys and all their friends were immediately recruited. Some returned with upward of 150 pounds of the 'red-haired' weed, a burden that fetched roughly $50,000 on the open market. 'Hiking for dollars' we called it, and in a week's time more than half a million dollars worth of booty had been hauled to light. . . . Climbers who a few weeks before

hadn't had two dimes to rub together, streamed back into the Valley and were spending cash with all the nonchalance of a Saudi prince. Good-bye Top Ramen. It was steak dinners and cognac all around."

Of course the contraband gold mine soon played out, and the money gained from the drug sales was quickly squandered on such things as high-stakes gambling and exotic clothes. For the climbers involved, it was back to living in the dirt and scrounging for leftovers. But such was the life of a Yosemite climber. The ups and downs of their lives were accepted and even embraced, for powerful feelings tied them to the rock, to each other, and to those who had come before them. "Back then," Long explained, "Yosemite was the focal point of world rock climbing, against which all other climbing areas were measured. And the Americans were the best. The very idea that some Frenchy could waltz into the Valley and show us how it was done was incomprehensible, and intolerable. If not invented, modern rock climbing was surely refined and defined in Yosemite, and all serious Yosemite climbers felt it a point of pride to carry on the tradition. . . . You, who probably pulled a D+ average in high school were now a torch bearer of a great tradition, a top dog. It was so outrageous and downright fun to be a part of it, that when you weren't you felt cheated and unfulfilled. You had to get back to Yosemite, back to Camp 4 and your main men, and get back up off the deck. In a hurry!"

If the locals ever needed an example of this mindset they had only to observe Bridwell. Just days after the exhausting Nose in a day ascent, he was back up on El Capitan. And not on some beat-out trade route. Instead, he was piecing together what would become the hardest big-wall route in the world.

Beginning back in 1974 Bridwell had scoped a tenuous line to the left of the North America Wall. He had previously completed a reconnaissance of the first ten pitches with Werner Braun. Dale Bard was also supposed to be part of the team, but he got caught stealing a loaf of bread from the Degnan's bakery truck and ended up cooling his heels in a Mariposa jail. Bridwell later returned to the route with Rik Reider, Mike Graham, and Billy Westbay. This attempt ended on the fifth pitch when Reider was hit by a large rock during a fall. The resulting skull fracture required emergency brain surgery in Fresno, and the red-haired fireball would never be the same.

Still intent on finishing the route, Bridwell and Westbay recruited Fred East and Jay Fiske to join them on El Cap. Westbay recalled, "After Rik's fall, it was really difficult trying to find people willing to go back up there with us. And even when we finally returned, and climbed past the spot where Rik got hurt, it was really weird because there was blood all over the rock."

Yet the team spent over a week on the wall and finished the route. Named *Pacific Ocean Wall* (VI 5.9 A5), the route was unprecedented at the time for its continuous difficulty—there were five A5 pitches on the first ascent. "The 6th, 8th, and 10th pitches were all really hard," said Bridwell, "especially the 8th. It was far and away the hardest pitch done at the time. It took 4½ hours to lead the thing. But that climb set a whole new standard for aid climbing. It probably changed me more than any other route. After that I knew that no matter how bad things looked that I could still do it." The difficulty also

made a huge impression on Westbay, who simply remarked, "That route was intense! Really intense!"

With this ascent, Bridwell shifted his focus back toward big, intimidating new routes on El Cap and Half Dome. The allure of the walls, with all of their triumphs and failures, was something that he surrendered to again and again. On the Big Stone he established *Mirage* (VI 5.9 A4) with Kim Schmitz and Jim Pettigrew, and then *Sea Of Dreams* (VI 5.9 A5) with Dale Bard and Dave Dieterman. The latter ascent was especially significant because the climb was the first Valley route to have an if-you-fall-you-die pitch. That section, dubbed the Hook or Book pitch (A5), still frays the nerves of many leaders and belayers alike. "With only 39 holes drilled, 9 pitches of A5, and lots of A4, that's the best route I ever did," Bridwell later said. He also put up *Bushido* (VI 5.10 A4) and *Zenith* (VI 5.9 A5) on Half Dome, and the *Bob Locke Memorial Buttress* (VI 5.11 A4) on Mt. Watkins.

Yosemite's big walls also received renewed attention by women climbers during this time. Although Bev Johnson and Sibylle Hectell had ascended the Triple Direct four years before, no team of women had been back to El Cap since. So in April 1977 Molly Higgins and Barb Eastman made an attempt at the first all-women's ascent of The Nose. They climbed the demanding cracks and airy pendulums of the lower section quickly, reaching El Cap Towers after a long, exhausting, but exhilarating first day. From this amazing perch, one of the most spectacular ledges in the Valley, Higgins could only marvel at the rock they had just climbed, especially Stoveleg Crack. "Those beloved Stovelegs," she exclaimed. "For the past two years every crack I'd climbed had been a gesture of training for those cracks. And I was sad that they were over. Now all we had to do was climb the upper 2000 feet of the route!" The pair went on to complete the route in four days.

The following year Bev Johnson returned to Yosemite and climbed the Dihedral Wall alone in eight days. In doing so she became the first woman, and only the fifth person ever, to solo El Capitan. It was a tremendous accomplishment—one that only climbers such as Royal Robbins, Tom Bauman, Jim Dunn, and Charlie Porter had achieved. Much of the lingering male chauvinism among the Yosemite locals was dramatically swept away by Johnson's bold ascent. Women had again shown themselves to be talented, competent climbers who were definitely up to the challenges of Yosemite. The petite former gymnast even helped out two male climbers who were struggling on an adjacent route, the West Buttress. In describing Johnson's impressive achievement, as well as writing a detailed list of previous coups by her and other women, Royal Robbins had this subtle message for the Camp 4 hardmen: "Read it and weep, lads."

Bev Johnson and Jim Bridwell, along with a handful of other determined climbers, always seemed to excel in the forbidding vertical desert of Yosemite's soaring walls. In fact a few climbers would totally dedicate themselves to a stark, monastic existence of sacrifice and discomfort on one huge wall after another.

This different breed of climbers became known as wall rats. John Long described them this way: "Many rats were extravagant characters, like the wandering prospectors of the Old West—fiercely private and independent. They cared little for supposed glory and nothing at all for fame. Having their exploits publicized or praised was considered poor form, because their game was like all obsessions: personal. However much they liked the hazards, toils, and long silences on the high crag, their climbing went beyond liking in almost all directions. What made them rats was who they became when they were pasted high above the world. They all seemed to do just a little better on the walls than on the ground. Their quest was their religion, and in religion, seeking is finding. The summit meant nothing, the wall everything."

The outrageous antics of these extraordinary outcasts often bordered on the unbelievable. Suspended in space and time, in a world that few knew and even fewer understood, they formed a wonderfully eclectic menagerie of humanity—sometimes dark and somber, sometimes loud and boisterous, but always intent on living life to the fullest.

On one occasion, after two climbers were killed near the Great Arch on El Cap's Tangerine Trip, an oppressive sense of death hung over the route. But then the wall rats took over. Greg Child recalled that a team "eager to shatter the aura rushed in where angels feared to tread, and crossed the tainted arch clad in Ghostbuster T-shirts and devil masks procured from a Fresno magic store."

One particularly memorable incident occurred when wall rats Hugh Burton and Steve Sutton carried a huge stash of stolen golf balls up El Capitan. "They teed up on El Cap Towers," recalled Long. "Along with 200 golf balls they brought a genuine three-iron, a driver, and a thatch of Astro-Turf, and spent a June afternoon banging great drives into the meadow far below. Several cars were struck, windshields shattered. The rangers closed the road down for three hours and fanned out on horseback looking for a sniper. Cars backed up, overheated, rammed each other, and tourists fought. There were several arrests. The case was never solved."

Burton and Sutton were in fact a frequent source of entertainment for the Yosemite locals. "Those two were inseparable, and absolutely bonkers," said George Meyers. "They were young and brash, and acted like it constantly. One time they came biking into camp late at night after some kegger, totally drunk, one pedaling the bike and the other sitting on the handlebars. They crashed right into their tent, snapped the center pole, and the whole thing collapsed on top of them. You could hear them both laugh, and then barf, and then pass out. And that's where we found them the next morning, lying in barf beneath their tent. But they were doing this kind of stuff all the time! They should've been dead a long time ago! For them, the hazards of climbing were the least of their worries!"

But while the wall rats sought enlightenment and escape amidst the great granite seas, a growing cadre of free climbers continued to open new horizons on an astonishing variety of routes throughout Yosemite. Two of the most productive free climbers were John Bachar and Ron Kauk.

Bachar was a young Southern Californian who started climbing at the tender age of 14. From his home near the L.A. Airport, he would pedal a beat-up bicycle all day to reach the tan sandstone outcrops at Stoney Point. This popular climbing area north of Los Angeles was instrumental in the early training of many prolific Yosemite climbers such as Royal Robbins, Yvon Chouinard, and TM Herbert. Bachar would soon join this elite group of Valley legends, leaving his own distinctive mark on the park's climbing lore.

But during these early years, reaching Stoney Point late in the day, the man who would become known as Johnny Rock only had time for about 30 minutes of bouldering before nightfall. Then it was back on his bike for the long ride home in the dark. Yet these marathon days paid handsome dividends when he reached Yosemite several years later.

Immediately after his high-school graduation ceremony Bachar jumped into his ramshackle car, already packed to the roof with climbing gear, and headed straight for the Valley. At that time it was still possible to drive right

John Bachar climbing Crack-A-Go-Go

into Camp 4 and park anywhere. So he did what everyone else did—picked a dusty spot among the pines, set up his stereo, and hung out for the summer.

It was there that he met Kauk. Together these titans formed an exceptional friendship and a powerful team. By the late 1970s they had established themselves as two of the best climbers in the country. Free ascents of Astro Man (5.11d) and Free Blast (5.11b) were behind them, they had climbed much of The Nose free, and they had made the first free ascent of *Hotline* (5.12a) in the Elephant Rock area, creating one of the early 5.12s in Yosemite. "We were right at each other's limit," Bachar recalled. "No one else was even close. It was just us pushing each other. I'd do something he couldn't do, then he'd do something I couldn't do. We'd each eventually get it, but it was great because we'd motivate each other. We just picked and chose whatever routes we wanted."

One of their most memorable efforts occurred in 1978 on Big Columbia Boulder, an immense block of rock that sits regally in the middle of Camp 4. All the legendary Yosemite climbers had strolled past the majestic boulder a thousand times. But it was Bachar and Kauk, acting on the suggestion of Valley madman John Yablonski, who thought they saw a possible route on the rock's overhanging east side. Despite the horrendous difficulties, Bachar and Kauk threw themselves at the problem with an avalanche of youthful energy for four months, relentlessly climbing up, falling off, and climbing up again.

After countless failures, Kauk finally muscled his way through the scary 5.13 crux high off the ground and reached the top. "I couldn't even believe it at first," he exclaimed, "I almost fell off just from excitement!" Bachar also

Ron Kauk climbing Midnight Lightning

solved the problem a short time later, despite the fact that a key hold broke off during his attempts. The route was named *Midnight Lightning,* and it became an instant classic in North American bouldering. As a measure of the route's difficulty and frightful appearance, it would be six years before anyone else but Kauk and Bachar could pull off the horrendous moves.

"Kauk and Bachar were the two people who literally exploded free climbing standards worldwide," marveled TM Herbert. "They were far ahead of anybody in the US, Europe, or anywhere else. Those two were way out there! They were the limits! They were doing 5.12s before they were 18 years old! By the time they were 20, they'd put up all kinds of vicious, cruel, nasty routes—and in a style that was far above anyone else."

The two climbers were also extremely successful working on projects separately. Kauk participated in free ascents of *Freestone* (5.11d), *Kaukulator* (5.11c), *Blind Faith* (5.11d), *Space Babble* (5.11a), the Rostrum's *North Face* (5.11d), *Separate Reality* (5.11d), and *Tales of Power* (5.12b). He also showed that he was no stranger to delicate aid work, participating in the first ascents of *Iron Hawk* (VI 5.9 A4) and *New Jersey Turnpike* (VI 5.10 A4+), two demanding new lines on El Cap's southeast face. "It's a heavy experience to be 17 years old and climb El Capitan," he said. "After being up there four or five days at a time you inevitably learn values, like how precious food and water are, and that any move you make must be carefully thought out. You lay there and look at the stars at night and get up with the sun in the morning. I found a deep connection with Nature through those experiences."

Bachar, meanwhile, was busy making a name for himself in a very different game—climbing completely on his own. Free soloing, climbing with no rope and no protection, began to exert an increasingly seductive allure which would ensnare him again and again. Only a select few had ever free soloed any of the Valley's major routes: Henry Barber started the trend with his 1973 solo of the *Steck-Salathé* (V 5.9) on Sentinel Rock, and Charlie Fowler raised eyebrows with his 1977 solo of the *Direct North Buttress* (V 5.10b) of Middle Cathedral Rock.

But in contrast to these climbers, Bachar began to solo constantly, often preferring to climb by himself. "I started soloing for a lot of reasons," he explained. "One is freedom. It's such a great feeling to be unhindered by gear, just moving. I also realized that I could do a lot more climbing. It's not challenging as far as figuring out new moves, but it's challenging spiritually and mentally. Soloing to some people was a crazy, taboo type of thing. But it seemed logical to me—lizards and frogs can crawl up El Cap without a rope, so why can't humans do that too?"

His ropeless escapades throughout Yosemite became more and more bold with each passing year. He worked out like an Olympic athlete, designed an overhanging rope ladder (now called a Bachar Ladder) for special finger training, and sometimes raced up one moderate climb after another to increase his endurance and stamina.

This high-powered training regime culminated in an audacious solo of one of Yosemite's most renowned routes. "I got the idea to solo New Dimensions because I thought it'd be fun," he said. "It's such a classic, pure crack climb, and it's such a big part of Yosemite history. I also knew it would blow some minds. I thought it would be great for climbing to reach that stage."

So with the nonchalance of someone casually jogging around the neighborhood, Bachar cruised up the 400-foot crack with uncanny ease. This outrageous new style, where a climber's life was literally on the line, did much more than just make people sit up and take notice. His accomplishment, the first 5.11 solo in Yosemite, was an inspirational model for climbers around the world.

It also changed Bachar himself. "Doing that route opened up a whole new realm for me," he said. "After that, I could see new stuff to solo all over the place. For me, that type of climbing is real free climbing—it's the real thing! Everything depends on you, not on your equipment. No rope, no knots, no belays. It's just like goofing around on the boulders, except that you get to keep on going. You're way up in the air and you're very clear about what's important, and what's right and wrong—like it's right to hang on and wrong to let go!"

He later upped the ante even more by soloing Butterballs (5.11c), a wickedly thin seam that soars up the Cookie Cliff's Nabisco Wall. Once again, the average mortal climber could only stand back in amazement at what this daring Southern Californian was capable of. TM Herbert summed up the feelings of many when he said, "Bachar is so bold, I don't even understand it!"

But for obvious reasons, free soloing was not embraced by the masses. A single mistake or accidental slip could doom a soloist to an existence as a cripple, or even result in a one-way ticket to the big basecamp in the sky. As Bachar himself observed, "You blow it once, and the penalty is severe. Way severe!"

Since virtually no one had the exceptional prowess and extraordinary confidence of John Bachar, the Valley locals pushed themselves as best they could using more conventional methods. Mark Hudson and Max Jones were particularly busy. They free climbed (with a rope) much of the Salathé Wall on El Cap, except for the daunting sections above the Ear and on the Headwall. The effort produced three pitches of spectacular 5.12 climbing, and a long string of demanding 5.11 pitches. They also freed most of Mt. Watkins' South Face, did the first ascent of the *Razor's Edge* (5.12), and later did a free ascent of Quarter Dome's North Face, renaming the free variation *Pegasus* (V 5.12). Half Dome's Northwest Face was the focus of attention for Jim Ericson and Art Higbee, who freed the entire route (5.12) except for a short section above

Thank God Ledge. Ericson later returned and freed this section on a toprope.

But in terms of pure technical difficulty, it was Ray Jardine who was really pushing the limits of free climbing during the late 1970s. He was slightly older than most of the Yosemite locals and he and his partner, John Lakey, pretty much kept to themselves. Yet this quiet pair continually searched out obscure, exceedingly difficult new routes to attempt. In doing so they raised the standards of the day ever closer to the coveted 5.13 level. Routes such as *Crimson Cringe* and *Hangdog Flyer,* both climbed in 1976 and rated 5.12, were typical of their early successes. They later teamed up to add *Dog's Roof* (5.12b), *Owl Roof* (5.12c), and *Elephant's Eliminate* (5.12d) to their growing list of desperate accomplishments.

Besides his climbing ability and fierce determination, Jardine applied an additional weapon to these impossible-looking routes—a revolutionary new form of climbing protection. Using the insight honed by years of experience as a NASA engineer, and with the help of a computer to fine-tune his ideas, he designed an array of spring-loaded camming devices that worked miracles on the rock. The new devices could fit in cracks of various sizes, would provide solid protection in those horrifying parallel-sided cracks, and could be placed quickly with just one hand. With their aluminum framework, circular holes, and ribbed cams, the new contraptions looked like psychedelic sculptures molded by some acid-tripping art student. But the novel gadgets, called Friends, gave Jardine the confidence he needed to attempt increasingly tenuous cracks.

The culmination of his efforts came in May 1977. Jardine was attracted to a gently curving but savagely hard hand

Ray Jardine with a prototype Friend on Phoenix

crack in the Cascade Falls area. "When I first laid eyes on [it], I knew it represented a whole new level," he explained. "It was absolutely stunning!" More than just stunning, the 140-foot crack turned out to be so difficult that it required repeated efforts over many days to complete.

During these early sessions, Jardine established a temporary belay station about halfway up the crack, and practiced only the upper part of the climb. "When we had finally completed the upper section, we pulled the belay station, repositioned it lower, and started over," he noted. "That's why we called

it the Phoenix—it rose from the ashes as a new, much tougher critter. We knew it was 5.13."

The crack was indeed 5.13—the first such route ever established in Yosemite. But instead of congratulations, he received ridicule for the landmark ascent. Many climbers were upset at the way he had done this and other routes. For the climbing style traditionally used in Yosemite required that when the leader accidentally fell during a first ascent, he would be lowered to the ground and start over. But the moves Jardine was attempting were so extreme, that he would rest on the rope after a fall and try again without starting from the bottom.

This approach of climbing up, rehearsing the exact sequence of moves, resting on the rope, and then climbing some more is called hang-dogging. And it infuriated many of Jardine's peers. "Everybody hang-dogs now in sport climbing," explained George Meyers, "but Ray was probably the first person in this country to climb that way. And everybody ragged on him for it. But I think what really got to people was his attitude—that he wouldn't tell people the style he was using. If he had just said, 'Hey, the moves are so hard I'm hanging on the rope,' then it probably wouldn't have been such a big deal. But he was very secretive about the whole thing. Obviously, what he was able to climb was amazing at that time. But he never got any respect for it."

Although acclaim would not be his, Jardine continued resolutely to leave his mark on Yosemite. In 1979, he and Bill Price achieved a major prize by climbing the West Face of El Capitan completely free (5.11d), the first time that El Cap had been ascended totally without aid. This ascent, combined with previous free ascents by other climbers of the Rostrum, Washington Column, and Half Dome, clearly showed the latent free-climbing potential that the Valley's big walls still possessed.

In the coming years, the ethical debate over climbing styles would escalate to increasingly virulent levels. Climbers would continue to wrestle with the meaning of routes like the Wall of the Early Morning Light and the Phoenix. Some would applaud them as visionary accomplishments, others would deride them as stylistic cop-outs.

The 1970s had begun with the vision and talents of Jim Bridwell and Royal Robbins, combined with the controversy surrounding Warren Harding.

They were now ending in an ironically similar way with the talents of Ron Kauk and John Bachar, combined with the controversy associated with Ray Jardine. Over those ten years, the climbing scene in the park had definitely been moving forward. In the process, however, it seemed to have lost much of its simplicity and innocence.

More than ever, the climbing community began to be segregated and polarized into different groups with different philosophies and different styles. But as climbers looked ahead to a new decade, there was one point that everyone could agree on: for better or worse, Yosemite climbing would never be the same.

John Bachar soloing in Tuolumne

7

A NEW GENERATION

*You can slander the Valley
and say that the climbers
there are screwed up, behind
the times. But climbers in
the Valley want to maintain
a certain kind of style.
Seriousness and danger
are difficulties that are as
deeply rooted in climbing
as technical difficulty. . . .
People just have to realize
that Yosemite is way ahead.
It's in a spiritual league
far beyond other areas.*

JOHN BACHAR

The dawn of the 1980s came with a rather strong sense of relief. For although the 1960s are commonly regarded as a time of tumultuous social upheaval in the US, it was in fact the 1970s that had seen an extraordinary number of pivotal events occur—and many people were glad that these events were behind them. For example, in August 1974 Richard Nixon resigned the Presidency in disgrace, becoming the only US president ever to resign from the nation's highest office. Then in the autumn of 1979, a militant group of Iranians seized the US Embassy in Tehran and took 53 Americans hostage. Now at the beginning of the '80s, the country quietly pondered what lay ahead.

Climbers in Yosemite were also immersed in some soul searching during this period. Would an explosion of bolts and non-traditional climbing styles ruin the adventure that had always characterized Yosemite? Would climbers strive to maintain the ethics of Muir, Salathé, Robbins, Herbert, and Chouinard? Did it even matter how a certain route was climbed, as long as it got climbed? The answers to these questions were not immediately apparent.

On the one hand, some excellent routes were put up in the early 1980s, in terms of both difficulty and climbing style. A case in point was *Cosmic Debris* (5.13), an outstanding new line established on the Chapel Wall by Bill Price. This severe route consisted of a sustained series of finger locks up a consistently overhanging crack. Another success was one by Tony Yaniro. This powerful climber was already well known for his landmark 1979 ascent of *Grand Illusion* (5.13c) in the Lake Tahoe area, which was the hardest rock climb in the world at that time. Now in Yosemite, he made an impressive variation at the very top of the Rostrum's north face called *Alien* (5.12b). El Capitan was also the scene of an important first, as Lynn Hill and Mari Gingery made the first female ascent of the Shield (VI 5.9 A4), once again showing the talent of women climbers. Ironically, in the near future Lynn Hill would achieve one of climbing's most historic accomplishments on this very same cliff. And John Bachar, the Johnny Rock of Yosemite climbing, free soloed the *Moratorium* (5.11b) before adding *Body And Soul* (5.12) to South Whizz Dome. As a measure of how significant these latter two feats were, the Moratorium ascent was the hardest on-sight free solo yet accomplished in Yosemite. In addition, his route Body And Soul was so difficult and scary that it would be five years before a team could muster the courage for the second ascent.

On the other hand, these accomplishments stood in marked contrast to several controversial climbs established on Glacier Point Apron and El Capitan. The first was *Hall Of Mirrors* (VI 5.12c), which ascended a hideously blank section up the center of the Apron. Chris Cantwell, Dave Austin, and Bruce Morris initially started up the polished rock in 1978, reaching a high point nine pitches up. With partners Scott Cole and Scott Burke, Cantwell returned repeatedly before completing the 16-pitch route in the fall of 1980.

The controversy of this ascent was generated by several factors. The first was the rating of the climb, for several pitches originally boasted a hefty 5.13 rating. Another part of the problem stemmed from the reputation of Cantwell himself. On some of his previous ascents, Cantwell had installed bolt ladders to protect sections of hard free climbing. This practice of drilling

his way up the rock and then later free climbing that section was regarded as cheating by other climbers. Plus the team intentionally avoided some natural lines of weakness in the rock, choosing instead to push the route up blanker and more challenging slabs. So rumors grew that this Mirrors route was irresponsibly over-rated, forced up a contrived line, and that the difficult sections hadn't even been freed.

The route's poor reputation caused it to fade into obscurity. At the time it was completed, the route was seen as a major blemish on the local climbing scene.

Also in this category was *Wings Of Steel* (VI 5.10 A4), an El Cap route completed two years later. This line ascended the blank Great Slab between the Aquarian and Dihedral walls. In a scene sadly reminiscent of the Dawn Wall fiasco, stories began to circulate that the climbing team of Richard Jensen and Mark Smith were simply drilling their way up the rock. Unsubstantiated rumors festered and grew about this cowardly demeaning of El Cap. Once again calls went out across Camp 4 to go up and deliberately chop the route.

So when the climbing team came down from the wall after fixing the first two pitches, a handful of outraged locals took matters into their own hands. "Several climbers jumared our fixed ropes, chopped the bolts, and then pulled down and defecated on our equipment," Smith recalled sadly. "The next night members of the Rescue Team boasted responsibility for the chopping, and spent the evening yelling degrading remarks across Camp 4 at Richard and me. It seemed as if the whole thing was a wild science fiction story! I couldn't believe what was unfolding!"

In spite of the harassment and ridicule, Jensen and Smith returned to the wall, reclimbed the first two pitches, and eventually completed the 13-pitch route. But the matter was far from over. For the pair spent 39 days finishing their line, far surpassing the 27-day record set by Harding and Caldwell on the Dawn Wall. Many climbers felt that 39 days was a ridiculously excessive amount of time, and was another indication that the pair had no business being on El Capitan.

But without a doubt, the biggest uproar occurred in 1981 when Ray Jardine attempted to make the first free ascent of The Nose. In order to avoid the bolt ladder and King Swing above El Cap Towers, Jardine forced a traverse left in an attempt to link up with an adjacent route called Grape Race. Regarding this traverse, Jardine later said, "It looked 5.11, but after several days of working the traverse, I determined that it was a lot harder. So I bought a chisel and made it 5.11." With hammer and chisel, Jardine hacked a series of holds into the rock to allow him to move across the traverse. When news of this got out, climbers in the Valley were horrified by his actions, and by his blatant disregard of traditional climbing ethics. Even Jardine himself became uncomfortable with his methods, and eventually gave up his all-free attempt. "Tooling those holds was an experiment," he later remarked. "Like everyone else, I was pretty appalled by the results. In retrospect, I should have experimented somewhere else."

These controversial ascents, and the people who established them, acquired ghastly reputations. The common sentiment was that these ascents had desecrated the ethics and traditions of Yosemite. A vocal group of climbers lamented the lack of adventure caused by a few gutless bozos.

In the midst of this confusion and controversy, the time was ripe for someone to step forward and make a clear statement about the future direction of Yosemite climbing. Not surprisingly, it was Johnny Rock who took that step.

Medlicott Dome: Bachar-Yerian

"Some climbers are content to climb the well-traveled and familiar paths of stone," observed Alan Nelson. "A few devotees seek less traveled and more difficult journeys. On rare occasions, a true master emerges—so inspired and creative as to transcend earthly considerations, thus establishing a brilliant new standard. To follow the path of the master demands fanatic dedication, power, and inspiration. One such master is John Bachar."

With his long blond hair, easy smile, and laid-back demeanor, Bachar had the look of a West Coast surfer intent on getting "tubed." Yet the adrenaline-charged rides he sought were not found on Oahu's North Shore, but rather on the incredible waves of vertical granite in the Tuolumne high country. For here, among the sparkling lakes and whispering pines of the High Sierra, Bachar found a spiritual home. Again and again he savored the adventure and the satisfaction that could be found only on Tuolumne's golden domes.

His solemn worship of these enchanted temples was proclaimed in the routes that he established here. His respect for the area compelled him to follow natural lines of weakness up the rock, and to place as few bolts as possible. His philosophy was simple: "Drilling a bolt is bogus! You're hacking the rock forever! So on my routes I put 'em in as few and far between as possible. And only when they were totally, absolutely necessary!" Because he had such an aversion to marring the rock with bolts, Bachar's routes quickly gained a reputation for being desperately "run-out", meaning that there was a long distance from one protection bolt to the next, so the potential for a long and dangerous leader fall was very high.

Not only did Bachar have immense respect for the rock, he also had great admiration for his predecessors, and for the ethics they had established in Yosemite. "Robbins did some unreal runouts in those horrendous Galibier boots!" Bachar exclaimed. "And Kamps did the same thing, putting up some wicked routes in clunky hiking boots. Those

guys were awesome! They just didn't fall! So I figured I'd push it too. Run-outs are an art!"

Two routes he established in 1981 exemplified this belief. The first was *You Asked For It* (5.10c), a desperately runout line which followed a black water streak on the western margin of Medlicott Dome. The first pitch had only two bolts to protect some very delicate 5.10c moves. The second pitch was almost as hard, but contained only one bolt in 80 feet.

This serious new route took its name from a rather whimsical source—an off-the-wall TV show. Bachar explained it this way: "People would write in to the TV station and say, 'We want to see the guy who rides his motorcycle away from a pole while still tied to the pole.' The announcer would read the letter on TV and then say, 'OK, you asked for it!' So some guy would tie a rope around his waist, tie the other end to a pole, and then go racing off on his motorcycle. After about 20 feet the rope would pull taut and he'd get ripped off the bike. And you'd just sit there and laugh! Or some other guy would get blasted out of a cannon. And they'd be doing this stuff all the time! It was just a classic, bizarre show! So when I did this Medlicott route it seemed like the same thing— you go up about 30 feet, the moves are hard, you still haven't reached the first bolt, and you're looking at a 60-foot screamer! So the name was obvious. You Asked For It!"

Then Bachar noticed an even steeper water streak to the left. The rock on this part of the dome looked hopelessly monolithic. But on closer inspection he noticed a glimmering array of feldspar knobs. The stunning crystals shot upward like a laser into the placid Tuolumne sky. The line actually seemed possible!

John Bachar on the Orangutan Arch

So he and Dave Yerian went to work. The first pitch began off a sloping platform at the base of the dome. Moderate climbing led upward to a difficult 5.11 section. About 60 feet above the belay, still with no protection in, Bachar began to place his first bolt.

Since he needed two hands to drill the hole, and since the footholds were small and tenuous, he draped a skyhook over a knob and then put his weight on it. Bachar was the first person in Yosemite to adopt this method of hanging off a hook to place protection bolts for free climbing. "I got the idea from Czech climbers," he later said. "They're real bold. They'll put up a 100-foot route that's only got three bolts on it. You gotta have big balls to do their routes! They really go for it!"

A few climbers questioned whether this was a legitimate way to protect a free climb. The normal method was to drill a bolt hole while balancing on footholds. To be a true free climb, some felt that the rope or other equipment should not support the climbers weight. But Bachar felt that the routes he was attempting were so difficult that they couldn't be free climbed in any other way. For although his weight was being held temporarily by the hook, he was still putting in the protection while actually leading the climb. And the hook could pop off the knob at any second, sending him plummeting head-first toward the ground. So he felt that the uncertainty and adventure of the route were not being degraded.

After placing two bolts to protect delicate 5.11c climbing, Bachar made a 30-foot runout before ending the pitch. Yerian then climbed up to the belay and the pair retreated for the day.

The next day Bachar reclimbed the first pitch and then started on the section above. Although the 5.11a moves were no walk in the park, the difficulty was much less than expected. So he moved quickly and confidently up the knobby rock without stopping to place protection. At a point almost 40 feet above the belay, still with no protection and looking at a potential 70-foot fall, he jokingly yelled down to Yerian about the frightful runout. His partner, however, was not amused. The thought of a 170-pound climber falling at terminal velocity directly onto his head did not titillate Yerian's sense of humor. He begged Bachar to put in a bolt. Johnny Rock finally relented. But he still kept the number of bolts on the 120-foot pitch down to just three.

Content with their progress the pair descended. Shortly thereafter they returned and climbed two additional pitches to finish the route. The third pitch was similar to the first two, containing only two bolts to protect 5.10d face climbing. The last pitch consisted of an easy 5.8 hand crack, and the pair quickly romped up the perfect cleft to the top of the dome.

The completion of the Bachar-Yerian was a landmark achievement in American climbing. Although other routes may have been longer or harder, never before had such a difficult climb been established with such serious runouts. "There's 13 bolts on the whole route, and that includes two 3-bolt anchors," Bachar explained. "So there's seven protection bolts spread out over four pitches. The whole route is runout! If you fell on the first pitch you could die! On the second pitch you probably wouldn't die, but you'd get really mangled if you fell. And the third pitch is the same thing—you could take some giant wingers!"

There were some in the climbing community who criticized Bachar for this route. They felt he had been reckless in making such extreme runouts, and that the route was unnecessarily dangerous. These feelings intensified after two separate teams tried but failed to make the second ascent. On one of these attempts, Wolfgang Gullich took a giant fall on the first pitch and nearly fell all the way to the ground. When his partner took several 40- and 50-foot falls on the second pitch, the climbers decided their efforts could best be spent elsewhere. At the time, Gullich was well known as one of Europe's top climbers. He would later make the first ascent of *Action Directe* (5.14d), which remains to this day one of the hardest routes in the world. Seeing such talented climbers fail caused many to wonder if the Bachar-Yerian would ever receive a second ascent.

But those who criticized the route failed to recognize what it really meant, and why it was established in that particular way. For every route is a reflection of the person who created it—a lasting declaration about a certain climber's hopes, fears, and aspirations. Consider, for example, the razor-sharp summit of Cathedral Peak. This regal mountain will always be associated with the impeccable style and mountain devotion of John Muir. In a similar way, to look at the Lost Arrow Chimney is to recall John Salathé, and the gutsy determination that it took to establish Yosemite's first big wall climbs. Likewise The Nose of El Capitan will forever be a tribute to Warren Harding, and his inspired ascent of the park's biggest cliff. In this case, the Bachar-Yerian bears the unmistakable stamp of John Bachar.

The route was a creation that perfectly mirrored his love and respect for Tuolumne, and for the remarkable climbers who came before him. It was not a stunt, nor was it based on reckless egotism. Instead the route was a profound, tangible statement about Bachar's deep personal beliefs. He fervently believed that the route deserved to be established in an adventurous style, with minimal damage done to the rock. "To climb that route and do the least amount of damage I used all the skills I've learned, trained for, and thought about over many years," he explained. "It can be viewed as an art—the art of admiring the mountain with the skillful use of bolts, and of respecting the rock by using as few as possible." The route stands today as a fitting monument to that lofty ideal.

There is only one chance to create a route in good style, and Bachar was determined to do it right the first time. "A first ascent is one of the highest statements you can make in the art of climbing," he noted. "You're going up on something that you know nothing about. The higher you get, the more things get thrown at you. And you have to respond immediately in a spontaneous and correct way if you're going to make it."

In this case Bachar did make it. And the result is a remarkable route that not only tests a climber's physical skill, but also their mental toughness. Peter Croft, who himself would become one of Yosemite's living legends, remarked, "I think it's great that John's routes test people in ways other than just how strong their forearms are." These sentiments were echoed by Steve Schneider, who noted emphatically, "The Bachar-Yerian remains the best known route in Tuolumne, a testpiece and a masterpiece. Aspiring hardmen from all over the world still come to pitch themselves against it each year."

Of all the climbers who try to repeat the route, only a handful are actually successful. The steep rock, dicey moves, and nerve-wracking runouts continue to take their toll. It is not uncommon for a team to approach the route, inspect the difficulties, shake their heads in disbelief, and then beat a hasty retreat. Success does not come easy. But this is hardly surprising, for it never is easy to follow the path of a master.

As the 1980s progressed, Yosemite climbers continued to scour the park for potential new routes. Interestingly enough, they were still able to piece together new lines on some of the park's most familiar landmarks, such as El Capitan.

Years before, Royal Robbins had remarked that about 20 separate routes would be a reasonable number for El Cap. But a motivated core of big wall veterans had other ideas. Jim Bridwell, now in his second decade as a Yosemite icon, continued to carry the torch by climbing *Zenyatta Mondatta* (VI 5.7 A5) with Peter Mayfield and Charlie Row. This demanding new line followed loose, minuscule seams to the left of Zodiac on El Cap's southeast face. Five consecutive A5 pitches were encountered on the first ascent, causing Bridwell to remark, "This was no place for those with a faint heart!" Regarding the potential for harrowing falls, and the fact that the overhanging wall prevented any thought of retreat, he later added, "Sometimes I feel that climbing is not so much a matter of courage as a function of adrenaline addiction!"

Greg Child was another climber who seemed to be addicted to El Capitan. He had previously made the first ascent of *Aurora* (VI 5.10 A5) with Mayfield,

The steep, smooth third pitch of The Nose

and the second ascents of *Iron Hawk* (VI 5.10 A4), *Magic Mushroom* (VI 5.10 A4), *Mescalito* (VI 5.9 A4), and *Zenith* (VI 5.10 A5). Now he and Randy Leavitt attacked a new line between Zenyatta Mondatta and Tangerine Trip.

The pair were determined to bag this prize, which they felt was one of the last good lines remaining on The Captain. "We headed directly to the base of El Cap to fix the first pitch," Child recalled, "mindfully avoiding the greatest single danger to the route—the Mountain Room Bar! Greater climbers than we had been sucked into this intellectual vacuum to spend all their money on drink, and talk nonsense for nights on end, only to see their ambitions and brains turned to mush."

Besides the difficulty of the climb, Child silently worried about two other factors. The first was comfort. So he and Leavitt made meticulous plans about precisely which "necessities" were needed. Child noted, "This hedonistic desire to attain unsurpassed levels of comfort in an overhanging environment accounted for the overkill wattage of our ghetto-blaster, pillows for portaledges, changes of underwear, shaving kit and premoistened towelettes, books, newspapers, gourmet food, and other excesses totaling 400 pounds. If we were going to live on a rock for ten days, we were going to do it in style!"

Child's other worry was his partner's arcane propensity for parachuting off of huge cliffs. Leavitt confessed, "I got the idea from Dale Bard. One time after we topped out on the Pacific Ocean Wall, Dale made a parachute for the haul bag out of the rainfly from his hammock. I remember watching the bag descend gracefully toward the meadow below and thinking, 'Hey, besides throwing your gear off, you could also throw yourself off!' What a classic idea!" Leavitt later acted on this idea and made several jumps off of El Capitan. Child's concern increased even more when Leavitt would say things like, "Nothing beats seeing the landmarks of El Cap that you know as a climber rush past at 32 feet per second squared. Free-fall; that's where it's at!" But despite Child's misgivings, the motivated pair managed to avoid any untimely free falls and climbed 12 new pitches of very exposed rock to create *Lost In America* (VI 5.10 A5).

Motivation was also not a problem for Charlie Cole. During 1984 and 1985 he established several impressive wall routes on El Cap and Half Dome. These included *False Shield* (VI 5.10c A4+), *Space* (VI 5.10 A4+), and *Queen Of Spades* (VI 5.9 A4+). This latter route, located on Half Dome's northwest face, was especially noteworthy because of its incredibly sustained difficulty—the route contains 14 A4 pitches in a row.

In addition, Cole teamed up with Rusty Reno and John Middendorf to climb an exceptional line called *Autobahn* (5.11+) on the clean southwest corner of Half Dome. The 12-pitch free route offers superb and runout face climbing in one of Yosemite's most spectacular locations. Middendorf led the crux pitch and later commented, "It's really 5.12!" Middendorf was feeling extremely fit at the time, having already made the first winter ascent of Zenyatta Mondatta and the first solo of *Never Never Land* (VI 5.9 A4). He also honed his skills with a rapid three-day ascent of the North America Wall, a one-day ascent of the Lost Arrow Direct, and a winter ascent of The Nose in a day.

His success in Yosemite was even more remarkable because of the physical handicaps he had previously overcome. Severe asthma had ravaged his body as a child, and a rare bone disease had left one of his legs several inches shorter than the other. But he worked through these challenges with the same determination that would later lead him up some of the scariest A5 pitches in the country.

The climax of his efforts came in September 1985 when he established the *Atlantic Ocean Wall* (VI 5.10 A5) on El Capitan with John Barbella. This demanding new line followed a series of overhanging corners, huge roofs, and expanding flakes for 15 pitches. The route consisted of some of the most delicate climbing they had ever done. Yet the pair kept the number of rivets and bolts down to 58. Middendorf noted, "The routes to the left and right required more drilling than our route. That was a rewarding aspect, because I think that's the name of the game— to follow natural lines."

The climbs that Middendorf completed during this period typified several trends which were prevalent in Yosemite. New routes, completely independent of previous lines, were increasingly difficult to find. So the locals embraced those methods that would keep the contest interesting. One such method was to solo the big walls.

Rob Slater was among those who succumbed to the call of Grade VI soloing. His early solo of the *Pacific Ocean Wall* (VI 5.9 A4) caught the attention of many in the Valley because this was one of the first solos of a big, hard aid route on El Capitan. His ascent was also exceptional because the longest aid pitch he had previously soloed was only 50 feet long. But he completed the route in five days, and then returned to the base in grand style by parachuting off the top.

Other significant solos were accomplished by Duane Raleigh on Zenyatta Mondatta, Walt Shipley on the North America Wall and Tis-sa-ack, and Sue Harrington's first female solo of Zodiac. Through these ascents, the big wall testpieces of the recent past began to seem a little less formidable.

Great energy was also focused on free climbing during the mid 1980s. Werner Braun, one of the pillars of the local climbing scene, was especially busy.

"Werner's kind of quiet and may not say much, but he's always striving for mastery," said Billy Westbay. "He's someone who feels that you can never really attain mastery, but you need to keep working toward it. And in his own way he's achieved that mastery. He's an outrageously good climber!"

Teaming up with Scott Cosgrove, Braun displayed that mastery by making the first free ascents of several established aid lines. Among these were *Power Point* (5.11c) on Higher Cathedral Rock, and *Thin Line* (5.11c) in the Ribbon Falls area. Cosgrove, no stranger himself to standard-pushing routes, also put up *Jack The Zipper* (5.12a) on Glacier Point Apron, and joined Steve Schneider on Daff Dome's *Cowabunga* (5.12c).

Kim Carrigan was another climber who made his presence known, focusing on the Rostrum. Although the North Face of this magnificent pillar was freed earlier by Ron Kauk (V 5.11c), Carrigan linked the lower cracks with the spectacular *Rostrum Roof* (5.12b) on the last pitch, thus establishing one of the Valley's most sustained free climbs. Ron Kauk added *Back To The Future* (5.12b) at Roadside Attraction, while Wolfgang Gullich made a no-rope ascent of the overhanging classic Separate Reality (5.12a). On Half Dome, Dave Schultz teamed up with Ken Yager and Jim Campbell to establish the desperate route *Karma* (V 5.11d Ao), where a fall at certain points could result in the rope being cut by a sharp dike. And in the high country, Kurt Smith would follow in the hallowed footsteps of John Bachar to create some runout horrors such as *Burning Down The House* (5.11c) and *Electric Africa* (5.12d).

But without a doubt some of the most

important contributions came from a young Canadian named Peter Croft. This incredibly gifted climber had first made his presence felt back in 1978 by establishing two short routes in the Royal Arches area: *Pigs In Space* (5.12) and *Peter's Out* (5.12). Four years later, on his home turf of Squamish Chief, he free-climbed the old aid route up the 1400-foot University Wall. At the time, this bold testpiece (V 5.12b) was one of the longest and hardest free climbs in the world. Yet Croft wasn't content to simply stop there.

By 1985 Croft was spending more time in Yosemite, and his familiarity with the area began to pay handsome dividends. What really began to astound the locals was Croft's bold and imaginative solos. He would think nothing of free soloing a multitude of hard climbs back to back, sometimes climbing 20 or 30 or more pitches up to a difficulty of 5.12 in a single day. And he would do these just for fun. For Croft it was just training. A typical training day might begin with a solo of the Northeast Buttress of Higher Cathedral Rock (IV 5.9), followed by the Steck-Salathé on Sentinel Rock (V 5.9), and finally end with an ascent of Snake Dike on Half Dome (5.7); over 30 pitches of climbing, and Croft would casually cruise it without a rope.

Yet his most noteworthy ascent was an amazing free solo of the Rostrum's *North Face* (V 5.11c). The intimidating route that had taken Warren Harding and Glen Denny days to complete back in 1962 required only a couple of hours of effort by Croft. He epitomized the daring attitude of the new generation—a generation that was completely demolishing the old barriers, and advancing the standards at an unbelievable pace.

Although many variables contributed

Peter Croft

to this situation, one particularly important factor was the introduction of a new climbing shoe. Known as Fires (pronounced fee-rays), the new shoes had remarkable soles made of sticky rubber that was originally developed for auto-racing tires. Climbers in America had heard rumors that the new European rubber worked miracles on a wide variety of rock. The shoes' notoriety increased when John Bachar was appointed as a technical consultant and distributor. Bachar was nearly mobbed when he brought the first batch of Fires to the Valley in 1983. Anxious climbers gobbled up his entire inventory in a single day. Even the steep price of $60 per pair didn't lessen the demand. About 13,000 shoes were sold the first year. "Fires blitzed the market," said Alison Osius. "Everybody bought a pair, and most bought more. On cliffs everywhere, the blue EBs gave way to the red and gray Fires. The adhesive soles made a radical difference— some said the new 'cheaters' made many routes a full grade easier. Today, when people ask why climbers are performing at standards so much higher than those dreamed of in the past, a stock answer is 'Improved training—and sticky shoes!'"

Bachar put the new shoes to good use during this period, establishing routes in his usual bold style. Free solos of *Edging Skills Or Hospital Bills* (5.10b) and *Tomb Of The Unknown Climber* (5.10b) showed that he still had the nerve for ropeless climbing. In addition, routes such as *The Believer* (5.12a), *Bombs Over Tokyo* (5.12c), and *Dale's Pin Job* (5.13) clearly indicated his mastery of the game.

One of Bachar's finer efforts was in the Reed's Pinnacle area where he made the first ascent of *Phantom* (5.13a). The route's daunting crack was formed by an extremely fragile flake, so Bachar relied on artificial nuts for climbing protection. But this made the crack extremely difficult to lead. "It took me three days to get the third nut in," he explained. "And then I spent 50 minutes on the move above the third nut, because I didn't think that it would ever hold a fall!"

Although Bachar was pleased with these routes, he was quietly thinking of a larger objective. In fact he was thinking of two big objectives, and of a climbing feat that had never been done before.

El Capitan And Half Dome In A Day

By 1986 it had been almost 30 years since Royal Robbins and Warren Harding had spearheaded efforts to first ascend the Northwest Face of Half Dome and The Nose of El Capitan. Over those decades, both routes had come to be revered as among the classic rock climbs of the world. Each had previously received a one-day ascent: Steve Roper and Jeff Foott made a one-day ascent of Half Dome in 1966, and Jim Bridwell teamed up with John Long and Billy Westbay for their one-day trip up El Cap in 1975. Yet many climbers still aspired to simply get up these routes any way they could, regardless of how long it took. Even among expert climbers, it was common to regard an ascent of either route as a highlight of one's career.

Very few people ever had the extreme audacity to consider climbing both Half Dome and El Capitan in a single day. The overwhelming nature of both walls meant that climbers approached these routes with a healthy dose of respect, and even a bit of fear. Most climbers considered a combined one-day ascent of both walls as a foolhardy dream, completely out of the question. But John Bachar never was among "most climbers"—he always was in a class by himself.

Bachar had been thinking about the El Cap/Half Dome combination for years. Although a few immortals like Bridwell and Long had toyed with the idea, no one had yet been spurred to action—and this was hardly surprising. For an attempt would involve nearly 60 pitches of climbing, with many sections of sustained 5.10 and 5.11 moves, all in a single day. It was indeed a daring thought. Anyone who would even ponder such a feat would have to be buoyantly optimistic, unbelievably fit, and supremely confident. In other words, someone like Johnny Rock.

While Bachar believed he was up to the challenge, he also knew that success would depend on finding the right partner. There certainly were a number of talented climbers in Yosemite at the time. But the project demanded a one-of-a-kind person as phenomenally gifted as Bachar himself. Only one person came to mind. So Bachar went to see Peter Croft.

Although Croft had also been thinking about this very idea, he was still honored that Bachar asked him. "At the time, Bachar was like the climbing god of Yosemite," said Croft. "He was the greatest—he could do anything, like Superman! So when we talked I felt like the hand of God had come up and tapped me on the shoulder!" Yet the divine Bachar also had tremendous respect for this young Canadian, declaring emphatically, "Croft is the best crack climber on the planet! Period! No doubt about it!"

Together they considered every aspect of the climb: what equipment would be needed, the order of doing the routes, and how to get from one climb to the next. They decided to start on The Nose at midnight, try to reach the summit by midmorning, jog over to the East Ledges descent route, rappel down to the Valley floor, jump in a car and drive to the horse stables, ride mountain bikes from there to Mirror Lake, scramble 3000 feet up steep slabs to the base of Half Dome, and then start up the Northwest Face. In the interest of speed they would take just one small rack of climbing gear, two ropes, a few morsels of food, and a couple of water bottles. No extra gear, no extra food or

water, and no rain parkas. Their margin of safety was incredibly slim. But they considered the whole thing as just another training day. And as a measure of their optimism, they even hoped to climb the Steck-Salathé on Sentinel Rock after reaching the top of Half Dome. Other climbers who heard of their plan could only shake their heads in utter disbelief.

On the chosen day they awoke at 11 P.M. to cloudy skies. Although thoughts of poor weather briefly flickered through their minds, both climbers were eager to get going. Croft was especially antsy. In order to be well rested, Bachar had insisted that each of them should avoid climbing for several days before the attempt. So now, bursting with energy, the two climbers began charging up The Nose at midnight.

The delicate light of their headlamps was in stark contrast to the stalwart monolith they were ascending. No climbers had ever approached El Capitan with such confidence and nonchalance. They moved with uncanny ease and speed. Higher and higher they climbed into the night sky, ascending toward the distant stars and their own lofty dreams.

They were already 1000 feet up the route when the sun started to rise. "I led the first bunch of pitches up to El Cap Towers and then Peter took over," said Bachar. But as Croft led upward and then began the King Swing, their second rope mysteriously became untied from his harness. The two climbers watched helplessly as it dropped to the ground. This could have been a major problem for a team of mere mortals. But they just shrugged it off and kept on going.

A short time later, however, a more serious glitch occurred. "John had just led a section," Croft recalled, "and I was getting ready to swing into the lead. Above Camp Six there was this big block of rock about five feet high. It looked pretty sturdy. So I grabbed it and started to pull back, and the whole thing began to come off! We'd just passed two parties down below—five people all together. If that block had fallen it would have ricocheted off the walls of the dihedral and killed someone for sure. In fact it would have been a miracle if only one person was killed! But Bachar leaped forward and pushed the block back into place. I was totally amazed, and I remember thinking, 'Man, this guy really is Superman!' "

They continued through the upper dihedral at an inspired rate. "It would take us about 10 or 15 minutes to do a pitch," Bachar explained. "You don't have to be frantic in your climbing, you just have to keep moving. Like we'd get to a belay and set it up in 20 seconds, instead of 2 or 3 minutes. Little things like that are the key."

They reached El Cap's summit shortly after 10 A.M. All told, they had passed four parties on The Nose. Those climbers would labor for several more days to get up the route. Bachar and Croft took slightly over 10 hours to do it. They had just completed one of the country's biggest Grade VI routes, 34 pitches of difficult climbing, in a single morning! And they weren't finished yet!

As planned they quickly made their way down the East Ledges and back to the Valley floor. Then they drove, biked, and hiked to the base of Half Dome, which they reached about 1 P.M. After a short lunch they started up the 24-pitch route.

In contrast to El Cap, a number of pitches on Half Dome had easy ratings of 5.6 to 5.8. So they were able to climb simultaneously (or simul-climb) for

much of the afternoon. The pair climbed at an astonishing pace and ended up passing seven parties on the route. Bachar recalled, "We'd come up to a party and say, 'Hey, is it cool if we pass? We just did The Nose this morning and we're kinda in a hurry.' At first some of them wouldn't believe us. But then they'd recognize us and let us go by."

Higher and higher they climbed. Connected by a single thin rope, they confidently moved together up the 2000-foot face. A slight wind began to rise and dark cumulus clouds gathered above the summit. But their world was a sea of magnificent gray stone. Hand jams, liebacks, pendulums, finger cracks, and chimneys completely captivated their senses. Each obstacle received an automatic, reflexive response. Their bodies were so attuned to the vertical world that each movement was smooth, effortless, and decisive. A graceful vertical dance was being performed on this colossal granite monolith. And their dance was so smooth that they weren't even tired. "We just kept on going and going," said Croft. "The higher we got, the stronger we got."

By late afternoon they reached Big Sandy Ledges, at the top of the 17th pitch. Croft was leading at the time and reached the ledges first. "Three Germans were on Big Sandy when I got there," he described. "At first they were totally excited because they thought I was Bachar. When I told them I wasn't they got really bummed. But then I said that Bachar was at the other end of the rope and would be here in a couple of minutes. And they were so thrilled! They were like little kids, so happy to meet Bachar up there, and so psyched for us!"

After some brief greetings Bachar and Croft continued upward through the Zigzags. Then four pitches from the top a fierce thunderstorm lashed out at them. "It was pretty bad," Bachar recalled. "It rained really hard and there was lightning everywhere. Our hair was sticking up from the lightning and the cracks were actually buzzing. We thought we were gonna get wasted, especially since all we had on were T-shirts and shorts!"

However, as the two climbers approached the top, they were relieved to see the storm die down. They scrambled onto the summit about 6 P.M. and found vibrant rainbows decorating the horizon. It was a wonderfully magic moment, and truly something special.

"Doing that was a real breakthrough for me," Croft commented. "No one was sure if it was even possible! So going out and actually doing it was a huge psychological breakthrough. And it's those kind of accomplishments that have real meaning."

Although their original plan now called for them to ascend Sentinel Rock, they decided that 58 pitches of climbing was enough for one day. "We really weren't that tired," Bachar noted, "but we knew we'd need headlamps for Sentinel. And I hate headlamps. So I said, 'Hey, let's just go to the bar!' After all, it was just a training day for us. We just did it for fun. We could have done it faster, but we just cruised and enjoyed the whole thing." Croft agreed, adding, "Neither of us felt pushed. It was just a fun day in the mountains, like we were just out cragging."

But even then, having just completed this monumental accomplishment, the wheels in Croft's mind began to turn— what was the next step? How could this landmark feat possibly be topped? He would find the answer four years later. And in the process, he would dramatically redefine the meaning of cragging.

The following year, Yosemite climbers continued to find new ways to challenge themselves in all realms of the sport. On the big walls, El Cap's southeast face was the scene of several new routes. Among these were *Heartland* (VI 5.10 A4+), *Native Son* (VI 5.9 A4+), and *Scorched Earth* (VI 5.11 A5).

The route Scorched Earth was the work of Randy Leavitt and Rob Slater. Both climbers had a knack for pulling off desperate aid climbs on the Big Stone. Two years before, Leavitt had pieced together Lost In America (VI

Peter Croft (bottom) nearing the summit of Half Dome after the first one-day ascent of El Capitan and Half Dome

5.9 A5), with its tenuous placements of shifting hooks and A5 rurps. And Slater had previously made the first ascent of *Wyoming Sheep Ranch* (VI 5.9 A5+). As a measure of Slater's tenacity, the 13th pitch of Sheep Ranch took him 15 tortuous hours to lead, during which he fought off wrenching fatigue and numbness in his legs. But he downplayed the severity of the route by leaving small curio toys from Wyoming at various spots. And to ensure that subsequent leaders remained focused, he even added an 18-inch skewer called the Cattleprod Pillar to the middle section of the climb.

Their new Scorched Earth featured A5 copperheads and an awesome 5.11 offwidth which they called the Leavittator. "Leading that pitch was like a religious experience!" Leavitt exclaimed. "At first I was able to aid it with big Friends and wooden blocks. But then it got too wide for that so I had to free climb. At one point I was runout about 50 feet above my last piece. I kept telling myself to just keep going, trying to convince myself that I'd eventually find someplace to put some pro in. So I kept getting suckered into climbing higher and higher. I had to really push myself on that pitch!"

They also pushed the idea of "cheater sticks" to a new level. Usually consisting of an old tree branch, cheater sticks are often carried along on certain routes to help climbers overcome long reaches between bolt or hook placements. For example, the Kor Roof on Washington Column's South Face was notorious for its distressingly long reaches. But Leavitt and Slater went a step further by making a 14-foot "Lovetron," consisting of a skinny tent pole with a skyhook on the end. "You have to be prepared to rake the wall with a hook on the end of a Lovetron and do

Half Dome seen from Glacier Point

other trickery," Leavitt explained. "If you're not willing to do that, then you shouldn't be on the climb." Scorched Earth remains one of the most difficult routes on El Capitan.

The northwest face of Half Dome also received additional attention. Jim Bridwell, Peter Mayfield, Steve Bosque, and Sean Plunkett took a direct line up overhanging white rock in the middle of the face to create the *Big Chill* (VI 5.9 A4). This route featured the debut of the Mayfield Big Wall Rating Scenario, which humorously discarded the traditional A1-A5 arrangement in favor of a simpler three-part rating system: NBD (meaning No Big Deal), NTB (Not Too Bad), and PDH (Pretty Darn Hard!). "Most of this route is solid PDH," Mayfield later said.

Speed climbing continued to attract a following, most notably from Jim Beyer. In an impressive 23-hour effort, Beyer climbed solo up the West Face of El Capitan. This ascent, the first one-day solo of El Cap, was even more remarkable because Beyer had not climbed the route before.

However, the biggest breakthroughs of 1987 occurred in free climbing. In June, British rock ace Jerry Moffatt visited Tuolumne and established *Clash Of The Titans* (5.13a) on Pywiack Dome. The holds on the route were so minuscule that Moffatt adopted the drilling method used on the Bachar-Yerian—drilling protection bolts while hanging from a hook. Although it was common for climbers in Europe to rappel down a route to place protection bolts, Moffatt respected the traditions of Tuolumne and drilled the bolts while actually leading the climb. At the time, this was the hardest face climb in the park.

That same month, Peter Croft decided to attempt a stunning free solo of Astro Man (V 5.11c). Like the inspired Stonemaster ascent of the route in 1975, Croft's vision was that it could be climbed in a challenging new way—free solo—and he wasn't about to pass up the challenge. So he casually walked up Washington Column with just his chalk bag and his thirst for adventure.

Although he had already soloed New Dimensions (5.11a) and the Nabisco Wall (5.11c) earlier in the day, he was feeling fit and up to the task. "I remember walking out into the forest past Curry Village and looking up at it, waiting for it to go into the shade," he recalled. "The route is mostly overhanging and it's on this beautiful orange granite. It's one of the most beautiful faces in the Valley. As I looked at it from the forest there, I started psyching myself up, getting it ingrained in my mind that this wasn't a dangerous thing, that I was totally ready for it, and that it would be a totally successful climb. I saw myself hiking up there, and saw myself climbing the whole thing. And then I started getting this overpowering urge to do it!"

Croft started the historic ascent about 5 P.M. "After the first pitch, I realized that I was going for it now and I started getting really jacked up," he described. "I had tons of adrenaline! I was climbing fast and hardly ever stopping to chalk up. I knew that I wasn't going to enjoy it if I kept climbing that quickly, so I got to a ledge a little more than halfway up and stopped, took off my shoes, wiggled my toes, and looked over at Half Dome. I sat there for a while enjoying the view, and then put my shoes back on and started climbing, but more slowly."

He reached the summit as the sun was about to set. "All my senses were incredibly sharp and my perception was super vivid," he remarked. "I could see everything in perfect definition and I was just amazed at how intensely beautiful everything looked. It was so much fun and totally worth the effort and risk. It was an adventure, a true adventure!"

Although the ascent was not at the top level of technical difficulty, it was an outstanding accomplishment. For nothing this serious had ever been soloed before. With this in mind Croft later explained, "Technical progress isn't as important as progress in adventure. The important thing is to push the limits of what's possible through intelligent boldness."

No one had ever accused Croft of lacking boldness. In fact, shortly after this ascent he went back to Washington Column and soloed Astro Man for a second time. But this time he started up the route after first soloing the Nabisco Wall (5.11c) and the Rostrum's North Face (V 5.11c). Also in June he free soloed *Mirage* (5.12a) and *Fish Crack* (5.12b), after making a no-falls flash ascent of *Cosmic Debris* (5.13a) earlier in the day. Two months later he soloed Astro Man for a third time, while also soloing the Rostrum and eight pitches of 5.11 at the Cookie Cliff, all in the same day. In all he climbed over 30 pitches of rock, without a rope, up to a difficulty of 5.11d, with little rest in between. "To put this in perspective," wrote John Steiger, "consider Henry Barber's 1973 blow to Valley standards when he free soloed the Steck-Salathé (V 5.9), prompting Royal Robbins to later call Barber's feat visionary. Fourteen years later, it appears Croft has leaped generations." Steve Roper added that Croft was "a hero to the old Camp 4 gang, a true 'Keeper of the Flame.' We need more climbers like Croft."

The approach of Peter Croft was always direct, unembellished, and uncompromising. His style of soloing did not permit mistakes, and his personality did not allow exaggeration. For him the climbing game was simple, and it deserved to stay that way.

Yet the following year, free climbing in Yosemite became much more complicated. During the spring Ron Kauk returned to the Valley and established a difficult new route at Arch Rock. This in itself was hardly surprising, for Kauk

was one of Yosemite's best all-around climbers. Besides his numerous accomplishments in the park, he had also completed outstanding routes in Canada and Europe, and had climbed the spectacular granite spire of Uli Biaho (19,957 feet) in Pakistan's Karakoram Range. "I always thought that Ron was the complete Yosemite climber," remarked Croft. "He'd done big wall climbing, the hardest free climbs, hard bouldering, everything. He'd done it all."

What made Kauk's new route so startling was the way it was established; he went to the top of Arch Rock and rappelled down, installing bolts along the way. In doing so he embraced the European style of "sport climbing," which permitted hang-dogging and rap-bolting in order to safely climb routes of incredible difficulty.

With the bolts now in, Kauk went to work. On the golden arete left of Entrance Exam he repeatedly practiced individual moves, rested on the rope, and then rehearsed the moves again. Eventually he learned the exact sequence of delicate movements necessary to climb the steep wall. He then led the pitch without resting his weight on the rope.

Kauk was certainly not the first person to protect a climb in this way. Rap-bolting had been used by Jim Bridwell back in 1971 prior to the first ascent of Wheat Thin (5.10c). Before that, Dave Rearick had added a rap-bolt to protect a 5.10 lieback on Split Pinnacle. But both of those climbs were regarded as exceptions to the rule. Neither route generated an uproar. Wheat Thin was tolerated because the rap-bolting was done to protect a delicate flake. And Split Pinnacle was a rather obscure formation, somewhat hidden by the forest near the western base of the Three Brothers.

However, these factors did not apply to Arch Rock. It was one of Yosemite's premiere free-climbing areas, with a rich history of traditional free ascents. So when news of Kauk's methods got out, a vocal group of Valley climbers were outraged.

John Bachar was especially furious. He and Kauk had once been extremely close friends. They were the dynamic duo of American free climbing during the late 1970s, always seeing eye to eye when it came to ethics. For Kauk to now resort to rap-bolting was an unbelievable turnaround. "Ron was such a staunch ground-up guy," said Bachar. "He always made fun of guys who couldn't run it out. So for him to start rap-bolting was just an incredible 180-degree change!"

But Kauk's ideas regarding acceptable climbing styles had recently undergone a major change. He had seen the amazing routes that French and German climbers were consistently putting up. And their acceptance of sport climbing methods had seemingly allowed them to completely surpass the rest of the world. Seeing these results, and not wanting to be left behind, Kauk decided that the ends were worth the means—even if it meant going against his previous beliefs. He explained, "I didn't feel that I had a responsibility to uphold something I no longer believed in, just because it was the way I had always climbed. The world to me is limitless. I don't see how people can impose limitations on things. I've seen people use their traditions to promote themselves and inflate their egos, saying their way is the best. To hide behind a curtain of tradition, and not have any good intentions, isn't any better than a guy who chips a hold to push a climb.

Each is insisting that everyone else play by his rules."

Bachar, however, vehemently believed in the rules against rap-bolting. To him, this new route was so detestable that there was only one possible response. So he went to the top of Arch Rock, rappelled down the face, and pried out all the bolts with a crowbar.

"Many would argue that the removal of rappel bolts is an offensive act," Bachar explained. "But it must be said that the placement of rappel bolts is just as offensive to the ground-up climber as the removal of rap-placed bolts is to the rap-bolter. If a top-down climber has the right to place rap-bolts on a ground-up climber's future route, then the ground-up climber has just as much right to remove those bolts."

In the ensuing days tempers escalated as accusations and insults were exchanged. The affair eventually reached an ugly climax in the Camp 4 parking lot. During a heated discussion, Mark Chapman, who had sided with Kauk, suddenly punched Bachar in the neck. The injury was serious enough that Bachar had to seek treatment in the hospital. As a result, the route became known as *Punchline* (5.12b).

The entire incident created a deep rift in the Yosemite climbing community. Some climbers felt that rap-bolting was the only way to keep up with the Europeans. After all, they had embraced sport climbing techniques and were at the forefront of doing the hardest routes in the world.

But other climbers had a simple response to this reasoning—so what! So what if some Europeans had lowered themselves to rap-bolting and taken the adventure out of climbing, all in a shallow pursuit of a harder rating. For climbers such as Bachar, it didn't matter what the Europeans did. Just

ABOVE. Climber searches anxiously for the next bolt on the Bachar-Yerian

PREVIOUS PAGE. Ron Kauk on Astro Man (5.11c)

Todd Skinner leading above El Cap Spire, Salathé Wall

ABOVE. Well-stocked bivouac on Long Ledge, Salathé Wall

FACING PAGE. John Bachar leading his Tuolumne classic, the Bachar-Yerian

Peter Croft on the traverse from Texas Flake to Boot Flake, The Nose

Steve Schneider on the seventh pitch (5.12d) on Excalibur, El Capitan

Ron Kauk fights his way up Tales of Power

because some French or German climbers reduced the sport to a rehearsed gymnastic routine, here in Yosemite the story was different. Yosemite was not Europe. And the traditions developed in the park deserved to be continued and respected. "The fact is that Yosemite produces some of the hardest ground-up routes in the world to date," said Bachar, "and the standards are increasing every year. Only because top-down routes are equated with traditional ground-up routes, via the usage of the same numeric rating system, do Yosemite-style ground-up first ascents appear inferior. After all what is harder, doing an on-sight, on-the-lead first ascent of a 5.13b, or doing a top-down, rehearsed, preprotected 5.14a? They are two different games, born of opposite approaches, and producing different results."

The controversy ended in something of a standoff. Bachar established Tuolumne's first 5.13 by leading *Love Supreme* (5.13a) in traditional style. Kauk countered by adding two more rap-bolted routes: *Love Sexy* (5.13b) and *European Vacation* (5.13b). Climbers continued to be polarized into different factions. The debate could easily have dominated the events of 1988— but one particular climb in the Valley soon prevented that.

El Capitan: The Free Salathé

Twenty-seven years is a long time in any sport. Incredible changes will typically occur during those decades. For a sport to remain healthy and vibrant, a relentless evolution must take place—especially in terms of attitude, ability, and equipment. This was certainly true in the sport of rock climbing.

Since 1961 an extraordinary number of advancements had occurred. Sticky shoes, gymnastic chalk, camming devices, and detailed climbing topos were only a few of the tools previously unavailable. A new generation embraced these tools and combined them with new ideas to accomplish routes of unbelievable difficulty. Not only did young climbers put up their own amazing testpieces, they also ascended established routes in ways never before imagined.

As the previous decades had shown, one of the most sought-after goals was to make a completely free ascent of some intimidating big wall. Since El Capitan clearly had the biggest routes around, it was the most obvious goal for aspiring free climbers. Ray Jardine had established the trend years before by making the first free ascent of El Cap's West Face (V 5.11c). Yet the two most classic lines—The Nose and the Salathé Wall—had repelled a previous generation of free climbers. The Salathé in particular was an exceptionally alluring objective.

By 1988 it had been 27 years since the legendary trio of Royal Robbins, Tom Frost, and Chuck Pratt had first climbed the Salathé Wall. The route was still commonly referred to as the greatest rock climb in the world. An ascent of the Salathé was a significant accomplishment in any climber's career. But no one had climbed the entire route without aid. Climbers of the 1970s had freed various parts of the route, and the first ten pitches could be done as a separate climb called Free Blast (5.11b). However, the daunting section below El Cap Spire, and especially the fearful pitches on the overhanging Headwall, had defeated all previous free-climbing efforts. Yet those defeats did nothing to dampen the enthusiasm of Todd Skinner and Paul Piana.

Both Skinner and Piana hailed from the rural outback of Wyoming. During

Todd Skinner on the 5.13a pitch below El Cap Spire

to rest and resupply, and then returning to the route. Such an approach would be a significant departure from the methods used on a typical free climb. But for Skinner and Piana, the Free Salathé was in no way typical. "We knew that we wouldn't be able to just fill a daypack with gear and be able to climb it free," noted Piana. "It would require an unheard-of amount of continually difficult climbing. . . . It was obvious that the Salathé Wall couldn't be touched without a lot of preparation."

With this in mind they embarked on a series of exploratory "camping trips." These trips consisted of climbing a short part of the route to practice and memorize the exact sequence of moves needed. Their reconnaissance excursions usually lasted about a week, after which they would return to the ground. They even hiked to the top of the cliff and rappelled down for several hundred feet to practice the intimidating moves through the Roof and the Headwall. "We marveled that at each impasse there was a sequence that worked, even if just barely," Piana described. "But we were appalled by the inhuman amount of difficult climbing that faced us. We were haunted by the specter of injury. Damage to a critical joint or tendon would finish our bid. A turn in the weather could be equally debilitating. Occasionally the mental strain of so many difficult sequences and unrelenting crux pitches became a burden that threatened to crush our dream." Yet in spite of the strain, after about a month of recons the two climbers set off on an all-out push.

The lower pitches through the Half Dollar, Mammoth Terraces, and Heart Ledges passed routinely. But the situation changed dramatically just above the Ear. A long and extremely steep

their early climbing years they dreamed of ascending some of the hallowed big wall routes of Yosemite Valley. As they became more experienced and confident, their emphasis shifted to climbing El Cap completely free. Not surprisingly, they soon fell under the seductive spell of the Salathé Wall. "Todd and I considered the Salathé to be the greatest free-climbing goal in the world," Piana explained. "There are a few [routes] here and there that may be tougher, but there is nothing even remotely as grand or sustained in difficulty."

Although others had failed, the two climbing cowboys from Wyoming had a plan for pulling off the ascent. The key would be a long period of preparation and rehearsal—going up on the route to work on specific sections, coming down

pitch started with wide 5.10d jamming. Liebacks and fingertip moves between pin scars were then required to finish the 5.13a pitch.

As the days passed they climbed ten more pitches, including two difficult leads up 5.12 cracks. Their efforts brought them to an airy and frightful belay directly below the dreaded Roof. Then Piana went to work on one of the most spectacular pitches in the world.

No one who has had the privilege of climbing the Roof can ever forget it. Eons of weathering along a horizontal joint system have fashioned a disconnected series of cracks and pockets shooting sideways through the multi-tiered overhangs. The Roof itself consists of several small overhangs jutting out into space for about 20 feet. Viewed from below it resembles a sinister, magnificent granite staircase tilted upside-down. Each small roof shoots farther out into the void than the one below. The leader must reach far to the right to climb sideways, then up, then sideways, then up again, all the while dangling precariously above 2500 feet of air. Those who follow the pitch enjoy their own experience, such as the unique thrill of sudden, distressing swings outward as pitons or cams are removed from the cracks. And through it all, climbers may suddenly be tossed left or right by violent wind gusts that often blast the upper part of El Cap. While leading or following on the Roof, more than a few climbers have implored a divine deity for mercy, pledging to begin a new and cleaner life if only the rope and anchors hold.

Since Skinner had led the desperate 5.12b section below, Piana had the pleasure of leading the Roof. Delicate footwork and a series of dynamic lunges carried him upward. The sloping 5.12

Paul Piana on the wild lead through the Roof

moves were exhilarating and exciting, not to mention terrifying. "What a place!" he wrote. "But if I fall I'm going to scream!"

Fortunately neither a fall nor a scream occurred as he finished the lead. He set up a belay at the upper lip of the Roof. Then Skinner came to grips with the first flared and runout 5.13 pitch up the Headwall. "So flaring were the jams that it was impossible to down-climb," Piana described, "and the slightest error, even a change in the blood pressure in his hand, would see the Salathé flick him off and send him screaming far below the Roof, until the force of the fall crashed onto my belay anchors. . . . We were both glad that he didn't fall."

Now at last they confronted their last major obstacles—the two remaining leads up the Headwall to Long Ledge. Both climbers silently worried about these two horrendous pitches. Yet they still could not ignore the majesty of their location. "The Headwall must be the grandest climb in the universe," marveled Piana, "a beautiful and inspiring crack system splitting the 100-degree sweep of golden wall at the top of El Capitan. The essence of the Salathé is distilled in this one incredible fissure. To be here, whether free or aid climbing, must be one of the most overwhelmingly good experiences a climber can have."

Although the Headwall inspired their spirits, the same could not be said for their battered bodies. The constant physical punishment had caused their hands and joints to be swollen into grotesque, blood-stained stumps that were too painful to close. And they ached in places that they didn't know they had. So far their fingers were being held together with Superglue and athletic tape, and they quaffed mega doses of ibuprofen to control the pain. But they couldn't keep it up much longer.

Two desperate leads, both sustained and polished 5.13, separated them from Long Ledge. A tired and gaunt Todd Skinner drew the first lead. From their earlier recons he knew that the 110-foot pitch would require a fiendish combination of power, technique, and endurance. Twice he threw himself at the crack, and twice it spit him out. After several 30-foot falls he was totally spent and was lowered to the belay.

The prospect of failure was now very real. In addition to their wasted frames, supplies of food and water were also seriously depleted. They desperately clung to their dream of freeing the Salathé, but that dream seemed increasingly farfetched. The thought of giving up was absolutely abhorrent, yet they also had to be honest with themselves.

After some discussion they decided to take a rest day. Skinner rested his mangled hands while Piana ascended a fixed line to practice the moves on the final pitch leading to Long Ledge. This initially sounded like a good idea. But after Piana had spent several frustrating hours repeatedly falling from the desperate moves, he returned to the belay solemn, depressed, and dejected. Both climbers spent a restless night tossing on their portaledges. They could see their chances of success slipping away.

"The next morning brought one of the longest breakfasts I have ever known," Piana later wrote. "After having put it off long enough, we started up the fixed lines to do battle with the Headwall. Todd felt a bit hesitant so early in the morning and needed to clear his mind. So he climbed 15 and then 20 feet above the piece he hung from, and then dramatically hurled himself into the void. He repeated this six or seven times until it became fun and the reluctance to go for it was completely gone. The sun hadn't hit the face yet and the winds on the Headwall were still. Todd flowed through the stillness and all the difficulties, slowing at the last few moves, taking care to make no mistakes. And then all was laughter as he clipped the belay and I started up to join him."

But it wasn't time yet to uncork the champagne. Now Piana had his own nightmare to deal with—the final stretch to Long Ledge. The previous day this pitch had completely humbled him. Piercing feelings of failure still clawed at his psyche. The success of the entire project—after over a month of effort, and countless hours of sweat and sacrifice—now rested with him. He summoned what confidence remained inside and tried to focus on preparing himself for the intricate moves above. He recalled, "Todd and I spent at least an hour cleaning my hands with alcohol, Superglueing the rents in my fingers, and then carefully applying a wrap of tape over the glue. Before starting I torqued my fingers in the crack to numb the pain. The morning's lethargy became adrenaline . . ."

Deliberately he climbed upward, rested a bit, tried to down-climb a short section, fell, and then fought his way back up. "It was a lonely, high-pressure situation," Skinner noted. "We'd worked on [this pitch] for five days before the final effort, and he was tired and beat up and suffering horribly. On the last move he made a wild lunge left and then a lunge right to a crazy fingerlock, and he caught it! And that effort was the best conquering of doubt I've ever witnessed, an effort that Yosemite climbers should enshrine!"

The pair rated this pitch 5.13b, making it the crux of the entire climb. Then they dispatched the few remaining pitches with enthusiasm and relief. Piana then led the final pitch to the summit. After 48 days of effort, they would claim that the Free Salathé was finally complete.

On reaching the top Piana anchored the rope to a huge granite block. The immense boulder was a familiar sight for climbers topping out on the Salathé. Hundreds of previous climbers had used it for an anchor. But just for grins, Piana decided to clip in to a few rusty pitons off to the side. As an afterthought he even inserted a small Friend into the crack. Then he started hauling up their gear.

Just as Skinner reached the lip of the cliff, dangling 3000 feet above the Valley floor, Piana was shocked to hear a weird grating sound. He turned in terror to see the huge block they were anchored to sliding directly toward him. "I am not clear about exactly what happened next," he later described. "Todd remembers me putting my hands out at the block and yelling 'NO!' I do recall the two of us being battered together and the horror of seeing my best friend knocked wildly off the edge. Then I felt a tremendous weight on my left leg as I was squeegied off the rim. There was a loud crack like a rifle shot, more pummeling, and suddenly everything stopped spinning and I could just peek over the edge. I was afraid to touch anything, and sick with the knowledge that Todd had probably just hit the talus. All of a sudden, a startling bass squeak sounded below me, followed by a desperate 'Grab the rope!'"

Skinner was alive. He slowly hauled his broken body up the only rope that remained uncut. The huge boulder had sliced through three other ropes with laser-like precision. Skinner's line escaped being cut by mere inches. They were both saved by the old fixed pins that Piana had casually clipped.

When Skinner reached the top they both just lay there for a long time. Piana had a severely broken leg, while Skinner had several broken ribs and was having trouble breathing. Slowly they summoned what little strength remained in their pitiful frames and started down the East Ledges. They endured seven painful hours of rappelling and scrambling until they finally reached the base. Although they looked much worse than the usual battered climbers who escape El Cap, they could now say that the Free Salathé was theirs.

Looking back on the whole affair Piana wrote, "We had dreamed, we had trained, and we had struggled. Even though the climb ended with a nightmare, we had triumphed. I'm sure that the ecstasy we feel now will live inside us forever."

But soon after the ascent their ecstasy began to vanish. It was replaced by anger and bitterness as accusations arose that they had cheated on the climb. Critics charged that Skinner and Piana were simply greedy liars whose thirst for publicity and sponsorship money had compelled them to make up the whole story. Rumors circulated that the climb was just a giant hoax. Part of the problem was Skinner and Piana themselves. Both men had a reputation for adding a few dramatic tidbits here and there to spice up their climbing stories. Because a few skeptics doubted the pair's credibility, the entire ascent was called into question.

This presented a unique and disturbing dilemma in the history of Yosemite climbing. For up until then, climbers were always taken at their word. If someone said they did a certain route, they were believed. Often this was a simple thing to check—either a person emerged at the top of a route or they didn't.

However, the Free Salathé presented a different situation. In this case two gifted climbers went after a spectacular prize. Success would surely mean fame, prestige, and a generous amount of money. In short, a lot was at stake. But what some people found especially troubling was that an unethical person could secretly grab a fixed pin or Friend and pull up on them, yet still insist that the climb was done completely free. In this case, skeptics had to be satisfied with the word of Skinner and Piana. For some, this was simply too much to ask. Whether because of skepticism or rivalry or jealousy, the two climbers

endured a constant stream of accusations and insults.

Besides the pair's own credibility, questions also arose regarding the likelihood of actually climbing such an extreme route. It was certainly true that the route was horrendously difficult. In over 30 pitches of climbing, it's sobering to consider that 17 pitches rated 5.10 or harder were encountered on the free ascent, plus 4 pitches rated 5.12, and 4 others rated 5.13. Some critics even said such a difficult route could never be done. Yet the history of climbing, not just in Yosemite but around the world, is filled with examples of "never" routes that were eventually climbed.

During all the controversy, Skinner and Piana stuck to their story that the Salathé was climbed completely free. "It takes a special breed of coward not to believe we did that climb," Skinner exclaimed. "We made it finally not because of our great skill, but because we were tenacious. If you refuse to fail, you eventually succeed. . . . It's a game of who can suffer the most. Whoever can suffer the most gets the most." Piana agreed, adding, "We worked harder than anyone else was willing to work, harder than we thought we could. We were willing to risk seeing our most shining goal become a tormenting failure. Yet we were prepared to fail and fail and fail until we could succeed."

It's a sad testimony of the times when the climbing community can't trust the word of its own members, especially considering that Skinner and Piana nearly lost their lives for this climb. But in the minds of many climbers, this ascent will always have a cloud of doubt over it.

Some climbing mysteries have an alluring romance to them. For example, did British climbers Mallory and Irvine reach the summit of Mt. Everest in 1924, 29 years before the first official ascent? Using only crude equipment, did the intrepid duo actually reach the top before they perished? No one will ever know for sure, since the two climbers were last seen at an altitude of over 28,000 feet before they disappeared behind swirling clouds. This remains one of the most puzzling questions in climbing. But in 1988 the Free Salathé controversy shared none of the romance of the Everest mystery.

The whole tangled controversy has recently died down, yet many doubts persist. Perhaps the most tragic outcome is that there should even be any doubts about something as important and historic as the first free ascent of the Salathé Wall. The future may shed some much needed light on the issue. Until then, many people will still harbor serious doubts.

The following year was marked by an explosion of climbing activity all over the park. This activity followed the familiar pattern established several years before: new big wall routes sandwiched between established lines, speed ascents of Grade Vs and VIs, and a multitude of incredibly hard new free routes.

On the wall scene El Capitan continued to be a coveted prize. Although the number of routes on the Big Stone was now well past 50, four new lines were pushed up the rock in 1989. These included *Octopussy* (VI 5.9 A3), *Genesis* (VI 5.11 A4+), *Central Scrutinizer* (VI 5.11c A4+), and *High Plains Dripper* (VI 5.11 A5).

Half Dome also had its share of activity. Much of the northwest face was closed to climbing for the season due to a peregrine-falcon nesting site. When the ban was lifted several new routes were established, including *Promised Land* (VI 5.10 A4), *Jet Stream* (VI 5.9 A4), and *Kali Yuga* (VI 5.10 A4).

The Kali Yuga ascent marked the return of John Middendorf to big wall climbing. After thriving on Yosemite's great cliffs during the mid 1980s, he had been conspicuously absent for the previous three years. This was no coincidence. Three years earlier a severe winter storm had trapped him, along with Mike Corbett and Steve Bosque, high on the South Face of Half Dome. In a scene remarkably similar to the epic tempest that Harding and Rowell had endured in 1968, the three climbers were forced to endure three days of extreme cold, iced ropes, and drenched sleeping bags. "It almost killed us!" Middendorf later explained. "We had a two-foot waterfall pounding down on us for a day and a half. Then it started to get cold and started snowing and sleeting on us. . . . The rock was basically covered with a four-inch sheet of ice. . . . That actually scared the shit out of me because we came so close to dying!" The three were eventually plucked off the face by helicopter. But their close brush with death prompted a hiatus in Middendorf's climbing. So when he returned to Half Dome in 1989, the Kali Yuga ascent (with Walt Shipley) provided an important boost to his bruised confidence.

The Bird was also back on Half Dome that year. Bridwell was joined by Cito Kirkpatrick, Charlie Row, and old pal Billy Westbay. The foursome completed a severe new line up the dark middle part of the northwest face. The route Shadows (VI PDH) was characterized by sinister black rock and delicate flakes. "I liked those thin piton flakes and corners," Bridwell explained. "They represent the last reserves of difficult aid climbing since the advent of copperheads and camming devices."

Both Half Dome and El Capitan were also the stage for some remarkably fast ascents. Valley local Steve Schneider authored two of these: a 21-hour solo of The Nose, and a 22-hour solo of Half Dome's Direct Northwest Face (VI 5.10 A3+). Werner Braun, Kevin Fosburg, and Rick Cashner then raced up El Cap's Zodiac (VI 5.11 A3+) in only 19 hours. All of these ascents indicated again just how casually the elite climbers were approaching big walls.

Schneider complemented his wall climbing with exceptional new free climbs. High-country routes such as *Helter Skelter* (5.13a), *You Ought To Be In Pictures* (5.13a), and *Bogey Meets Mr. Porcupine* (5.13b) were some of the hardest lines yet climbed in California. His achievements were even more impressive since he established these routes in traditional ground-up style.

Another ground-up virtuoso, Peter Croft, added his own testpiece to Pennyroyal Arches. He climbed a wickedly thin, overhanging crack to establish *Whippersnapper* (5.13a). As always, he led the route in traditional style with natural protection.

Other climbers active in creating new free routes were Dave Schultz, Ron Kauk, and Tom Herbert. However, the routes established by these climbers were rap-bolted, and therefore became controversial. Schultz ruffled the feathers of some people by bolting two lines at the Cookie Cliff: *Cookie Cutter* (5.13b) and *Meat Grinder Arete* (5.13a). But the uproar in the Valley was nothing compared to what happened in the high country.

In Tuolumne, the venerable Kauk

stirred up a proverbial hornet's nest when he installed rappel bolts on *Rap It Up* (5.12d) and *Super Sonic* (5.13b). The former route ascended a golden, knobby wall on Hammer Dome for 80 feet of forearm-wrenching effort. Super Sonic was similar in nature, but its location, on the same wall as John Bachar's runout classic Body And Soul (5.12b), was considered a desecration of Tuolumne ethics.

Despite the controversy, an uneasy truce was maintained for most of the summer between traditional climbers and rap-bolters. Although the top-down style of climbing was not appreciated by many in the climbing community, the situation did not immediately disintegrate into bolt chopping. But arguments grew hotter as more rap-bolted routes were established.

Ironically, Tom Herbert was one of the principal activists adding more top-down routes. As the son of Yosemite legend TM Herbert, Tom occupied a unique position in terms of climbing philosophy. His father was a staunch traditionalist, always adhering to the ground-up style of climbing. For a time the younger Herbert followed his father's example. He noted, "When I first started climbing I either placed my own pro on the lead, or else just ran it out like everyone else." As a 16-year-old teenager, he even shared leads with his father on an ascent of Half Dome's Northwest Face, becoming one of the youngest climbers ever to climb the route.

But as Tom Herbert took a closer look at sport climbing, and the level of difficulty that was being achieved, his ideas began to change. "When I was 18 I went to Smith Rocks [Oregon] and saw what was going on," he said. "The climbers there weren't any better than in Yosemite, but the Oregon guys were

Tom Herbert

doing harder routes because of the new style." As a result, Herbert started to wonder what amazing new routes might lay undeveloped in Yosemite.

More than most climbers, Tom Herbert felt the conflicting pull of two different eras—a past filled with the rich traditions of ground-up climbing, and a tantalizing future filled with visions of extremely beautiful sport routes. His personal dilemma mirrored the vexing question facing Yosemite climbing: should the park remain a stronghold of traditional ethics, or should climbers surrender to the new wave of sport climbing?

Herbert spent considerable time deciding which path to follow. Although he was good friends with Kauk, climbs such as Rap It Up and European Vacation represented an unsettling new philosophy. "At first I was really against those routes," he recalled. "I thought Ron had blown it, and that it'd cause all the cliffs to be littered with bolts." However, his opinion changed when he began to repeat these fierce new lines himself. He observed, "When I got on those routes, I realized that Ron had single-handedly raised the standards of Yosemite climbing. So after he introduced it, I started to put up hard rap-bolted routes too."

Herbert proved to be extremely energetic during the summer of 1989, establishing sport routes such as *Ice* (5.13a), *Carcass* (5.12b), and *Sudden Impact* (5.13a). All three required a demanding series of intricate movements up some of the steepest and prettiest cliffs in the Meadows.

But in contrast to the aesthetic location, criticisms were voiced about the methods used. In late autumn the summer's tenuous truce finally vanished when an anonymous climber chopped the bolts from several sport routes,

including Ice. Herbert recalled sadly, "Although Ron introduced rap-bolting to Tuolumne, he wasn't around at the time. So everybody came down on me instead. And I took a lot of shit for it! I had hoped that people would see what I'd done and have fun on those routes. And I hoped that they'd want to work up to those routes and get better. The lines are really good. No way are they bolt ladders. But the repeat ascents never came."

The season of 1989 could easily have been remembered as another ugly summer marred by dissension, disgust, and disillusionment among the local climbers. But the unbridled spirit and gutsy determination of two particular climbers helped to erase the aura of bitterness—replacing it instead with an inspirational example of teamwork and personal achievement.

El Capitan: Four Arms, Two Legs, And One Dream

Boundaries are made to be broken. If the history of Yosemite climbing has taught us anything, it has repeatedly revealed how the vision and sacrifice of even one person can lead to the shattering of perceived barriers. But more importantly, the boundary itself can mark the gateway into an exciting new world. To confront that turning point and move confidently forward into the unknown requires a gifted and courageous person. Fortunately for us, Yosemite has been blessed with a generous number of such people. Climbers such as John Muir, John Salathé, Royal Robbins, Jim Bridwell, Henry Barber, Bev Johnson, John Bachar, and Peter Croft have risen above the existing limitations of their day, each in their own way. In the process, they have awakened the aspirations and dreams of

entire generations. Because of their efforts, obsolete views have been cast
aside and our true potential has begun
to be realized.

Yet every adventure requires taking
that crucial first step. A person must
refuse to be satisfied with the status quo
set by personal limitations. The trend-
setters in Yosemite have always had this
mindset. Mark Wellman also had this
mindset.

Raised in the Bay Area community
of Palo Alto, Wellman showed an early
interest in the outdoors. He participated in Boy Scout outings as a youth,
scrambled up Lassen Peak (10,457 feet)
at the age of ten, and later graduated to
climbing Mont Blanc (15,775 feet), the
highest peak in the Alps.

Like others who have left their mark
in Yosemite, Wellman fell victim to
some unforeseen circumstances that forever changed the course of his life. But
his path was more painful than most.
He endured excruciating setbacks in
the process of reaching for his dreams.
Those setbacks began in 1982.

In August of that year he was on a
routine ascent of Seven Gables (13,075
feet), a massive peak in the southern
Sierra. Late in the day while descending down the mountain's west face, he
accidentally slipped and plummeted
100 feet down a steep, rocky chute.
When he stopped bouncing and finally
came to rest, his entire body screamed
in pain. The most serious injury was to
his back—the fall had crushed two verte-
brae in his spine. Never again would his
legs carry him up a remote, windswept
mountain. From now on his mode of
transportation would be a wheelchair.
As a result of those few terrifying seconds of falling, Wellman was now a
paraplegic.

Twenty-four hours after the accident
Wellman was rescued by a US Navy helicopter. He then began a tortuous two

years of rehabilitation and physical ther-
apy. Initially he languished in an abyss
of despair. His legs remained paralyzed,
he grew faint just trying to sit up in bed,
and he suffered the embarrassment of
having no control of his bowels. Slowly
his hope and dignity were stripped
away. "I would never walk again," he
mourned. "I would never climb another
mountain. I would never ski again. I
would never hike or play tennis or ride a
bike or paddle a kayak. I'd never stroll
along the beach with my girlfriend or
make love or have children. For the rest
of my life, I'd be different from everyone else. I'd be less than whole."

But the passage of time gradually
changed his outlook. Ultimately, he
accepted his situation and resolved to
make the best of it. Although his legs
were paralyzed, he began to exercise
his upper body with a passionate fervor.
He lifted weights with fanatic intensity,
swam laps in a pool, and became a
nationally-ranked player on the wheelchair tennis circuit. He also enrolled in
college to pursue a degree in park management, hoping to eventually land a
job with the National Park Service.

His efforts were rewarded in 1986
when he obtained a job as a park ranger
in Yosemite. His first assignment was at
the Big Oak Flat entrance station. He
made the most of the opportunity and
explored as much of the park as he
could. During the winter he used a sit-
ski to whisk down the slopes of the Bad-
ger Pass ski area, and the rest of the year
he cruised around the Valley floor in his
wheelchair.

Although he found the job and lifestyle fulfilling, he also began to desire
something more. In particular, he
started to pay more attention to the tattered horde of offbeat bums in Camp 4.
"Watching them at a distance in my
wheelchair, I felt an almost physical
yearning to join them," he explained,

"to touch the stone again, to sense the fresh air beneath my toes. I knew it was crazy. Climbing took my legs away from me. But as I sat there, I found myself once again feeling the strange attraction that motivates climbers to risk everything for those glorious moments high above the everyday world. I longed to struggle toward a summit again, to feel the thrill that comes from living on the edge in a high and wild place. I envied those guys, and I wanted to join them."

Remarkably, he was indeed able to join them after a chance encounter with big wall master Mike Corbett. By the late 1980s Corbett had climbed El Capitan an amazing 41 times, by 25 different routes. Although the Camp 4 climbers were always guarded in bestowing nicknames, Corbett earned a title that clearly reflected their respect for him. Around the Valley he was known simply as Mr. El Cap.

One evening in January 1989, Corbett and Wellman were enjoying a beer in the Mountain Room Bar, talking in general terms about climbing. Wellman shared his feelings about wanting to climb again: "If I'd learned one thing since my accident, it was that a lot of sweat, determination, and positive thinking would allow me to accomplish things that might have seemed impossible. I had built a nice life for myself as a ranger, but I yearned to throw myself into something big and uncertain, with no turning back. I wanted to face new adversity and challenge, and to live and breathe with it every day until I overcame it. As far as I knew, no paraplegic had even tried to scale any of the big walls in Yosemite. And to me, that made the idea nearly irresistible. How many things are there in life that you can be the first to do?"

As Corbett thought about the idea his face suddenly brightened. Impetuously he looked Wellman in the eye and said, "Climb El Cap with me!" Corbett's generous, spur-of-the-moment offer was based on some deep-seated feelings. He later explained, "I liked the challenge of engineering a way up El Capitan with Mark. I almost think that I had gotten a little bored with El Cap. I'd climbed it so many times that every time I walked up to the base of it, I knew I'd make it to the top. I think I was feeling a little cocky. Not only could I climb El Cap, I could climb it with a guy who couldn't walk."

Wellman immediately accepted the invitation and the two men set about planning the ascent. The strategy would place a huge burden on the sturdy shoulders of Corbett. He would have to lead every pitch of the climb, anchor the rope at the top of the pitch, rappel back down to the belay, jumar back up the rope and remove all the pitons, winch one of their haul bags up to the new belay, rappel back down once more, attach a rope to the other haul bag, and then raise it up to their stance. So each pitch would require him to yo-yo up and down multiple times. Then he'd have to repeat the grueling process all over again on the very next pitch. As a result, he would end up ascending the cliff not just once or even twice, but rather three times!

While all this was going on, Wellman would slowly jumar to the top of the pitch on a separate rope. To accomplish this they modified a jumar ascender and fitted it with a pull-up bar so that Wellman could use both arms simultaneously to lift himself up the rope. Another ascender was attached to his waist harness. By alternating his weight on the rope between these two ascenders, Wellman could pull himself up about six inches at a time, shift his weight to the waist ascender, slide the top ascender farther up the rope, and then do another pull-up.

They spent several months perfecting their technique while hanging from trees and small cliffs in the Valley. After many tries they hit upon a system that functioned smoothly. However, a crucial, troubling question remained. For ascending an oak tree is one thing, but ascending El Capitan is quite another. They made a rough estimate that Wellman would have to do about 7000 pull-ups to get up the cliff. Could it really be done?

To answer this troubling question they embarked on a rehearsal climb in April. Corbett and a companion first climbed up to Heart Ledge, on the lower part of the Salathé Wall. Then they rappelled back down to the Valley floor leaving several fixed ropes in place, a common tactic used by climbers on this route. Soon after Corbett returned to the rock with Wellman. Then after rigging up their ascent system, Wellman started up the cliff, using only his arms.

Slowly, six inches at a time, Wellman heaved himself higher. Imperceptibly at first, the forest floor began to recede beneath his atrophied legs. The stalwart pines became smaller and smaller as he entered that magical world of rock and sky. A relentless tide of fatigue swept over his arms and shoulders. His upper body rebelled against the strain. But he doggedly kept cranking pull-ups, one after the other. The tedious repetition could easily have broken a weaker person. Wellman, however, would not be defeated.

After four hours of pull-ups he finally reached Heart Ledge, 900 feet above

Mike Corbett leading one of the final pitches on the Shield, El Capitan

the ground. He reveled in the spectacular view, and even sun-bathed on the warm rock. A short time later Corbett joined him on the ledge and the two climbers enjoyed a gourmet dinner of Gatorade and Beanie Weenies. Although they munched their food in silence, Wellman was filled with exhilaration. "I don't think I ever drifted off to sleep that night," he recalled. "I lay awake, watching the constellations ticking off time on the celestial clock, and thinking about how far I'd come in the years since my accident. . . . And I knew for sure that even bigger adventures were just around the corner."

Having shown that their system really was feasible, they rappelled back to the Valley floor the next morning. Then they began making final preparations for a full El Cap ascent. Their target date was July 19.

The specific route they would attempt was the Shield, Charlie Porter's classic, direct line up the southwest face. They chose this route, one of the straightest lines on the cliff, because they wished to avoid complex and time-consuming traverses.

The next three months passed in a blur of preparations, setbacks, solutions, and anticipation. A multitude of nagging problems appeared, but Corbett and Wellman devised an answer for each one. On the eve of their departure, they spent a final sleepless night tossing and turning in their beds, each wrestling with his own individual hopes and fears.

The adventure began the following morning at 8 A.M. Wellman attached his mechanical ascenders to the rope, slid protective chaps over his legs, checked every knot one last time, and then took a quick glance at his feet. The boots he was wearing were the same ones he had worn years earlier, during that fateful

afternoon on Seven Gables. His life had been changed forever while wearing them. Now, with those very same boots on his feet, and looking up at the hardest mountain he had ever attempted, he hoped his life would again be changed.

With all of his equipment in place, Wellman finally started up the fixed rope. He was happy to be away from the reporters who had come to interview them. Now at last it was just him, his partner, and El Capitan.

The fixed rope snaked skyward to Mammoth Terraces. Corbett had previously reclimbed the lower section of the Salathé Wall to reach this commodious ledge. Here, 1000 feet above the ground, they would spend their first night. Besides leaving ropes in place Corbett had also cached two haul bags filled with the supplies they would need: food, sleeping bags, rain gear, portaledges, and 100 pounds of water.

As always, the water would be one of their most precious resources. Since the beginning of big wall climbing in Yosemite, water has figured prominently in virtually all pilgrimages through the vertical desert. The Corbett/Wellman ascent would be no different. For not only were they climbing in summer, they would also be enduring the fierce July heat. "Hardly anybody climbs El Capitan in the middle of summer—for good reason!" Corbett explained. "The glacier-polished granite acts as a big reflecting oven, and as a climber, you feel like an ant scaling the side of a cast-iron skillet. But I didn't want to be in anyone's way, and I didn' t want anybody else in our way. I knew that in July we could have the place pretty much to ourselves. Besides, both Mark and I had experienced our worst moments as climbers in the cold. For us, heat was the lesser evil."

Wellman reached Mammoth Terraces

four and a half hours later. Although both climbers were pleased with their progress, the ferocious heat had drained them. They would go no further that day.

Their real work began the next morning. Corbett started methodically nailing the Muir Wall section of the route. These pitches required several days of tedious effort to ascend.

Throughout those days, both climbers tried to avoid looking too closely at the Shield Roof above them. But the horrendous obstacle, jutting out from the rock for 25 feet, could not be ignored. To surmount it they would have to hang backwards above 1900 feet of turbulent air. Yet the physical difficulties and fearful exposure were not the only factors that worried them. "The Shield Roof also marked the point of no return," Wellman explained. "Once we surmounted the overhang, retreat would be all but impossible. Our rappel ropes would be left dangling out in space, 25 feet away from the wall. We would have no choice but to continue to the summit. And if we ran into trouble above this point of no return—a sudden storm, a fall, an injury—well, neither one of us wanted to think about it. The Shield Roof was the psychological crux of our climb. . . . Corbett tried to act calm and self-assured, but I could see the strain beginning to show on his face. His worry lines were caked with dried sweat, and in his eyes I could see a reflection of my own concern."

They reached the ominous roof on the afternoon of their fourth day. Corbett climbed up to the belay station atop the 17th pitch, just at the point where the sinister roof shot out perpendicular from the cliff. He anchored the ropes there and rappelled down to his partner. The roof itself would wait until tomorrow.

After a restless night hanging in portaledges, Corbett attacked the dreaded roof. Both climbers had looked forward to this day with a mixture of excitement and fear. However, Corbett made the pitch look routine as he applied total concentration to the textured gray rock immediately in front of him. He moved with controlled, calculating motions that had been burned into his memory long ago. Whether hammering a piton, resting in slings, selecting a cam, or testing a copperhead, Corbett was at home here. El Capitan had mercilessly flogged him in the past whenever a mistake was made. But that abuse was invaluable—for it had forged a climber who now moved with ruthless efficiency up one of the most demanding mountains in the world. He was indeed Mr. El Cap.

Corbett made short work of the dank roof and the A3 crack above. He reached the end of the pitch and breathed a huge sigh of relief. The burden of the Shield Roof was now behind them. He was even happy that retreat was now impossible. "You'd think it would be frightening to pass the point of no return, but the opposite was true," he noted. "Psychologically, it was as if a weight had been lifted off our shoulders. Now we were committed to the top; there could be no more doubt or indecision. Once the bridge was burned behind us, once we had no choice but to move forward, the picture became clear and focused."

Over the next two days they focused on the monolithic, overhanging rock which gives the Shield its name. The climbing here was still difficult and fearsomely exposed. Yet the hardy pair, who referred to themselves as "the climbing bum and the gimp ranger," kept moving upward with stubborn determination.

The morning of their eighth day saw them only five pitches from the top. The climbing was easier than what they had already ascended, and both men were eager to finish those five pitches. "Mike attacked them like a man possessed," Wellman recalled. "He was in a mad rush to get to the top—not the least because he had run out of cigarettes!"

The pair reached the top of El Capitan to find a small army of friends and journalists. Hugs were exchanged and champagne flowed. But although the praise and the congratulations felt good, nothing compared with the inner satisfaction that both climbers felt.

Over the preceding six months, Corbett and Wellman had each wrestled with his own faults, strengths, worries, and hopes. However, each man had qualities that complemented the other's. Corbett had the unequaled ability and generosity to make the climb happen. No one could match the experience and big wall savvy of Mr. El Cap. Yet he saw and appreciated The Captain in a new way because of Wellman's dream. The unquenchable spirit of the quiet park ranger provided a perfect complement to Corbett's experience.

Perhaps the climb's most important result was the statement that it made regarding handicaps. Wellman noted, "Each of us is handicapped in one way or another. . . . The important thing is that [we] recognize these handicaps and understand that we have within ourselves the power to transcend them." He clearly showed that "disability" does not mean "inability."

Like the all-female ascent of the Triple Direct in 1973, the Corbett/Wellman climb was not an achievement that shattered the record books. It wasn't the longest, hardest, or fastest ascent of El Capitan. But it was a triumph of the human spirit. Wellman was not willing to take the easy way out. He would not allow himself to sit idly and let his dreams evaporate. Instead he summoned the courage to confront uncertainty and the fear of failure. He and Corbett had shared the slogan "four arms and two legs." But they also shared a common dream—to reach for something beyond their grasp.

Such a reach always brings risks. But the fleeting chance of success can overshadow the risk. Just having the courage to make an attempt can itself bring an invaluable experience. Such was the case for Wellman. Sitting on top of El Capitan after his ascent, he put it this way: "I knew I'd soon be settling back into my wheelchair. I also knew that the person sitting in it would never be the same as the one who had left it eight days earlier."

A formidable barrier had indeed been broken.

"If you couldn't improve on what had been done before, like doing a route faster or doing more of it free, than what was the point of doing it at all?"

These sentiments, expressed by Jim Bridwell in the early 1990s, could well be the credo for all of the present decade. For although the ideals of "fast and free" have been around in Yosemite for years, the current decade of the 1990s has seen these ideals become entrenched as never before.

The tone for the new decade was set immediately in the early summer of 1990. High-powered climber Rick Lovelace came storming out of Nevada and attacked El Capitan like a savage, hungry predator. He first made a winter ascent of Zenyatta Mondatta (VI 5.7 A5) and then soloed a new route called the *Shortest Straw* (VI 5.10 A3+) on the same face. Then, while Eric Kohl and Walt Shipley were working on their new route *Surgeon General* (VI 5.9 A5), Lovelace started up that route solo and went on to complete the second ascent. In addition to the A5 grade, the route received the additional rating of "YDFS," meaning that if the leader fell, "You're Dead For Sure!"

With this training behind him, Lovelace then made the first one-day solo of Zodiac (VI 5.11 A3+), reaching the summit in a remarkable time of 23 hours and 47 minutes. Shortly thereafter he teamed up with Kevin Fosburg to make a rapid ascent of the Shield (VI 5.9 A3+) in 23 hours, 9 minutes. This was also the first one-day ascent.

Not content to stop there, Lovelace then pounced on one of El Cap's most historic aid lines—the *North America Wall* (VI 5.8 A3). With partners Steve Gerberding and Scott Stowe, he raced up the fearsome route in 24¹/₂ hours. Peter Croft called this "one of the most awesome speed ascents that has been done!" The trio climbed right on the edge between boldness and insanity, as they simul-climbed in the dark and free-climbed steep sections of A3 nailing. One heart-stopping moment occurred high on the route when Lovelace, simul-climbing with Gerberding, suddenly fell. Although he caught himself before the rope became taut, Gerberding came dangerously close to being yanked off the cliff along with the plummeting Lovelace.

Although the ascent was a remarkable achievement, it clearly showed the slim margin of safety that modern climbers were now willing to accept. Lovelace himself just shrugged off the risks by stating, "When you're going that fast, you're not being that safe anyway."

But without a doubt, the most extraordinary speed ascents of 1990 were accomplished by Peter Croft and Dave Schultz. During the summer this honed pair demolished the old speed records for both The Nose and the Salathé Wall.

Up to that point, the fastest ascent of The Nose had taken just over 8 hours. Steve Schneider and Hans Florine had accomplished this impressive ascent that very spring. However, in June, Croft and Schultz sliced nearly two hours from the record, reaching the top in 6 hours and 40 minutes, even though they had climbed most of the route in the dark.

Amazingly, they weren't even trying for the speed record on The Nose—they were actually trying to combine ascents of both The Nose and the Salathé Wall in the same day. They started the attempt at midnight and used headlamps all the way to Camp Six. The pair carried only one rope and a bare minimum of hardware, and they simul-climbed much of the route. But on reaching the top of The Nose, Schultz was just too sleepy to continue, so they called it a day and returned to the Valley floor.

Four days later, they made another attempt at climbing two El Cap routes in a day, this time starting with the Salathé Wall. The route commonly referred to as the greatest rock climb in the world was blitzed by the pair in just 10 hours and 6 minutes. But again they didn't feel up to continuing once they had reached the summit.

The next month they prepared for a third try. Interestingly enough, Croft had first gotten the idea for this climax back in 1986. Standing atop Half Dome after the first ascent of two Grade VI routes in a single day (El Cap and Half Dome), he immediately began thinking about the next possible step. He recalled, "I remember thinking that the next thing to do was The Nose and the Salathé in a day."

To combine these two colossal routes in the same day would require about 70 pitches of climbing, up to a difficulty of hard 5.11, in one 24-hour period. But Croft's previous combination (or enchainment) of The Nose and Half Dome's Northwest Face had convinced him that such extreme combinations really were possible. And his rapid ascents in June demonstrated that in Schultz, he had finally found the right partner.

Ironically, the clean-cut Schultz had come from a rather questionable background. "I was what you might call a juvenile delinquent," he admitted. "I was arrested maybe 23 times before I turned 18—auto theft, burglary, ripping off jewelry stores, whatever. I'd probably be in prison right now if it wasn't for climbing."

Schultz showed an early knack for climbing and eventually put up some of the hardest and scariest routes in the Valley. His route *Meat Grinder Arete* (5.13b) was near the top of the standards, and his 1988 route on Half Dome, *Southern Belle* (V 5.12d), was one of the most runout and severe lines in the country. Regarding this latter route he explained, "It's only 14 pitches, but it's horrendous! There are no more than four bolts per pitch!" However, the one route he was especially known for was *Karma* (V 5.11d), also on the south face of Half Dome. "It makes any other scary climb look like a picnic!" Schultz later stated. "Mandatory 60-foot runouts. There are two pitches on it which would be death if you fell, since the route traverses along this Ginsu knife-like dike. . . . It was so scary! It was a first ascent and it hasn't been repeated!"

Croft felt confident that both he and Schultz were up to the challenge of two El Cap routes in a day. And he was pleased to know that he'd be sharing the rope with Schultz. He noted, "You can't compare Dave to anyone else. He's totally unique, and one of the funniest guys I know! As a climber, he wasn't the first to do 5.13 in the Valley, but he firmly established it through the routes he put up. He deserves a lot of credit."

The formidable pair started their audacious enchainment with The Nose on July 6 at midnight. "We mostly simul-climbed, with some pitches [lasting for] 1500 feet without stopping," Schultz described. "The dangerous part would be if the second would fall, with the top guy 60 feet out or so. There is no way the top climber could hold the bottom guy. The leader would be pulled like a vacuum towards the last piece. We used a nine-millimeter rope. There's no telling what would happen. So we didn't fall!"

They reached the summit around 6 A.M. "We were both so totally happy," Croft recalled. "It was like being a couple of little kids! It was still nice and cool, we had plenty of time, and we were both so totally psyched! So we skipped down the descent slabs, just having a great time, and then cranked the rappels back to the ground."

Seven and a half hours after leaving, they returned to their car. After a short rest and a recharge of coffee and sandwiches, they nonchalantly set off for the Salathé Wall.

As before, Croft did most of the leading and they simul-climbed most of the route. "We moved together all the way to Mammoth Terraces," Croft explained. "We did the rappels to Heart Ledge and then moved together all the way to the top of the Ear. At that point we started to get a bit tired."

After climbing about 52 pitches of demanding vertical rock, even an elite climber would have felt much more than just "a bit tired." But Croft and Schultz had molded their physiques into climbing machines. They devoured the route with relentless intensity, climbing an additional 17 pitches before reaching the top at 6:50 P.M.

For the first time in the history of Yosemite climbing, a team scrambled onto the rounded crest of El Capitan for the second time in the same day. Both climbers were utterly elated. "It was outrageous!" Schultz exclaimed. But he also admitted, "It was the most tired I've ever been. We almost hit the wall!"

From the time the two climbers first started up The Nose, to the time they returned to the ground after completing the Salathé Wall, only 20½ hours had gone by. To put this in perspective, it is not unusual for a team to spend 20 hours just getting to Dolt Tower on the lower part of The Nose. Some parties have even been known to spend 20 hours just sorting their gear in El Cap

At the lip of the Roof, Salathé Wall

Meadow. To fire off both routes in one day was nothing short of historic. Schultz summed up the whole experience by stating, "Climbing The Nose and the Salathé in the same day was a once-in-a-lifetime deal. . . . It was way more fun [than crime], and you don't have to go to jail!"

Other climbers who were having a lot of fun during this period were Tom Herbert and Steve Schneider. Both climbers focused on free ascents of hideously difficult routes around Tuolumne Meadows. On the small dome of Canopy World, Herbert climbed a short and severely overhanging face to establish *Grapevine* (5.13a). He also re-established the bolts on *Ice* (5.12d), which had previously been chopped. At the same time Schneider went on a tear through the high country, putting up dozens of new routes. The coup de grace of his summer romp was *Raging Waters* (5.13c), a steep face climb on the golden west face of Medlicott Dome.

These routes continued the trend started by Ron Kauk years before—using sport-climbing ethics to create clean, safe lines up some of Tuolumne's most flawless cliffs. "Once known for runouts on holdless granite slabs that made even experienced leaders wince, Tuolumne now hosts many challenging yet safe climbs," explained Chris Falkenstein. "The new generation is looking at Tuolumne through eyes not clouded by traditional beliefs."

This latter point continued to be a source of division in the climbing community. New sport routes in Tuolumne itself, the original bastion of traditional ground-up climbing, clearly illustrated that the region was drifting further and further from its roots.

Although a few climbers felt it was time to go out and start chopping routes again, the tide of sport climbing now seemed overwhelming. There was no arguing that the new lines were challenging, safe, and aesthetic in their own way. The argument was whether the style of the first ascent should take precedence over the route's quality.

Previous generations had virtually worshipped Yosemite's great cliffs. Those traditional climbers now felt that too many of the younger climbers were only concerned with high ratings, punk haircuts, multiple earrings, pierced noses, and neon lycra. Feelings intensified that Yosemite had become simply a crowded, pathetic, outdoor gymnasium. Yet since no one felt like making the first move with hammer and chisel, the new sport routes were not erased. Younger climbers enjoyed the physical challenge of the new routes, while the old guard grudgingly tolerated their existence.

However, there were no grudges when it came to the big walls. A handful of brilliant climbers continued to make inspired ascents of Yosemite's most revered routes. Hans Florine and Andres Puhvel were especially busy. In June 1991 they raced up The Nose in a record time of just over six hours. Later in the month they completed the Salathé Wall in 8 hours and 56 minutes. Another speedy team was Steve Gerberding and Banny Root. Gerberding had already participated in a 26-hour ascent of Tangerine Trip (VI 5.9 A3+) and a 15-hour ascent of Zodiac (VI 5.11 A3+). In September he and Root, together with Dan Osman, climbed Lurking Fear (VI 5.10 A3) in 15 hours and 26 minutes. Ascents such as these demonstrated just how comfortable the current wall masters were on the Valley's huge walls.

Ironically, one of the year's most noteworthy ascents was also one of the slowest. For during the middle of September, Mike Corbett and paraplegic Mark Wellman returned to the vertical world. This time the focus of their efforts was Half Dome. The hardy pair took the lessons they had previously learned on El Capitan and applied them to the fearsome route Tis-sa-ack (VI 5.9 A4). Over a tedious 13 days they struggled up a route notorious for delicate nailing and dangerously loose rock. They emerged on the summit six days late, and distressingly low on food, water, and emotional reserves. "It was the toughest climb of my life!" Corbett exclaimed. "I was at my absolute limit!"

Yet limits did not seem to be a problem for Peter Croft and Hans Florine. Two years later, in the early summer of 1993, the two speed demons sprinted up The Nose in an amazing 4 hours and 22 minutes. Croft explained, "I'd just gotten back from a road trip where I was traveling around giving slide shows, and I was just happy to be back in the Valley. I felt like doing El Cap again, so we went up on The Nose because it's my favorite route. Going for a record wasn't a big deal, but I did want to do it fast." His traveling must have agreed with him, for this ascent indicated how fit he really was. But he kept it all in perspective as just another way to enjoy himself in Yosemite. "The fun thing for me is that by doing it fast I hardly have to take anything—just a tiny bit of water and maybe a PowerBar," he noted. "I'm not really up there long enough for it to be a big issue. During the ascent I really wasn't pushing that hard. So when we got down I went over and soloed the Steck-Salathé on Sentinel."

Such exemplary climbing was nothing new for Croft. By this time he was world-famous for his bold solos, for the enchainments of El Cap and Half Dome in a day, and for doing two El Cap routes in a day. But less publicized excursions indicated just how much he loved climbing, loved the challenge, and loved Yosemite.

On one occasion, he and Dave Schultz decided it would be fun to try climbing four Grade V routes in one day. Their plan called for back-to-back ascents of the North Face of the Rostrum (5.12b), Crucifix on Higher Cathedral Rock (5.12b), the West Face of El Capitan (5.11c), and finally Astro Man on Washington Column (5.11c). But as if about 50 pitches of climbing weren't enough, they decided to add a special little twist to the Rostrum—a 5.13b finish at the top of the route called the Excellent Adventure. They succeeded in climbing the first three routes as planned. But the difficulty of the Excellent Adventure slowed them down. Their fatigue caught up with them on their final route Astro Man. They managed the first few pitches and then realized they were just too tired to finish safely. So they called it a day and rappelled off. "It may seem like a failure," Croft later said. "But we failed because we really wanted to push it! We didn't want to just do the Rostrum the easy way, we wanted to do it with the Excellent Adventure finish. And we were doing it all for fun anyway."

Other fun-seekers, such as Steve Schneider, Bill Price, and Jeff Schoen set their sights on a free ascent of El Cap's Excalibur (VI 5.10 A4). The wide, desperate cracks on the eighth and ninth pitches are legendary among big wall climbers—they require a bizarre combination of huge pitons and sawed-off blocks of wooden 2×4s to ascend. With a gaping span of nine inches in places, these cracks were, according to Schneider, "some of the most human-devouring offwidths ever attempted!" The trio climbed about 75% of the route free, with numerous pitches of 5.12 climbing, plus a 5.13a thin crack on the 21st pitch. "A big wall

doesn't have to be 100% free to make it a 'free climb'," Schneider explained. "Excalibur is one such climb—predominantly free, immensely difficult, and totally outstanding!"

Schneider also participated in Todd Skinner's project to make the first free ascent of Half Dome's Direct Northwest Face (VI 5.10 A3+). Skinner went through a slew of partners during his 61-day siege, including Schneider, Paul Piana, Galen Rowell, Scott Franklin, Nancy Feagin, Steve Bechtel, and Chris Oates. As in his effort on the Free Salathé, Skinner made numerous forays up the wall to toprope specific sections and add bolts to various pitches.

Because some climbers still remembered the Free Salathé controversy, Skinner's Half Dome ascent was subject to extremely close scrutiny. Galen Rowell noted, "Todd was so scared that the Yosemite locals would denigrate him, that he underrated the hardest pitch so that someone could not later accuse him of exaggeration. Instead of 5.13c/d, it is probably 5.14a/b, since it took him weeks to work out the moves and no other top climber has yet to repeat it." Rowell acknowledged that Skinner's ascent "may be rightfully controversial because of its sport-climbing style." Still, Rowell was emphatic in his assessment of the climb: "Todd Skinner did the most continuously difficult free climbing ever done on a big rock face in history."

Another key player of 1993 was Hans Florine. During the summer he made a 14-hour roped solo of The Nose, which was the fastest solo yet done there. He also teamed up with two talented women climbers, both of whom would make a huge impact that year.

The first was Nancy Feagin, who joined Florine on a rapid 12-hour ascent of the Salathé Wall. Besides her involvement with Skinner's Half Dome project, Feagin also joined Sue McDevitt on The Nose. The five-foot, 100-pound McDevitt was herself a giant on the Yosemite climbing scene, having already climbed El Cap 14 times and participated in the first all-female ascent of Astro Man. Now on The Nose, the two gifted women went on to become the first female team to make a one-day ascent of the route. Their climb required just 17 hours.

Then Lynn Hill stepped to the forefront. She and Florine climbed The Nose in 8 hours and 17 minutes, the fastest ascent ever for a male/female team. After that Hill began to focus not on speed but rather on pure free climbing.

Although small in stature, she was a giant in terms of determination and talent. And that very summer Hill would attempt one of the world's most coveted free-climbing prizes.

El Capitan: The Nose Free

When Lynn Hill walks down the street, virtually no one ever suspects that she is a world-class climber. At five feet, two inches tall, and weighing in at a slender 100 pounds, she is petite and charming, and graced with a gentle spirit. Yet Hill is a powerhouse in terms of athletics, and climbing in particular comes naturally to her.

While bopping around Joshua Tree as a teenager she happened to run into John Long. The fabled Stonemaster vividly recalled the incident this way: "Bachar and I were standing below an obscure boulder, our fingertips shredded, arguing whether a certain problem was B1 or B2. Then 'Little Lynny' (as we later styled her) showed up. . . . She climbed the goddam boulder problem on her second try. 'I guess it's only B1,' I carped to Bachar. Hard to say, though, because I couldn't do it, then or ever!"

Hill eventually began dating Long,

Climbing up toward Sickle Ledge, The Nose

and became one of the local inhabitants in Camp 4. "It seemed like we were a bunch of oddballs," she recalled. "But we were really like a family since we shared such a passion for climbing." She climbed, trained, and lived the typical penniless life of a Yosemite climber. Although quiet and easy-going by nature, she took on some rather unusual jobs in order to make ends meet. "Perhaps the most embarrassing way I made money was boxing other women at a local bar," she explained. "I was so poor that it was worth the 20 bucks to pummel some girl who was trying to pummel me. . . . But the money fed John and I for quite a while."

Hill's residency in the Valley gave her a firm foundation in traditional Yosemite climbing, and that gave her an important advantage in many types of climbing. In the course of her travels she became the first woman ever to climb a 5.14 route (France's Masse Critique in 1990), and dominated the competition climbing circuit for years, becoming a permanent fixture in the winner's circle. Yet she never forgot her Yosemite roots.

Like most other Valley climbers she tried to sample everything on the park's climbing menu: hard cracks, runout slabs, and soaring big walls. Ascents of both El Capitan and Half Dome ingrained in her the majesty and splendor of the high granite kingdom. And like her peers, she was extremely interested in trying to climb El Cap completely free.

By 1993 it had been five years since Todd Skinner and Paul Piana had claimed the first free ascent of the Salathé Wall. Yet the original El Cap testpiece, The Nose, had so far resisted all free attempts. But not because people hadn't tried. Jim Bridwell had freed the Stovelegs in 1967, then rappelled to the ground. During the early 1980s Ray Jardine had traversed left below El Cap Towers to avoid the bolt ladder and pendulum above, but only by the destructive method of chiseling his own handholds. Then John Bachar and Ron Kauk had freed sections of the upper dihedral in the later 1980s. However, no one had ever free climbed through the intimidating Great Roof, or the desperately smooth crack above Camp Six. The best male climbers in the world, with their imposing physiques and bulging muscles, had never mastered the intricate moves that these horrendous obstacles demanded. So Lynn Hill, all 100 pounds of her, waltzed up to the rock and went to work.

In September Hill started up the route with British climber Simon Nadin. The lower pitches passed routinely until they reached the first big obstacle—the Great Roof. A 5.11d slot led up to the crux where the crack curved to the right beneath the oppressive roof. She charged up the crack and threw herself into a series of fingertip underclings and sketchy liebacks. However, the warm temperatures of Indian summer caused her sweaty fingers to slowly ooze out of the vicious crack with alarming regularity. "I gave it a really good effort," she described. "But at one point I almost fell off! My foot was frictioning on the face and I was just about to dive my fingers into the crack when my foot suddenly slipped! But I went for it anyway and managed to sink my fingers into the crack and hold on."

A separate team of Croatian climbers was watching all of this from above, and they were completely awed by what they saw. "The Croatian guys were looking at me wide-eyed and couldn't believe it!" Hill recalled. "They were just trying to get up the route any way they could! They really couldn't understand this crazy woman trying to free it!"

After an exhausting effort Hill managed to free the 5.13 pitch. She and Nadin then continued upward to Camp Five ledge, where they called it a day. Early the next morning, still sore and stiff from the day before, Hill confronted a heinous 5.12d corner. She struggled with the daunting problem and eventually was able to surmount it. The two climbers then continued on to Camp Six.

At this point, however, the relentless difficulty of the climb began to overwhelm their thrashed bodies. "Because our planning was a little off, we often arrived at the hardest pitches first thing in the morning, when it was difficult to get warmed up for hard free climbing," she admitted. "We also neglected to carry a hammer which, as it turned out, we needed to remove a broken piton." With their limbs screaming for rest, and a busted piton clogging up the only climbable crack, they gave up the attempt and ascended to the rim without exclusively free climbing.

A short time later Hill returned to the wall with Brooke Sandahl. They hiked to the rim and rappelled down so that Hill could refine her techniques and prepare for a final attempt. She again worked the moves on the Great Roof pitch, then set about devising some way through the daunting corner above Camp Six. She first hammered out the broken pin that had stopped her before. Then she reached into her bag of tricks and pulled out the arcane array of unorthodox techniques needed to finesse and muscle her way up the vicious dihedral. She described the pitch this way: "You climb up a crack, throw your hand out to an arete, then throw your foot onto the face and hope that it stays! Then match hands on the arete and get over into the corner. From there it's all strange climbing and weird stemming. Just to get started required all kinds of strange opposition, and a weird arm-bar higher up." She and Sandahl spent several days on the upper part of the route before returning to the Valley floor. They rested and geared up for their final attempt.

That effort began on September 12. The two climbers moved easily through the lower pitches, reaching the base of the Stovelegs on their first day. From there they rappelled to the ground and took a day off for rest, then returned to the campaign on the following day.

Through the Stovelegs, past Dolt Tower, and across the Jardine Traverse they climbed, their vision fixed ever upward. They scrutinized every inch of the rock above, perusing an ever-changing tapestry of micro edges and bold cracks. They also pondered their own chances of success. All the pitches were known to them, so there shouldn't be any surprises. But the climbing was so extreme that it was in no way a sure thing. And if this attempt should fail they were unsure when they could compose themselves for another try. So they felt a definite sense of urgency.

They made their first bivouac on Camp Four ledge, beneath the glaring ferocity of the Great Roof. The next day Hill again wrestled with the desperate stems and power underclings beneath the roof. As before, her petite stature and small fingers were a distinct advantage here, allowing her to cross terrain that had defeated several generations of the world's hottest free climbers.

After an uneventful night at Camp Five, the two climbers continued upward and Hill confronted the nightmarish corner above Camp Six. From her previous attempts she had a good idea what the pitch demanded. So without hesitation she launched herself into a series of peculiar twists and bends that would have made any circus contortionist proud: her back against one wall, her left hand probing a delicate seam far above her head, her other hand plastered against the rock chimney-fashion behind her back, while her feet groped for upward progress on some of the smoothest and steepest rock in Yosemite. Down at the belay, Sandahl could only watch in amazement as this climbing titan fought her way up. "It was totally wicked!" he later remarked, adding that Hill was "doing stuff that I've never even seen before!"

When Hill reached the top of the pitch there was little time for celebrating the completion of one of the most severe leads in California (5.13b).

The weather had suddenly taken a turn for the worse. Knowing that a sudden rainstorm would cripple their free-climbing effort, the two climbers made a desperate attempt to finish the route. A short time later, with the weather still holding and the rock mercifully dry, Hill led the final 5.12c pitch through the overhanging summit roofs.

As she scrambled onto the easy slabs above and emerged onto the summit, she couldn't suppress a huge smile. Her eyes sparkled at the sight of friends there to greet her. Sandahl soon joined her and the group relaxed and laughed around a small campfire. But far from being exhausted, Hill had an indescribable feeling of exhilaration. Her dream was finally realized: The Nose was now free.

Was it a surprise that Hill was the first one—and so far the only one!—to succeed on this monumental challenge? For the people who know her, it was no surprise at all. John Long expressed the views of many climbers when he wrote, "There's not so much mystery why Lynn Hill is such a splendid climber. She simply came into the world with more natural gifts than the rest of us."

Although Hill had traveled and climbed in some of the most exotic locations in the world, and had recently made her home in France, it was particularly satisfying for her to return to the Sierra. For this sublime mountain landscape always had held a special allure for her, as did the regal splendor of El Capitan. She later explained, "It was great coming back to Yosemite and completing the circle of my climbing career. It was a way of communicating something about free climbing."

Like many of the legendary figures in Yosemite climbing, Hill was a quiet person who let her actions speak for her. But when those actions spoke, everyone was definitely listening.

In the aftermath of this climbing milestone, El Capitan continued to dominate the aspirations of many top climbers. Speed ascents and free ascents remained the prime objectives for many of the climbing elite. Argentinian climber Rolando Garibotti typified the speed trend, going on an absolute tear up some of El Cap's finest routes. In late May 1994, he and Jon Rosemengy blasted up Lurking Fear (VI 5.10 A3) in slightly under 13 hours. Four days later, Garibotti was joined by Rob Slater on The Nose, which they climbed in 5 hours and 48 minutes. After a few rest days, Garibotti and Adam Wainwright cruised the Triple Direct (VI 5.9 A2) in 8 hours and 20 minutes, followed three days later by an ascent of the Shield (VI 5.9 A3+) in 18 hours and 20 minutes.

Local hardman Steve Schneider was another climber who had some notable outings on the Big Stone. With various partners he climbed the West Buttress (VI 5.10 A3+) in 18 hours, Chinese Water Torture (VI 5.11 A4) in 17 hours and 15 minutes, and the Dihedral Wall (VI 5.9 A3) in 27 hours and 38 minutes. He also made a determined effort to do the first free ascent of Lurking Fear; most of the route went free up to a difficulty of 5.13a.

Then in mid June, El Capitan was the scene of a bizarre soap opera involving three climbers and the National Park Service. Scott Cosgrove, Kurt Smith, and Greg Epperson spent over 20 days (spread over two months) trying to free the Muir Wall (VI 5.10 A3). During the ascent, they used a power drill to add protection bolts to certain pitches, and to replace some corroded belay anchors on the 29-year-old route. This use of a power drill was technically illegal. According to the Wilderness Act of 1964, motorized equipment was prohibited in federal wilderness areas,

Evening alpenglow on Fairview Dome

which includes all the big walls of Yosemite Valley. Although they were breaking the law, the team was unconcerned since the Park Service had always been lax in enforcing it.

This time, however, things were different. After freeing 31 of the route's 34 pitches, the tired climbers reached the top on June 12. Another climbing team happened to be on the summit, so the two groups swapped stories about their respective ascents. The Muir Wall team described the difficulties of their route, the vagaries of the weather they had endured, and their use of a power drill. The other two climbers seemed unusually inquisitive about the details of the Muir Wall ascent. The reason for their curiosity soon became apparent, for the other climbers were actually park rangers in disguise. Cosgrove, Smith, and Epperson were cited for violation of a federal statute, their gear and film were confiscated, and they were ordered to appear before a federal judge for sentencing.

Although their gear was later returned, and they were subject to only a minor fine, the incident made a huge impact throughout the climbing community. The relationship between climbers and rangers had often been a contentious one, but in the aftermath of the

Muir Wall bust it became even more antagonistic. Some climbers accused the rangers of prejudice in their heavy-handed behavior, while others defended the Park Service as simply enforcing the law. The rangers claimed that the Wilderness Act would be rigorously enforced in the future. It remains to be seen if this will be true, and how it will affect such important safety concerns as the replacement of old anchor bolts on Yosemite's popular routes.

Despite the antagonism and division that this incident created, the bitterness was thankfully overshadowed by two inspired ascents that occurred several months later. The first was another accomplishment by Lynn Hill, who made history by completing the first one-day/all-free ascent of The Nose. Relying on her intimate knowledge of the route, Hill started her landmark climb at 10 P.M. on September 19. With Valley wall master Steve Sutton doing the belaying, Hill climbed through the night, reached the Great Roof in the morning, climbed the horrible 5.13b corner above Camp Six that afternoon, then surmounted the 5.12c summit overhangs in the dark. The indomitable Hill led every pitch, yet took only 23 hours for the entire ascent. In terms of physical endurance and technical difficulty, this ascent was simply unprecedented— ranking as one of the most astonishing climbing feats ever accomplished. It clearly showed, beyond any doubt, that Lynn Hill was truly in a class by herself.

A similar statement could be made regarding Steve Schneider and Hans Florine, who completed the other inspired ascent of 1994. One month after Hill's superb climb, Schneider and Florine completed an amazing three El Cap routes in the same day. With surprisingly little effort they raced up The

Nose in 5 hours and 42 minutes, Lurking Fear in 8 hours and 52 minutes, and the West Face in 4 hours and 31 minutes. The pair swapped leads on The Nose, Schneider led all of Lurking Fear, and Florine led all of the West Face. Since the focus of their effort was speed, they didn't try to climb each route completely free—they used whatever method (free climbing or aid climbing) was quickest. In order to descend back to the Valley floor between climbs, they utilized fixed ropes which had previously been strung on Lurking Fear. The entire jaunt lasted only 23 hours, even though it involved an unheard-of 72 pitches of climbing.

This El Cap trilogy, along with Lynn Hill's all-free ascent of The Nose in a day, provides fitting testimony about the continuing challenges that Yosemite still offers. Although the Valley walls are extremely familiar to generations of climbers, they continue to offer priceless opportunities for cleansing the spirit and for changing one's life. Even after all these years, and countless ascents of El Capitan and Half Dome, the vertical world continues to provide pathways for greater self awareness and appreciation of Nature.

The main players of the "new generation" were well aware of this fact.

Throughout the 1980s and early 1990s, they forged ahead with new climbing objectives while still maintaining a crucial link to Yosemite's past traditions. Climbers such as John Bachar, Peter Croft, Mark Wellman, and Lynn Hill were cut from the classic mold of their adventurous predecessors. Their speech may sound modern, but their words resonate with the inherent philosophies of Muir, Salathé, Robbins, and Chouinard. For all these climbers, the mountains were always more than just platforms to perform on.

As we end our examination of the past, there is much that provides encouragement and inspiration. Climbers of the last 15 years definitely contributed to the ongoing evolution of Yosemite climbing, and their contributions will serve as stepping stones for even more remarkable achievements, which are sure to come in the future.

Yet achievements are not the essence of rock climbing—the essence is firmly rooted in friendship, humility, adventure, and respect for the natural world. If we maintain these ideals as we venture outdoors, the cliffs of Yosemite will continue to teach us valuable lessons. For as John Muir noted over 70 years ago, "In every walk with Nature, one receives far more than one seeks."

Climber and sunset, El Capitan

8

BEYOND THE HORIZON

Climb the mountains and get their good tidings. Nature's peace will flow into you as sunshine flows into trees. The winds will blow their own freshness into you, and the storms their energy, while cares drop off like autumn leaves.

JOHN MUIR

The story of Yosemite climbing is many things: humorous, tragic, worrisome, and inspiring. It has involved some of the most bitter controversies in modern mountaineering, as well as some of the most important achievements. And the story will go on—significant chapters are still to be written in the future.

As this book goes to press in 1995, it is appropriate to consider how the past could influence what tomorrow might hold. Armed with the many lessons that history can offer, perhaps future climbers will avoid some of the pitfalls that the unknown always holds.

One of the most contentious topics these days remains the controversy surrounding rap-bolting. Few topics generate the intense feelings that sport climbing and rap-bolting do. For some climbers the issue is clear. "Anybody can rap-bolt," exclaimed John Bachar. "You might as well go bowling or play golf, they're harder! Especially golf!"

A comparable view is held by Royal Robbins, who stated emphatically, "Sport climbing has a place, and it's not in Yosemite! Our generation had a clear definition of how to play the game—the way you do it counts. You avoid bolts whenever you can, any bolts placed are from a natural stance, and the rock is sacred so you don't change it. These standards guided the actions of Yosemite climbers since the 1940s, and what we're seeing now is a collapse of any ethical stylistic standards in favor of gymnastic pleasure in climbing. . . . What's essentially happened is that traditions are being overturned. They were fine the way they were. They preserved standards and ethics and the best in American adventure climbing. Sport climbing came in and set a tone for athleticism over adventure. This is fine as far as it goes but you have to ask, 'What have we lost?' You've lost something pretty precious. You've lost adventure!"

Many prominent climbers around the world hold a similar belief. The renowned British climber Doug Scott noted, "We set off on our climbs expecting a degree of commitment. But if there are bolts every two meters, there is no commitment. Nor is there elation from stepping out into the unknown, as you do when you challenge your ability and imagination to protect yourself on a hard route. How could climbers deny themselves that pleasure? . . . We should be raising our standards to meet the rock, not reducing the rock to meet us."

When looking at the modern climbing scene it is easy to focus on the sport-climbing controversy, as well as other problems such as crowding, trash, access, and competition. But the Yosemite that we see today is by no means dominated by gloom and doom. Yosemite can still mean what it has always meant, as long as we maximize our respect for the rock and climb in the best possible style.

Here are the views expressed by some of the giants of Yosemite climbing:

HENRY BARBER: *"Style matters in life. I think that tomorrow is another day. We should leave some of these gems of climbs and real challenges for climbers who will be really inspired to do them in the best possible style. And if you can't do it, leave it for someone else."*

YVON CHOUINARD: *"Are we willing to compromise our ethics and style, all for the sake of raising [numeric ratings]? If so, the climbers coming after us will have to grind off our chipped holds, plug up our bolt holes, and wash away our chalk marks in order to raise their own standards. It seems to me that climbing would be better off if we just learned to hold back a bit, and take an attitude of 'each climb has its time.'"*

LYNN HILL: *"The purpose of climbing is to adapt yourself to the rock. You work on yourself to overcome the obstacle of the rock. . . . And if a route doesn't go, so what? Not every square inch of rock needs to be climbed."*

PETER CROFT: *"It seems that every generation gets a generous portion of sports heroes who believe that their species has evolved as far as it's going to go, and who (along with their fans) fail to understand that puppet strings link them to the past. To reach beyond what you are . . . might mean that you adopt a far tighter code of conduct to ensure the necessary level of intensity and adventure."*

Adventure—maintaining some of the unknowns in climbing—lies at the heart of the issue. Although feelings persist among some climbers that the ends justify the means, it is important to remember that climbing can be much more than just a rehearsed sequence of gymnastic moves. It's really a question of accepting some limits and leaving some routes, some "impossibles," for the future. The Himalayan guru Reinhold Messner put it in these terms: "If we use more technical tricks we will destroy the impossible, and without the impossible, climbing will lose the most important motivation. Nobody can do the impossible, but we can go near the impossible. And if we destroy the impossible with bolts or technical tricks, we destroy climbing."

So in terms of the future, the climbers of tomorrow can make the most meaningful contributions by respecting the traditions of Yosemite climbing. Yet this respect should not be viewed as a hindrance. As Peter Croft noted, "I can feel the history here and it's not a burden! I get inspiration from it. I don't think of the history as holding me back in any way. . . . The past is more than just rules or guidelines. It's also the spirit of adventure you can get from those guys!"

In this day of satellite photos and electron microscopes, of fiber-optic wires and CD-ROM, it's easy to lament that all the important "firsts" have already been done. It's considered chic today to restrict "real adventure" to such grandiose projects as the south face of Lhotse in Nepal or the east face of Great Trango Tower in Pakistan. But

Gary Arce relaxes on Hollow Flake Ledge, Salathé Wall

the future has always been kind to those with the vision and insight to recognize new opportunities. And meaningful climbs certainly remain to be done in Yosemite.

Just because El Cap is crisscrossed with routes doesn't mean that no adventure exists there. Royal Robbins once remarked, "Although some of the early aura is gone, and climbers are approaching El Cap with more confidence these days, an ascent of its walls will always be one of the more life-giving experiences a climber can seek." We can't go back to the days when this great cliff was unexplored, just like the footloose days of the American West are forever gone. Yet adventure can still be found in Yosemite's granite kingdom, and the flame of Yosemite climbing continues to burn brightly. "The spirit of this place is something you can't describe," said Tom Frost. "You have to go out and experience it for yourself."

So what is there still to do? "There's an incredible amount to do," noted Peter Croft. "The more imagination that you have, the more you can find to do in Yosemite. And it's not important that what you do is the latest and greatest. It's just as important that you have fun and really enjoy what you're doing. The best way to push yourself the hardest and do the most amazing things is by having fun—not going up on something because someone said it would be impressive, but because you can't imagine any other place on the planet you'd rather be!"

If we take these words to heart, Yosemite will enrich us in ways never dreamed of. One person who made a huge contribution to Yosemite climbing, and received much in return, was Chuck Pratt. In the aftermath of the 1964 ascent of Mt. Watkins' South Face, he expressed these emotions, which speak volumes about the true Yosemite experience:

In the vanishing twilight, the Valley of the Yosemite seemed to me more beautiful than I had ever seen it, more serene than I had ever known it before. For five days the South Face of Mt. Watkins had dominated our lives as only Nature can dominate the lives of men. With the struggle over and our goal achieved, I was conscious of an inner calm which I had experienced only on El Capitan. I thought of my incomparable friend Chouinard, and of our unique friendship, a friendship now shared with Warren. For we were united by a bond far stronger and more lasting than any we could find in the world below. I wondered what thoughts were passing the minds of my companions during the final moments. My own thoughts rambled back through the entire history of Yosemite climbing—from that indomitable Scotsman Anderson, who first climbed Half Dome, to John Salathé, whose philosophy and climbing ethics have dominated Yosemite climbing for nearly 20 years, to Mark Powell, Salathé's successor, who showed us all that climbing can be a way of life and the basis for a philosophy. These men,

like ourselves, had come to the Valley of Light with a restless spirit and the desire to share an adventure with their comrades. We had come as strangers, full of apprehension and doubt. Having given all we had to the climb, we had been enriched by a physical and spiritual experience few men can know. Having accepted the hardships as a natural consequence of our endeavor, we were rewarded with a gift of victory and fulfillment for which we would be forever grateful. It was for this that each of us had come to Yosemite, and it was for this that we would return, season after season.

Friendship, humility, adventure. These represent the soul of Yosemite climbing in the past, and they need to remain central to Yosemite climbing in the future. If we keep this in mind as we organize our racks and coil our ropes, the mountains will bless us with a bountiful procession of unique and precious experiences. For as John Muir noted, "The mountains are fountains not only of rivers and fertile soils, but also of men. Therefore we are all, in some sense, mountaineers—and going to the mountains is going home."

REFERENCES AND FURTHER READING

Ament, P., 1991: High Endeavors. Mountain N' Air Books, La Crescenta, CA, 172 pp.

Bachar, J., 1988: "Biased and Destructive Reporting". Mountain magazine, Sheffield, UK, July/Aug., p. 50.

Benge, M., 1990: "Hot Flashes". Climbing magazine, Carbondale, CO, Oct./Nov., p. 39.

Benge, M., 1994: "The Nose Goes". Climbing magazine, Carbondale, CO, Dec./Jan., p. 56–57.

Birkett, B., and B. Peascod, 1989: Women Climbing. The Mountaineers, Seattle, WA, 192 pp.

Bocarde, G., 1974: "Up the Shield". Climbing magazine, Carbondale, CO, winter issue, p. 24–26.

Bracksieck, G., 1993: "Charlie Porter". Rock & Ice magazine, Boulder, CO, Jan./Feb., p. 23–29.

Brewer, W., 1966: Up and Down California. University of California Press, Berkeley, CA, 583 pp.

Bridwell, J., 1974: "Brave New World". Mountain magazine, Sheffield, UK, p. 26

Bridwell, J., 1991: "Largo's Apprenticeship". Rock & Ice magazine, Boulder, Co, Nov./Dec., p. 14–15.

Bridwell, J., 1992: Climbing Adventures. ICS Books, Merrillville, IN, 208 pp.

Chapman, M., 1993: "Charlie Porter". Rock & Ice magazine, Boulder, CO, Jan./Feb., p. 22.

Child, G., 1987: "Lost in America". Climbing magazine, Carbondale, CO, June.

Chouinard, Y., 1961: "Sentinel Rock, West Face". American Alpine Journal, New York, NY, p. 369.

Chouinard, Y., 1963: Modern Yosemite Climbing. American Alpine Journal, New York, NY.

Chouinard, Y., 1965: "Muir Wall—El Capitan". American Alpine Journal, New York, NY.

Chouinard, Y., 1987: "Coonyard Mouths Off—Part II". Climbing magazine, Carbondale, CO, Feb., p. 44–48.

Croft, P., 1990: "Bat Wings and Puppet Strings". Climbing magazine, Carbondale, CO, April/May, p. 77–78.

Falkenstein, C., 1991: "Riding the Crest". Climbing magazine, Carbondale, CO, Feb./Mar., p. 22.

Farquhar, F. P., 1965: History of the Sierra Nevada. University of California Press, Berkeley, CA, 262 pp.

Haan, P., 1972: "The Salathé Wall Solo". American Alpine Journal, New York, NY, p. 74–75.

Harding, W., 1959: "El Capitan". American Alpine Journal, New York, NY.

Harding, W., 1971: "Reflections of a Broken-Down Climber". Ascent, San Francisco, CA.

Harding, W., 1975. Downward Bound—A Mad Guide to Rock Climbing. Menasha Ridge Press, Birmingham, AL, 197 pp.

Herbert, TM, 1971: "Comment on Two Ascents of the Wall of the Morning Light". American Alpine Journal, New York, NY, p. 361.

Higgins, T., 1974: "Fairview Dome's West Face". American Alpine Journal, New York, NY, p. 66–70.

King, C., 1970: Mountaineering in the Sierra Nevada. University of Nebraska Press, Lincoln, NB, 292 pp.

Kroger, C., 1971: "El Capitan—Heart Route". Climbing magazine, Carbondale, CO, Jan., p. 7–9.

Leonard, R., and D. Brower, 1940: Climber's Guide to the High Sierra. Sierra Club Bulletin, v. 25, p. 41.

Long, J., 1990: "DNB". Climbing magazine, Carbondale, CO, Feb./March, p. 86–89.

Long, J., 1990: "Three Little Fish". Climbing magazine, Carbondale, CO, Apr./May, p. 145.

Long, J., 1991: "The Nose". Climbing magazine, Carbondale, CO, June/July, p. 60–64.

Long, J., 1991: "Back Then". Rock & Ice magazine, Boulder, CO, Nov./Dec., p. 16–17.

Long, J., 1992: "Little Lynny". Rock & Ice magazine, Boulder, CO, May/June, p. 20.

Long, J., 1994: "The Bird's Boys". Rock & Ice magazine, Boulder, CO, May/June, p. 37–40.

Macdonald, A., 1962: "Realm of the Over-hang". Sierra Club Bulletin, San Francisco, CA.

Matthes, F. E., 1950: The Incomparable Valley. University of California Press, Berkeley, CA, 160 pp.

Meyers, G., 1979: Yosemite Climber. Diadem Books/Robbins Mountain Letters, Modesto, CA, 96 pp.

Morgan, L., 1994: "Hammer Time". Climbing magazine, Carbondale, CO, Aug./Sept., p. 152.

Moser, S., 1988: "The Golden Age of Yosemite Climbing". Rock & Ice magazine, Boulder, CO, March/Apr., p. 14–25.

Nelson, Alan, 1982: "Tuolumne Expose". Climbing magazine, Carbondale, CO, July, p. 32–33.

Nelson, Alan, 1984: "The Path of the Master—Tuolumne". American Alpine Journal, New York, NY, p. 109–115.

Nelson, Anton, 1948: "Five Days and Nights on the Lost Arrow". Sierra Club Bulletin, San Francisco, CA.

O'Connell, N., 1993: Beyond Risk—Conversations With Climbers. The Mountaineers, Seattle, WA, 300 pp.

Osius, A., 1987: "From Rock Bottom to Passion". Summit magazine, July/Aug., p. 27.

Osius, A., 1989: "Four Desert Pioneers". Climbing magazine, Carbondale, CO, April, p. 74.

Piana, P., 1989: "The Free Salathé". American Alpine Journal, New York, NY, p. 94–103.

Pratt, C., 1965: "The South Face of Mt. Watkins". American Alpine Journal, New York, NY.

Pratt, C., 1965: "Ribbon Falls East Portal". American Alpine Journal, New York, NY, p. 413.

Prichard, N., 1991: "Hot Henry Barber". Rock & Ice magazine, Boulder, CO, Mar./Apr., p. 24–30.

Prichard, N., 1991: "Playing the Game—Conversation with Ron Kauk". Rock & Ice magazine, Boulder, CO, Nov./Dec., p. 24–30.

Prichard, N., 1991: "Speed Thrills—Dave Schultz and the Fastest Rope in the West". Rock & Ice magazine, Boulder, CO, Nov./Dec., p. 52–57.

Prichard, N., 1992: "An Interview with Lynn Hill". Rock & Ice magazine, Boulder, CO, May/June, p. 16–22.

Robbins, R., 1963: "The Salathé Wall of El Capitan". American Alpine Journal, New York, NY.

Robbins, R., 1965: "The North America Wall". American Alpine Journal, New York, NY.

Robbins, R., 1968: "Interview". Summit magazine, Nov./Dec., p. 12–17, 26–27.

Robbins, R., 1969: "Alone on the John Muir Wall, El Capitan". American Alpine Journal, New York, NY.

Robbins, R., 1970: "Tis-sa-ack". American Alpine Journal, New York, NY, p. 8

Robbins, R., 1970: "Dawn Wall". Summit magazine, Dec., p. 31.

Robbins, R., 1971: "Arcturus". American Alpine Journal, New York, NY, p. 358

Robbins, R., 1972: "Chocks". Summit magazine, Oct., p. 9.

Robinson, B., 1934: "The First Ascent of Higher Cathedral Spire". Sierra Club Bulletin, San Francisco, CA.

Robinson, D., 1969: "Camp 4". Mountain magazine, Sheffield, UK.

Robinson, D., 1978: "Grand Sieges and Fast Attacks". Mariah/Outside magazine, Chicago, IL, p. 22–33.

Roper, S., 1994: Camp 4—Recollections of a Yosemite Rockclimber. The Mountaineers, Seattle, WA, 255 pp.

Rowell, G., 1969: "Rescue on the South Face of Half Dome". Summit magazine, May.

Ryan, G., 1993: "Free At Last". Rock & Ice magazine, Boulder, CO, Nov./Dec., p. 30–32.

Schneider, S., 1991: "Sea of Domes". Climbing magazine, Carbondale, CO, Aug./Sept., p. 60–66, 128–132.

Schneider, S., 1993: "Excalibur—Freeing the Sword from the Stone". Climbing magazine, Carbondale, CO, Oct./Nov., p. 84.

Scott, D., 1994: "Bolts from the Blue". Rock & Ice magazine, Boulder, CO, Nov./Dec., p. 6–9.

Sherman, J., 1991: "Life Without a Net". Climbing magazine, Carbondale, CO, Feb./March, p. 130.

Sherrick, M., 1958: "The Northwest Face of Half Dome". Sierra Club Bulletin, San Francisco, CA.

Smith, M., 1983: "Wings of Steel". Climbing magazine, Carbondale, CO, June, p. 34.

Steck, A., 1951: "Ordeal By Piton". Sierra Club Bulletin, San Francisco, CA.

Steiger, J., 1986: "Johnny Rock". Climbing magazine, Carbondale, CO, Oct., p. 30–39.

Steiger, J., 1987: "Basecamp". Climbing magazine, Carbondale, CO, Oct., p. 3

Vause, M., 1990: Rock and Roses. Mountain N' Air Books, La Crescenta, CA, 144 pp.

Vetter, C., 1986: "John Bachar Hangs On". Outside magazine, Chicago, IL, April.

Vetter, C., 1992: "Limestone Cowboys". Outside magazine, Chicago, IL, April, p. 62, 169.

Walling, R., 1991: "Death Valley Days". Rock & Ice magazine, Boulder, CO, Nov./Dec., p. 48–51.

Wellman, M., and J. Flinn, 1992: Climbing Back. WRS Publishing, Waco, TX, 254 pp.

Wilson, K., Steck, A., and G. Rowell, 1971: "Interview with Royal Robbins". Mountain magazine, Sheffield, UK.

Woodward, J., 1994: "Smoke and Mirrors". Climbing magazine, Carbondale, CO, Dec./Jan., p. 104.

Worrall, K., 1994: "Rockin' the Cradle— A New Age in Old Camp 4". Climbing magazine, Carbondale, CO, May/June, p. 81.

GLOSSARY

AAC: abbreviation for the American Alpine Club.

Aid: climbing in which mechanical devices are used at least part of the time to support the weight of the climber. Aid climbing is subdivided from A1, which is the easiest, to A5, which is the hardest. Aid climbing is also known as Class 6 climbing.

Angle piton: a type of piton designed for cracks larger than ½ inch wide.

Arete: a narrow glaciated ridge, or the outside edge of a corner system.

Belay: (verb) to carefully feed out rope to the lead climber, so that the rope could catch the leader in the event of a fall. Also (noun) a place where a climber temporarily stops, the end of a Pitch.

Bivouac (or bivy): (verb) to pass the night out in the open during a climb. Also (noun) a place for passing the night, such as a ledge.

Bolt: a small piece of metal, resembling a small blunt nail, which is hammered into a drilled hole in the rock. Bolts are used for anchors as well as for upward progress in aid climbing.

Buttress: a prominent projection on a mountain or a cliff face.

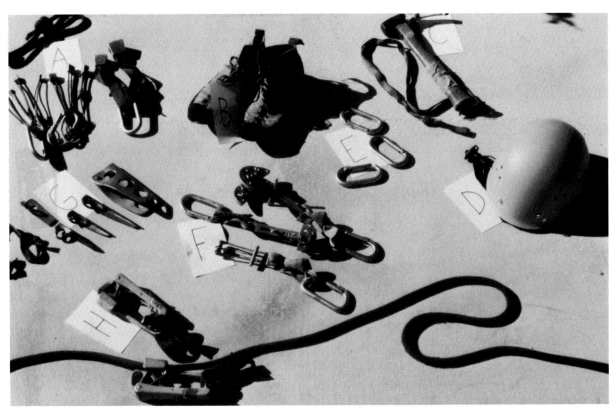

Tools of the trade for rock climbing: A = chocks, B = climbing shoes, C = hammer, D = helmet, E = carabiners, F = Friends and other camming devices, G = pitons, H = jumars.

Bong: a large piton used in cracks several inches wide.

Carabiner: a metal snap link, usually oval-shaped, used for attaching different pieces of equipment together.

Chimney: a wide crack which may resemble the inside of a fireplace chimney. A climber ascends the chimney by climbing directly inside it using counter-pressure. An extremely narrow chimney is called a squeeze chimney.

Chocks: small pieces of aluminum, which come in various shapes, used in cracks instead of pitons or other devices. Hexagonal-shaped chocks are called Hexentrics or hexes, and tapering chocks are called stoppers.

Class: (see also Ratings definitions in the front of this book) describes the difficulty of a particular mountaineering route. Class is subdivided as follows: Class 1—extremely easy, such as walking along a trail; Class 2—rugged hiking, with some scrambling over boulders and ledges; Class 3—climbing which is technically easy, so ropes and other equipment are generally not needed; Class 4—exposed climbing up a steep cliff, ropes and other equipment may be needed; Class 5—technical rock climbing where ropes and equipment, plus knowledge of belays, are needed for safety. Rock climbing routes currently range from 5.0 (easiest) to 5.14d (most difficult); Class 6—see Aid.

Clean climbing: an ascent using chocks or camming devices instead of pitons.

Cliffhanger: see Skyhook.

Dihedral: an inside corner where two rock walls converge. It resembles a partly-open book.

Direct aid: see Aid.

Expansion bolt: see Bolt.

Face climbing: using small handholds and footholds to ascend a rock face devoid of cracks.

Fixed rope: a rope left in place after a section of rock is climbed. This permits a section of rock to be ascended quickly once fixed ropes are in place, since subsequent ascents just climb up the rope instead of reclimbing the rock.

Flake: a semi-detached piece of rock which protrudes from the surrounding rock face.

Flash: to climb a route on the first try, without previous practice.

Free climbing: an ascent where mechanical devices are not used for upward progress, and a rope is only used to stop a climber in the event of a fall.

Free solo: technical rock climbing where a person climbs alone, without the protection of ropes or other equipment. Since the climber is completely unprotected, a fall can result in serious injury or death. Also known as a ropeless or no-rope ascent.

Friction climbing: to ascend a smooth rock face, devoid of obvious handholds or footholds, using only the friction of shoes and hands upon the rock.

Friend: a spring-loaded camming device which can be inserted quickly into cracks of varying sizes.

Hand traverse: to traverse sideways below a small ledge while hanging from the hands.

Haul bag: a large duffel bag used to carry all the provisions needed on a multiday rock climb.

Headlamp: a device used for night climbing which resembles a small flashlight that can be strapped around the head, leaving the hands free to climb.

Hook: see Skyhook.

Jam crack: a crack which is ascended by jamming various body parts, such as feet, hands, or fingers into the fissure.

Jumar: a mechanical device used to quickly ascend a rope. The jumar slides easily up the rope, but grips tightly when pulled downward.

Lieback: to ascend a vertical crack by pulling with the hands and pushing with the feet.

Nailing: slang for Aid climbing.

Nuts: see Chocks.

Offwidth: a fissure wider than a Jam crack but narrower than a Chimney.

Pendulum: a method of traversing across a blank wall in which the leader is lowered some distance on the rope, then swings back and forth from a single pivot point in order to reach easier terrain off to the side. A double pendulum is similar except that two separate pivot points, some distance apart, are used.

Pin: a Piton.

Pitch: a particular section of a rock wall, usually the distance that can be covered in one rope-length. Pitches may be as short as 40 feet, or as long as 165 feet, depending on the difficulty of the climb and the availability of suitable places or ledges to stop.

Piton: a metal spike that can be hammered into a crack. Also called a Pin.

Protection: any device (a Bolt, a Friend, a Piton) inserted into the rock to catch a climber in the event of a fall. Also known as pro.

Prusik: a special type of knot used to ascend a rope. The knot slides up the rope, but grips tightly when pulled downward. Prusik knots have been replaced by Jumars and other mechanical ascenders.

Rack: an assortment of equipment carried by the leader on an ascent, which may include Pitons, Friends, and Carabiners.

Rap-bolting: to descend down a rope, drilling holes into the rock and inserting bolts along the way.

Rappel: to descend down a rope.

Roof: an overhang that protrudes from a cliff face at a sharp angle.

Runout: (adjective, noun) a large distance between protection points on a Pitch.

Also (verb) to climb a Pitch that has a large distance between protection points. When the protection points are widely-spaced, the leader risks a long and dangerous fall.

Rurp: a flat, tiny Piton used for Aid climbing up extremely small cracks. The name is an abbreviation for Realized Ultimate Reality Piton.

Skyhook: a small metal hook used for Aid climbing.

Sling: a loop of nylon webbing used in a variety of ways, such as attaching to pitons or chocks to make the rope run straighter, tying equipment to the rock, or making stirrups for climbers to stand in for Aid climbing.

Talus: loose rocks and boulders at the base of a cliff.

Toprope: a fixed rope that protects a climber from above. Also (verb) to climb a route with a toprope in place.

Traverse: to climb sideways.

Undercling: to use counter pressure to traverse beneath a protruding Flake.

CHRONOLOGY OF SELECTED CLIMBS
IN YOSEMITE AND THE HIGH SIERRA

1863 *Mount Hoffmann*. Southeast slopes. Josiah Whitney, William Brewer, Charles Hoffmann.
Mount Dana. Northwest slopes. William Brewer, Charles Hoffmann.

1864 *Mount Brewer*. Southwest slopes. William Brewer, Charles Hoffmann.
Mount Tyndall. North slopes. Clarence King, Richard Cotter.

1866 *Mount Clark*. Southeast arete. Clarence King, James Gardiner.
Mount Conness. Southeast slopes. Clarence King, James Gardiner.

1869 *Cathedral Peak*. East and south slopes. John Muir.

1871 *Mount Lyell*. Northwest Ridge. John Tileston.

1872 *Mount Ritter*. Northern slopes. John Muir.

1873 *Mount Whitney*. Western slopes. A. H. Johnson, C. P. Begole, J. Lucas.
Mount Whitney. Mountaineer's Route. John Muir.

1875 *Half Dome*. Northeast face. George Anderson.

1877 *Mount Starr King*. Southeast slopes . George Anderson, James Hutchings, John Lembert.

1896 *Mount Clarence King*. Southern slopes. Bolton Brown.

1899 *Matterhorn Peak*. Western slopes. James Hutchinson, Lincoln Hutchinson, M. R. Dempster, Charles Noble.

1903 *North Palisade*. Southwest slopes. James Hutchinson, Joseph N. LeConte. J. K. Moffitt.

1931 *Mount Whitney*. East Face. Robert Underhill, Norman Clyde, Jules Eichorn, Glen Dawson.

1933 *Washington Column*. Lunch Ledge. Richard Leonard, Jules Eichorn, Bestor Robinson, Hervey Voge.

1934 *Higher Cathedral Spire*. Southwest Face. Richard Leonard, Jules Eichorn, Bestor Robinson.
Lower Cathedral Spire. South Face. Richard Leonard, Jules Eichorn, Bestor Robinson.

1936 *Royal Arches*. Morgan Harris, Ken Adam, Kenneth Davis.

1946 *Half Dome*. Southwest Face. John Salathé, Anton Nelson.

1947 *Lost Arrow Chimney*. John Salathé, Anton Nelson.

1950 *Sentinel Rock*. Steck-Salathé Route. Allen Steck, John Salathé.

1952 *Yosemite Point Buttress*. Allen Steck, Bob Swift.

1953 *El Capitan*. East Buttress. Allen Steck, Will Siri, Willi Unsoeld, Bill Long.

1954 *Middle Cathedral Rock*. North Buttress. Warren Harding, Frank Tarver, Craig Holden, John Whitmer.
Middle Cathedral Rock. East Buttress. Warren Harding, Jack Davis, Bob Swift.

1956 *Lower Cathedral Rock*. East Buttress. Mark Powell, Jerry Gallwas, Don Wilson.
Liberty Cap. South Face. Mark Powell, Royal Robbins, Joe Fitschen.
Arrowhead Arete. Mark Powell, Bill Feuerer.

1957 *Half Dome.* Northwest Face. Royal Robbins, Jerry Gallwas, Mike Sherrick.
Middle Cathedral Rock. Powell-Reed Route. Mark Powell, Wally Reed.
North Dome. South Face. Mark Powell, Wally Reed.

1958 *Fairview Dome.* North Face. Wally Reed, Chuck Pratt.
El Capitan. The Nose. Warren Harding, Wayne Merry, George Whitmore,
Mark Powell, Bill Feuerer.

1959 *Washington Column.* East Face. Warren Harding, Glen Denny, Chuck Pratt.

1960 *Kat Pinnacle.* Southwest Corner. Yvon Chouinard, Tom Frost.
Sentinel Rock. West Face. Yvon Chouinard, Tom Frost.
Rixon's Pinnacle. East Chimney (First free ascent). Royal Robbins, Dave Rearick.
Arches Direct. Royal Robbins, Joe Fitschen.
El Capitan. The Nose (First continuous ascent). Royal Robbins, Tom Frost,
Chuck Pratt, Joe Fitschen.

1961 *El Capitan.* Salathé Wall. Royal Robbins, Tom Frost, Chuck Pratt.
Elephant Rock. Crack of Doom. Chuck Pratt, Mort Hempel.
Leaning Tower. West Face. Warren Harding, Glen Denny, Al Macdonald.

1962 *El Capitan.* Dihedral Wall. Ed Cooper, Jim Baldwin, Glen Denny.
Rostrum. North Face. Warren Harding, Glen Denny.
Middle Cathedral Rock. Direct North Buttress. Yvon Chouinard, Steve Roper.

1963 *El Capitan.* West Buttress. Layton Kor, Steve Roper, Eric Beck.
Leaning Tower. West Face (First solo of Grade V). Royal Robbins.
Half Dome. Direct Northwest Face. Royal Robbins, Dick McCracken.

1964 *Lost Arrow Chimney (First free ascent).* Frank Sacherer, Chuck Pratt.
Higher Cathedral Rock. Northeast Buttress (First free ascent). Frank Sacherer,
Jeff Dozier.
Half Dome. Southwest Face (First free ascent). Frank Sacherer, Bob Kamps,
Andy Lichtman.
Washington Column. South Face. Layton Kor, Chris Fredericks.
Mount Watkins. South Face. Warren Harding, Chuck Pratt, Yvon Chouinard.
El Capitan. North America Wall. Royal Robbins, Tom Frost, Chuck Pratt,
Yvon Chouinard.

1965 *El Capitan.* Muir Wall. Yvon Chouinard, TM Herbert.
Middle Cathedral Rock. Direct North Buttress (First free ascent). Frank Sacherer,
Eric Beck.
Middle Cathedral Rock. East Buttress (First free ascent). Frank Sacherer, Ed Leeper.
Arch Rock. Entrance Exam. Chuck Pratt, Chris Fredericks.
Cookie Cliff. Twilight Zone. Chuck Pratt, Chris Fredericks.

1966 *Half Dome.* Northwest Face (First one-day ascent). Jeff Foott, Steve Roper.
Half Dome. Northwest Face (First solo of Half Dome). Eric Beck.

1967 *Manure Pile Buttress.* The Nutcracker. Royal Robbins, Liz Robbins.
El Capitan. West Face. Royal Robbins, TM Herbert.
Half Dome. Northwest Face (First female ascent of a Grade VI). Royal Robbins,
Liz Robbins.
El Capitan. Stoveleg Crack (First free ascent). Jim Bridwell, Jim Stanton.

1968 *El Capitan.* Muir Wall (First solo of El Cap). Royal Robbins.

1969 *Washington Column.* The Prow. Royal Robbins, Glen Denny.
Half Dome. Tis-sa-ack. Royal Robbins, Don Peterson.

1970 *El Capitan.* Heart Route. Chuck Kroger, Scott Davis.
Arch Rock. New Dimensions. Jim Bridwell, Mark Klemens.
Sentinel Rock. In Cold Blood (First solo of new Grade V) . Royal Robbins.
Half Dome. Arcturus. Royal Robbins, Dick Dorworth.
Half Dome. South Face. Warren Harding, Galen Rowell.
El Capitan. Wall of the Early Morning Light. Warren Harding, Dean Caldwell.

1971 *El Capitan.* Salathé Wall (First solo). Peter Haan.

1972 *El Capitan.* Cosmos (First solo of new El Cap route). Jim Dunn.
El Capitan. The Shield. Charlie Porter, Gary Bocarde.
El Capitan. Zodiac. Charlie Porter.

1973 *Sentinel Rock.* Steck-Salathé Route (Free solo). Henry Barber.
Cookie Cliff. Butterballs. Henry Barber, George Meyers.
Fairview Dome. Fairest of All. Tom Higgins, Mike Irwin.
El Capitan. Triple Direct (First all-female ascent of El Cap). Bev Johnson,
Sibylle Hectell.

1975 *El Capitan.* Free Blast. Jim Bridwell, John Long, Kevin Worrall, Mike Graham,
John Bachar, Ron Kauk.
Washington Column. Astro Man. John Long, John Bachar, Ron Kauk.
El Capitan. The Nose in a day. Jim Bridwell, John Long, Billy Westbay.
El Capitan. Pacific Ocean Wall. Jim Bridwell, Billy Westbay, Fred East, Jay Fiske.
Cascade Falls. Fish Crack. Henry Barber.

1976 *Half Dome.* Northwest Face (First free ascent). Art Higbee, Jim Erickson.

1977 *El Capitan.* The Nose (First all-female ascent). Molly Higgins, Barb Eastman
Cascade Falls. Phoenix. Ray Jardine, John Lakey.

1978 *El Capitan.* Dihedral Wall (First female solo of El Cap). Bev Johnson.
Big Columbia Boulder. Midnight Lightning. Ron Kauk, John Bachar.

1979 *El Capitan.* West Face (First free ascent of El Cap). Ray Jardine, Bill Price.

1980 *El Capitan.* The Shield (All-female ascent). Lynn Hill, Mari Gingery.
Chapel Wall. Cosmic Debris. Bill Price.
Glacier Point Apron. Hall of Mirrors. Chris Cantwell, Scott Cole, Scott Burke,
Dave Austin, Bruce Morris.

1981 *Medlicott Dome.* Bachar-Yerian Route. John Bachar, Dave Yerian.
El Capitan. Zenyatta Mondatta. Jim Bridwell, Peter Mayfield, Charlie Row.

1985 *El Capitan.* Atlantic Ocean Wall. John Middendorf, John Barbella.

1986 *Reed's Pinnacle.* Phantom. John Bachar.
El Capitan and Half Dome in a day (The Nose and the Northwest Face). John Bachar,
Peter Croft.

1987 *El Capitan.* West Face (First one-day El Cap solo). Jim Beyer.
Washington Column. Astro Man (Free solo). Peter Croft.

1988 *Arch Rock.* Punchline. Ron Kauk.
Whizz Dome. Love Sexy. Ron Kauk.
Whizz Dome. European Vacation. Ron Kauk.
El Capitan. Salathé Wall (First free ascent [Free Salathé]). Todd Skinner, Paul Piana.

1989 *El Capitan.* The Shield (Paraplegic ascent). Mike Corbett, Mark Wellman.

1990 *El Capitan.* North America Wall ("One-day" ascent in 24¹/₂ hours). Steve Gerberding,
Scott Stowe.
El Capitan. The Nose and Salathé Wall in a day (20¹/₂ hours). Peter Croft,
Dave Schultz.

1991 *Half Dome.* Tis-sa-ack (Paraplegic ascent). Mike Corbett, Mark Wellman.

1993 *El Capitan.* The Nose (Speed ascent in 4 hr. and 22 min.). Peter Croft, Hans Florine.
El Capitan. The Nose (First free ascent). Lynn Hill, Brooke Sandahl.

1994 *El Capitan.* The Nose (First one-day/all-free ascent). Lynn Hill, Steve Sutton.
El Capitan. The Nose/Lurking Fear/West Face in a day (23 hours). Steve Schneider,
Hans Florine.

PHOTO CREDITS

Numbers preceded by a C are color-page numbers.

Gary Arce xiv, 4, 20, 24, 26, 41, 57, 61, 70, 80, 101, 102, 135, 165, 168, 172, 182, C10, C11
Courtesy Bancroft Library 7, 10
Phil Bard 123, 128, 142, front cover (all copyright © Phil Bard)
Greg Epperson C15 (copyright © Greg Epperson)
Bill Feuerer/Don Lauria Collection 44, 45, 75, 98
Chris Falkenstein 109, 138, 155, C7, C8, C9, C12, C14, back cover (all copyright
    © Chris Falkenstein)
Tom Frost 36, 37, 49, 50, 52, 53, 54, 55, 63, 64, 69, 91
Tom Frost Collection 65 (left and right), 66, 68
Bill Hatcher 148, 149, C16 (all copyright © Bill Hatcher)
Don Lauria ii, 56, 85, 90
Don Lauria Collection 15
Richard Leonard 22
Jay Mather 159 (copyright © Jay Mather)
George Meyers 96, 118, 122, 126, 132, C2, C4, C5, C6 (all copyright © George Meyers)
Ruben Minjarez 177
Chuck Pratt/Tom Frost Collection 67
Galen Rowell 42, 83, 84, 174, C1, C3, C13 (all copyright © Galen Rowell/Mountain Light)
Jeffrey P. Schaffer 12
Allen Steck 29, 32
Steck/Salathé Collection 33
Billy Westbay 117
Billy Westbay Collection 114
Thomas Winnett 21, 143

INDEX

Route names are italicized when first mentioned in the text;
they are italicized here as well.